# Buckinghamshire
# Within Living Memory

To Barbara
   Hope you enjoy this book
 — like you it covers 60 years!
       Happy birthday.
            Love
         Jan and Brian.
            25 November 1993.

# WITHIN LIVING MEMORY SERIES

# Buckinghamshire Within Living Memory

Compiled by the Buckinghamshire
Federation of Women's Institutes

Published jointly by
Countryside Books, Newbury
and the BFWI, High Wycombe

First Published 1993
© Buckinghamshire Federation of Women's Institutes 1993

COUNTRYSIDE BOOKS
3 Catherine Road
Newbury, Berkshire

ISBN 1 85306 251 0

The cover photograph was taken in 1911 and has
been kindly supplied by Mrs K. Myall of
Long Crendon Institute.

Designed by Mon Mohan

Produced through MRM Associates Ltd, Reading
Phototypeset by The Midlands Book Typesetting Company,
Loughborough
Printed in England

# Contents

# Acknowledgements

Modern technology in the form of typewriters, word processors and photocopiers has made easy the task of assembling these memories of the days of slates, sand trays, chewed pencils and dipping pens in inkwells. However we do appreciate the time and effort freely given by the members of the Buckinghamshire Federation of Women's Institutes to create a book such as this.

Thanks are also due to: Betty Bunce and Margaret Scott for their line drawings; Thelma Coughtrey for help with typing; Ann Spalton, Chairman and members of the Publications Committee and the staff at the BFWI County Office; Irma Dolphin for making available the script of her booklet of her village, Hyde Heath; Elizabeth Knight for making available her booklet, in aid of the Cowper & Newton Museum in Olney, on Harry Armstrong and the Bucks Cottage Workers' Agency; the Headmaster of Cokethorpe School for allowing us to use part of an article from his school magazine; Rowley Bird for information on farming for Brian Edgley's article in the Parish Magazine, Clarion Five; Mr L J Mayes for making available his recorded stories; Mr Bill Rockall for making available printed material about his Father's life as a bodger; the Wycombe Local History and Chair Museum, Buckinghamshire County Council Surveyor's Department and to all those unknown to me who have encouraged their fellow members to record treasured memories.

Nancy Brazier
Co-ordinator

# List of Contributing W.I.s

Contributions were received from the following Buckinghamshire Women's Institutes:

Amersham Morning, Ashley Green, Ballinger Evening, Bellingdon & Asheridge, Bledlow, Booker Evening, Bourne End, Buckingham, Buckingham Morning, Buckland & Drayton Beauchamp & Aston Clinton, Chalfont Common, Chalfont St Giles, Chalfont St Peter, Cheddington, Chenies & Latimer, Chesham, Chesham Bois, Claydons, Coleshill, Cuddington, Downley Evening, Downley Village Evening, Drayton Parslow, Dunsmore, Edlesborough, Flackwell Heath Evening, Forty Green, Frieth, Fulmer, Great Brickhill, Great Hampden, Great Horwood & Singleborough, Great Linford, Haddenham, Hambleden, Hedgerley, High Wycombe Morning, Horn Hill, Hughenden, Hyde Heath Evening, Iver Heath, Kimble & Ellesborough, Lane End Evening, Ley Hill, Little Chalfont, Little Chalfont Evening, Little Kingshill, Little Kingshill Morning, Long Crendon, Longwick Evening, Loosley Row & Lacey Green, Marlow Bottom, Marlow Common, Marsh Gibbon, Marsworth, Medmenham, Monks Risborough, Naphill, Nash, Newport Pagnell, Newton Longville, Oakley, Olney, Padbury, Penn & Tylers Green, Penn & Tylers Green Evening, Penn Street, Preston Bissett, Prestwood, Prestwood Evening, Princes Risborough Evening, Quainton, Seer Green & Jordans, Simpson Village, Slapton, Southcourt, Speen, Stoke Hammond, Stoke Mandeville, Stokenchurch, Stoke Poges & Wexham, Stony Stratford, Taplow & Hitcham, Templewood, Terriers & Totteridge, The Lee, Thornborough & Thornton, Tingewick, Two Mile Ash, Waddesdon, Water Eaton, Wendover, Wendover Evening, Weston Turville, West Wycombe, Wheeler End, Wing, Wingrave, Winslow and Wooburn.

# Foreword

The County of Buckinghamshire stretches about 70 miles from north to south and between 1900 and 1960 was bordered by no fewer than seven other Counties.

However, two recent events altered the balance of the population of Bucks. Under the 1975 Government Reorganisation, Slough, in the south was lost to Berkshire whilst at the same time, the new city of Milton Keynes was rapidly growing in the north. Such dramatic changes in just 20 years show how important it is to catalogue the past whilst it is within living memory and before it is lost for ever.

Memories can play strange tricks. Were summers really always long and hot? Did it always snow in winter? Did fresh strawberries taste better than they do today and were pea pods always plump and juicy? Probably not! A record such as the one contained in this book shows hardships and harsh reality along with happy childhood and adult reminiscences.

It is full of memories of an age when perhaps there was more time to appreciate the world around us. Many of us lead such busy lives these days but let's forget about the hustle and bustle outside and take a little time out from this hectic world to wander through 'leafy Bucks' with memories gathered by the members of the Buckinghamshire Federation of Women's Institutes.

Kay M Bradley
County Chairman

N

OLNEY

NEWPORT PAGNELL

NORTHAMPTONSHIRE

STONY STRATFORD

THORNBOROUGH

MILTON KEYNES

BEDFORDSHIRE

BUCKINGHAM

STEEPLE CLAYDON

WINSLOW

MARSH GIBBON

QUAINTON

WINGRAVE

EDLESBOROUGH

AYLESBURY

LONG CRENDON

HADDENHAM

HERTFORDSHIRE

WENDOVER

OXFORDSHIRE

PRINCES RISBOROUGH

GREAT MISSENDEN

BLEDLOW

CHESHAM

PRESTWOOD

AMERSHAM

TURVILLE HEATH

HIGH WYCOMBE

THE CHALFONTS

LANE END

BEACONSFIELD

MARLOW

BURNHAM BEECHES

MIDDLESEX

STOKE POGES

BERKSHIRE

SURREY

| 1993 County boundary
: pre 1960 County boundary

**COUNTY OF BUCKINGHAMSHIRE**

# TOWN & COUNTRY LIFE

# SOME TOWNS AND VILLAGES
# AS THEY WERE

**The muffin man on the streets of High Wycombe; a horse-drawn fire engine rushing to an emergency in Aylesbury; taking the Sunday joint to be cooked at the bakery at Quainton; building a new house at Stony Stratford for £1,830 – how long ago it seems, but all within living memory. Here is just a flavour of some of Buckinghamshire's towns and villages as they used to be.**

## HIGH WYCOMBE

'I was born in 1915 in White Hart Street, High Wycombe in the flat over my father's butcher's shop. Still standing on each end are two stone pigs, thankfully protected by preservation orders.

At the end of White Hart Street was Newlands. This was a horrible slum area – the children used to go up and down White Hart Street poorly clad, often without knickers and shoes, and always very dirty, hoping to find something to eat or to find an old coin in the gutter.

At this time Wycombe was a very Liberal town and most of the well-off chair masters were Liberals, Baptists and teetotallers. I well remember when an election was to take place Lady Terrington, the Liberal candidate for Wycombe, walked up and down our street picking up these dirty children, kissing them and blowing their noses.

At the end of the street there was the church school rooms, where I went to Sunday school. In the summer we had a Sunday school treat and were all taken in carts to the Abbey Ground where we had races, lemonade, buns and other unusual eats. The highlight to me was the scramble for sweets. A man stood in a cart and threw hundreds of sweets to the children standing below. At Christmas we had wonderful parties in the school room. My enjoyment of the Sunday school was cut short as I caught ringworm and my parents were sure I caught it there as my class-mates were always trying on my hats. I was banished to London to my grandparents and had my hair shaved off and was given x-ray treatment. I stayed there for months until my hair grew again. Ringworm was a dreadful disgrace.

There were only a few schools in High Wycombe. Godstowe was

for the well-off. The Abbey School was only for children of titled birth and then I remember when they lowered the standards and allowed the children of doctors and the Church to go. There was the Convent for the Roman Catholics, Priory Road School, the Church of England school, and much later Haddows in Oxford Road. About 1925 Wycombe Preparatory School was held at the Baptist chapel, Easton Street.

About 1917, through my father-in-law and two other parents who could not afford Godstowe, and who as nonconformists couldn't allow their children to go to a Roman Catholic school, a Miss Mary Freeman of 143 London Road was asked if she would teach their children, and from this small beginning came Whitwell House School, opening in September 1917. It became a very well known prep school. There were always 40 to 50 children attending at once. Many well known Wycombe men and women were educated here until they passed the entrance exam to the Wycombe High School and Royal Grammar School at ten years of age. Two bedrooms were used as classrooms, one with a coal fire in the front room and a round valor oil stove in the back room. Singing and exercises were taken in the drawing room on the ground floor. We were so happy there and the teaching must have been good as almost all of us went on to the High School and Royal Grammar. One boy was expelled for smoking on the railway bank.

We walked backwards and forwards twice a day and thought nothing of it. Mrs Bristowe, whose husband had the chemist's shop in Desborough Road, used to walk with Ian and push her twins, Monica and Sheila, backwards and forwards in a huge twin pram and we used to trot along with her. Also, to make up the party, there was my friend Muriel James whose parents were manager and manageress of McIlroys Departmental Store.

Sometimes we called for Ernest Slade whose father kept a tobacconist's shop in Easton Street near the Baptist church. Mr Slade used to wear the most elaborate velvet jacket and smoker's hat with a long tassel. We thought the shop sheer magic.

We lived over our butcher's shop and the slaughterhouse was at the back, so when the shop was closed the cattle were driven through and housed until the morning when they were slaughtered. From our back door (upstairs) there was a wooden bridge going to a huge wooden barn and from there you could go down to the stalls and the slaughterhouse. As children we thought nothing of standing on the bridge and watching the animals being slaughtered.

At the back of White Hart Street, you will realize it is like a circle. In my childhood all the buildings at the back were wooden store rooms and barns, highly dangerous when there was a fire. Lansdale, the chemist, had a fire once and it was absolutely terrifying. Many little chair factories were close to the centre of the town and we seemed to have lots of fires in the 1920s. There were few, if any, safety rules and regulations, and with the polish and wood and cane they were at great risk. Great lumps of burning debris used to float about and this put us and all the wooden buildings in danger. As soon as there was a fire the police would come along and wake us all up. We would be dressed, wrapped in rugs and went and sat in the kitchen until it was all over. We were then given a drop of brandy in an egg cup with hot water to warm us up. I used to adore this.

Market days were very exciting. The stallholders kept their stalls (more like barrows on wheels) somewhere in Newlands, and they would come down White Hart Street on the way to the High Street. Children from the slum would run along behind hoping for things to drop off and they would rush off with free fruit. The fruit stalls were packed high with colourful fruit, and how I longed for a pomegranate, but we were never allowed one of these as it was considered not quite nice because of spitting the pips out. How I loved Mr J. K. Taylor's sweet stall, and to watch him standing with apron on throwing the humbug mixture over and over a steel hook and then making the humbugs. When darkness came, the stalls were illuminated with naphthalene lamps, with their naked flames flashing, making everything warm and exciting.

Opposite our shop was The White Hart Hotel, where on market days the farmers, butchers, corn merchants and others connected with farming met and had their midday dinner. I used to know all the farmers as I would go with my father to the farms in our pony and trap (sometimes I was allowed to drive) and watch him buy sheep and cattle. Most of the time animals were driven along the roads and streets to the slaughterhouses. It was fun for me to watch the farmers coming in and out of The White Hart. My favourite farmer was Frank Kember of Hughenden Farm.

We used to go to all the horse shows – Thame and Tring were my favourites. My father competed in the Tradesmen's Turnout with his high trotters. He was well known for his high stepping trotters and later his hackney horses. He won many prizes; it was a very competitive time.

We had a pony and trap which was housed at the back of our butcher's shop in Easton Street. Every Wednesday we went to tea with our grandparents at Prestwood. Cryers Hill was very, very steep in those days. My father would get out of the trap at the bottom to lighten the load and lead the horse up. When it rained we had a huge umbrella which we huddled under, it covered most of the trap.

*A Christmas display of poultry hanging outside Aldridges in White Hart Street, High Wycombe in 1931, reflects a more matter-of-fact attitude to butchery.*

The excitement when we had a crystal set! We used to sit around it, chained by our head sets, while my parents fiddled with the whisker and little wire.

The next great excitement was our first car. One Saturday night, when the shop was closed at about 10 pm, my father went off to Pugh's Garage, West Wycombe Road and bought a bull-nosed Morris Cowley. He sat in the car with Mr Pugh for ten minutes and was told what to do, then he drove home. He drove until he was 80 and never had an accident. How simple it was in the 1920s.

I couldn't wait to get to school on Monday to tell my friends. The car was housed at the back of our Easton Street shop and after church on Sunday my parents, my little sister and I went down there to go for a ride in our new car. It was a thrill. I sat in the dicky, tucked up in a rug.

Meat was delivered to hotels, pubs and cafes in the town by men carrying a long wooden tray with two handles at each end and meat piled high. They carried these on their shoulders and most butchers developed one shoulder higher than the other because of this. My father had to have the jackets of suits made up with a padded right shoulder to make him look right.

In my early days, until we had a van, meat was delivered twice weekly to places like Flackwell Heath, Loudwater, Hazlemere etc. Some was delivered by boys on bikes with a basket in front piled high with meat, sausages, bacon etc. These men never finished delivering and returning to White Hart Street before 9.30 pm or ten o'clock. Then they had to book in their takings, put in next week's orders, then the shop was cleaned and scrubbed ready for Monday. In those days there were only wooden blocks and they did take hard scrubbing with steel brushes and a gallon of boiling water from the copper out at the back. There were always errand boys in those days and at least two apprentices who paid for the privilege of training for the trade. They were often the sons of well-known farmers and my father usually had a waiting list.

Where the Law Courts are now were several cottages whose owners were allowed to graze a cow on the Rye. It was not unusual to see cows coming back from the Rye driven through the front door and through the house to a shed at the back to be milked and stay for the night.

During the depression of the 1920s, when there was much unemployment, we used to get buskers and actors coming from London hoping to earn a penny or two. These were a great thrill to watch; jugglers, musicians and magic men in our streets was something quite new.

In the spring at the time of the General Strike and no trains running, we moved to the top of Amersham Hill. No tennis court or large garden compensated me for the thrill of White Hart Street and all High Wycombe was in those days.'

'When buses first appeared they were very much under-powered, as all roads leading out of Wycombe meant ascending a hill. The last bus at 11 pm on a Saturday night to Downley was absolutely crammed full, with people standing in the aisle and on the steps. It never could manage Downley pitch and used to "conk out" halfway up. Everyone had to get off and push the bus to the top of the hill.

The muffin man was a regular sight on Wycombe's streets, with his four caps on his head, the last two upside down to make a level support for the tray of muffins, one hand reaching up to steady the tray while with the other hand ringing a huge brass bell. Muffins were much larger and whiter than those made today.

Another common sight was women sitting outside their doors, a small frame between their legs and piles of rushes laid in long tin baths of water, very busy caning the seats of chairs. A boy with a long-handled barrow would collect them when the chairs were ready. In the 1920s, during the chairmakers lock-out, or strike, there

16

would be queues of women holding white jugs, waiting for them to be filled with a brown nourishing soup dished out by the Salvation Army. Any help was gladly received.

Several "characters" roamed the streets, quite harmless. There was Banana Anne, with her stockings always wrinkled around her ankles, and Old Willy with his wooden cart wheeling his worldly goods around, living on any old scraps he could find.

Friday and Saturday nights there would be piano playing and singing in the pubs. When turning out time came, the singing continued in the streets for hours, often ending in fights. The Friday and Saturday markets were lit by flaring gas jets. The tarpaulin sides of the stalls flapped in the rain and the wind, adding to the excitement of being out in the dusk, as much later hours were kept then.'

## AYLESBURY

'I was born in Aylesbury and lived in the town centre. My parents had a fruit and florist shop. In my younger days all shopkeepers lived on their premises.

Aylesbury was a lovely country town. I remember when the villagers brought their wares into the town for sale. It was one side of the cattle market which was the venue – under cover. It consisted of garden and dairy produce, milk, butter and new laid eggs in abundance. Pets could also be bought, tame mice, puppies, kittens and rabbits particularly.

On the opposite side of the market were pens full of sheep, pigs and calves. Cows and bulls were also there. They went inside to be sold. The farmers all gathered round on stands and it was a treat if we could catch a sight of the auctioneer on his dais, high and lifted up. We never understood what he was saying. It was very noisy.

At the bottom of the market horses would be sold. Their owners would trot them through the arches by what was the Town Hall and past what is now the Civic Centre. That was a corn merchant's then.

The canal was an interesting place, too. At the Basin End was a coal yard. Barges were busy all the time and many goods were transported this way. Nestle had their own loading bay. Chocolate was the main product then, and cocoa. It was a lovely smell we had when we passed on our way to school. Many times I stood on the bridge and watched them loading. The barges were all very gay, and there would be a horse towing the barge along, as it walked along the tow-path.

Very few people had bathrooms. We used to go once a week to

the public baths. Lashings of hot water and half an hour allowed for threepence. For sixpence you could have a towel and soap provided. This was after we were too big to have a tub in front of the fire.

The fire brigade was housed next to the baths. It was always very exciting when the fire alarm sounded. The engine was horse drawn. We used to love to rush up, and see if we could arrive before the firemen and see the horses harnessed up. Off they would go, clanging the bell. We followed as far as we could. I will never forget one fire which happened on my birthday. It was over a shoe shop. The smoke and the flames took a long time to control and sadly the proprietor's wife died in that fire. I didn't realise the severity at the time.

It was a special event when the fair came to town. There would be big roundabouts, and little roundabouts, and hoopla, and coconut shies. I loved the swinging boats. Another great feature was the rock they used to make. They had gas lights on their stalls to make the rock. After cooking, in some sort of cauldron, it had to be stretched over a hook and looped over again and again as it was pulled into shape. A brown substance was put on it, and as it was stretched it made a stripe. When cool enough shears cut it in bars. It smelled lovely and tasted lovely too.

Down Cambridge Street there was a gipsy encampment. The Fire Brigade now occupies that site. Their caravans were all very ornate and the people were colourful too. Many of them were quite illiterate, except for money. Many times they came to my mother to decipher letters.

Tramps were seen daily, traipsing up to the workhouse. They had a casual ward where they could stay overnight. I believe they had some chore to perform in the morning before they left. They were harmless enough. Sometimes they asked for their billycans to be filled with hot water.'

'In 1939 the town had a visit from Oswald Mosley's Blackshirts. They started to harangue the crowd in the Market Square, but I am glad to say that the good people of Aylesbury would have none of them. They were heckled and booed. Mr Parminter, a local butcher, clad in his striped apron and boater, really discomfited them, and they soon left never to return!

In 1940 Aylesbury received its only bombs, probably ditched on the way back from bombing the Midlands. A stick of bombs fell on Walton Road near the pond. It demolished several cottages and the old Grange. One man was killed and damage was extensive. All the shop windows in the High Street were shattered, and a lot of houses lost windows too, but my home in King Edward Avenue stayed intact although the heavy velvet curtains blew out at right angles to the french windows. Another bomb fell in Bicester Road where it blew all the leaves off the hedges, but thankfully no one was hurt. Another small bomb landed between King Edward Avenue and Limes Avenue but it fortunately missed the houses and made a large hole in a field.

During the Second World War I was a Red Cross nurse at Stoke Mandeville Hospital. It was then half servicemen and the other half overflow from the Middlesex Hospital. Many of the patients were long stay geriatrics, very sick children and plastic surgery cases. There were regular bus loads of casualties from the bombing of London. The servicemen were sometimes flown from North Africa with gunshot wounds covered with plaster. We spent a lot of time carefully removing the plaster to dress the wounds, sometimes setting the bones. We also had a ward of amputees, several of whom were prisoners of war. The Italians were treated in a friendly manner by the others, but the Germans were "sent to Coventry". Opposite the hospital were fields – Churchill Avenue didn't exist.'

## HADDENHAM

'My father was a butcher and our shop was on Church End Green, Haddenham. We called the green the hub of Haddenham. Milking cows were driven across it, and horses and carts, and we were near the old station which was much used. Corn and hay merchants used to collect their goods from the station, as it was cheaper than Princes Risborough. Haddenham was a very self-contained village and didn't alter much until the last war. Even if you wanted a suit you could be measured in The Beehive (the village general stores and post office) and the order could be sent off. There were many little farms (closes) where there would be one field and one cow. It was a long while before there was a regular milk delivery, you just went where there was milk to spare.

We raised some meat ourselves, or bought the animals from Thame market. This was reckoned to have better quality beasts than Aylesbury. There was no cattle transport in the 1920s so they had to be brought back by the drover. It was a great sight for the children if a herd was driven past the school. There was no drover at Aylesbury market, you had to use unemployed labour and they expected to be given a meal of cold meat, bread and beer on arrival. After all, they did have the long walk back. The killing went on in the yard and seemed nothing out of the way to us.

We were very popular when a pig was killed – the children wanted the bladder for a football. Children walked to Haddenham school from Aston Sandford and Scotsgrove in their old boots. One of my lasting memories is the smell of wet coats hung along the guard rail round the school stove on wet days. The children only brought bread and dripping for lunch, and had nothing to drink all day.

In church the big farmers sat in the front pews. Everybody had their particular place. The vicar did a lot for the village and his daughter took books and sewing round for the villagers to do in Scotsgrove. The Victorian age lingered on in Haddenham.

A lot of men from Haddenham went to fight in the First World War and some families found it hard afterwards to make ends meet on a widow's pension. The children had to work on smallholdings to help. Even a captain's pension was not very much. Soldiers returning from the war used to come back on the milk/paper train early in the morning. The bigger farms had contracts to send their milk in churns up to London, and the men waited to get lifts out to the particular farms. Only farm work was available when they got back and not much of that. A few emigrated.

The green was used for the schoolchildren to play on. My father used to buy horses at Thame Horse Fair in October and train them on a leading rein on the green. I remember the old poor widows going "a-Thomassing" on 4th December every year, going round the bigger houses begging for old clothes and food.

We had a little voluntary fire brigade based in the old cottage in Banks Park. Once they went to a fire in a pair of cottages and pumped water down the wrong chimney onto the old couple beneath and into the cauldron cooking their food, washing ash everywhere.'

THE NEWTON LONGVILLE FIRE ENGINE

'I was born in Newton Longville in 1921 and vividly recall seeing the village fire engine in action when I was about five years old.

It was an unusual thing for a village to have and the inhabitants were justly proud of it. "Bessie", as it was called, was not modern by any means and as I remember was an oblong box with a funnel on top. This was then placed on two wheels. A large handle was attached to each side of it to pump the water, the hosepipe being fitted into the funnel. The inside of the box must have been a tank of some sort to hold the water which was pumped out by working the handles up and down.

On the day I saw Bessie, a thatched cottage in London End had a very bad chimney fire. This was very serious as there were several thatched houses nearby.

The village shopkeeper got the fire engine out and with the help of neighbours trundled it to the fire – he had also sent some schoolboys to the local brickyard for some men to come and help; my father was among them.

The fire was soon put out and the thatch made safe by giving it a good soaking. Bessie was then taken back to her home, a tin hut in the garden of a house opposite the church for which the parish paid one shilling a year rent. The hut was painted red with "Newton Longville Fire Engine" in white letters on the front. It was kept there until the war, when I believe it was sent for scrap. Although newcomers to the village say a film company bought it, I can remember my father, who was the Parish Clerk, writing an "Obituary to Bessie" in the Parish Book – which he could not have done if she had still been alive!'

## STOKE POGES

'The village was truly rural in the mid 1930s. There was no public telephone apart from one inside the post office. When it was shut one could in an emergency ask for help from the landlord of The Dog and Pot public house. Very few ordinary folk were "subscribers", as they were called in those days.

However, all the tradespeople were most obliging. The butcher called every morning for orders and delivered. The dairyman called at 7 am, 10 am and midday, and the post and papers arrived punctually at 7 am. There were two village bakers and one also came up from Slough. There were three grocers and a newsagent, tobacconist and sweetshop. The fishmonger from Gerrards Cross called, as did a greengrocer who lived in the village but had no shop.

Villagers thought nothing of walking to Slough (three miles) or Uxbridge (seven miles) pushing their perambulators to do the shopping. The bus service was better than it is now – more frequent and it ran later in the evenings. At weekends there was a very late bus from Windsor which made a detour to Slough station to pick up late theatregoers and "night out on the town" travellers. Of course, very few folk had their own car in those days.

As to education, there was only the one school in School Lane and children spent their whole school life there. Some youngsters won scholarships and went to Slough Grammar School for boys or Slough High for girls. Others went to Slough Technical School or Wycombe Technical, and some to Sir William Borlase School at Marlow. There was no school transport.

The village hall was built around 1912 by public subscription and was always much used and valued. Where the car park is now situated there used to be a roomy hut used by Scouts and Guides. A barber cycled up from Slough on Saturday mornings to hold a very busy session here for the men and lads of the village.

In 1935 Stoke Court was in use as a residential country club and during the Second World War was the home of many celebrities. We were lucky and suffered very little from enemy action – the worst happening was the arrival in the small hours one morning of a V2 rocket on the common which left a big crater and broken windows all over the area. Sefton Park was taken over by the military. It was occupied at one time by the 51st Highland Division and the skirl of the bagpipes could be heard continuously it seemed. Later the American GIs came to take up residence in the Nissen huts dotted around the park. All these soldiers made themselves very much at home here.

In the 1940s the village had a very successful and popular Dramatic Society which was led by Mr Marsden and school headmaster Mr Harman. Television was in its infancy so the live productions of the Eden Phillpotts and Noel Coward plays attracted large and enthusiastic audiences. As to television, my family was the only household to have one, as far as I know, and I have great memories of having a living room full of people to watch such events as the wedding of Princess Elizabeth and Prince Philip in 1947 and the 1948 Olympics from the White City.'

CHESHAM

'There used to be an old town crier in Chesham and his main job seems to have been to warn people when the water would be turned off – a frequent occurrence. He would cry "Oy, Oy, the water will be turned off from 'arf past two to 'arf past four." It always seemed to be 'arf past.

The Regent Street lights were made in Chesham and there was always an air of excitement when they left on the backs of lorries for London. Lucky children, as an annual treat, were taken to London, dressed in their best, to see them illuminated.

On my daily walk to school we would see the horse-drawn timber haulage carts off to the woods to collect the trees felled by the woodmen, to be followed on our return from school by the sight of the carts fully laden. They would halt at the top of the hill and fit what I thought were very strange metal blocks to the back wheels, but this, of course, was the brake system. Trees are still felled but how the transport has changed.

The Town Hall was once the Friday and Saturday meeting point of so many people. The market was held outside and late on Saturday all fruits and vegetables left were sold off very cheaply or given away. As the Second World War started, the scene gradually changed. The market traders were called up into the services, their wares became in short supply, and the children's favourite stall was unable to continue. This was run by the "Pennyanorse Lady" (penny a horse) – that was the cry used to attract the children, but in fact everything she sold cost a penny.

The Town Hall itself became a much used building. The ground floor was the communications centre for the ARP where the air raid alerts were received and the all clear sirens were sounded. In the upper part of the building a floor was covered with a complete map of the Chesham district, used by the incident officer to control the movements of Fire Rescue, Ambulance and the Gas Officer. Fortunately, this service was only used for a few minor incidents. At the end of the war the Town Hall stood empty and was for a time taken over as a factory where silk braids and tassels were made.

Chesham High Street was at one time laid with a special surface of wooden blocks, intended to lessen the noise of the traffic. Sadly, one very heavy downpour unseated the wooden blocks and it was quite a sight to see the High Street floating away.

Between the wars there were many woodenware factories and mills in Chesham. Some were quite small, the owner working with two or three men, while others had a much larger workforce. All these buildings had one thing in common, though – they frequently caught fire!

These fires were a great source of entertainment to the whole town. The word would go round that "Beechwoods is on fire" or "Wrights is on fire" and everybody would make their way to the scene. Most of the buildings were open sided so there was never any danger to life, but being built of wood they burned well so we could all enjoy a spectacle. I can remember one particularly large fire at Beechwoods when I was unfortunately in bed with measles. Because of this my mother had to stay with me while most of the rest of the family went to the fire and she was quite put out at missing the excitement.

A friend recalls one time when the fire siren went at about 11.45 on a Saturday morning, and she was at work due to finish at 12 noon. This posed a problem. Should they all leave early to go to the fire, or wait until the end of the morning's work when their week's wages were due to be paid? This time the fire came second. They waited to be paid and then rushed into town to see the end of the fire.

Much later, I think in the early 1950s, Canada Works, another woodenware factory, caught fire. We all turned out and were enjoying ourselves as usual when word went round that the factory

23

cat was missing. This sobered us up, but within a few minutes a fireman appeared at the front of the building holding up the cat! A rousing cheer went up and we all went back to enjoying ourselves.

On the morning of what was possibly the last of the factory fires, the milkman remarked to the wife of the owner, "That was a good fire last night. Haven't had such a good show since the Blitz." She was not amused.'


## A NEW LIFE IN STONY STRATFORD 1950

'My first sight of Wolverton was from the train I arrived on one spring morning in 1950. I can even remember what I was wearing – my New Look petrel blue costume with straight skirt almost to my ankles and jacket with padded shoulders, white blouse and white straw flower-trimmed hat (borrowed from my sister).

My husband, Ted, could not meet me. He was working at Lampitts as a television engineer and I had strict instructions to make my way there. "Go out of the station, turn right and keep walking till you see Lampitts radio and television shop on your left".

Nobody had warned me that the wall surrounding Wolverton works looks like a prison so that it had the well-deserved nickname "Sing-Sing". It was a daunting prospect but I was young and the sun was shining.

Ted had been working as a television engineer for about six months, only coming home occasionally to Walton-on-Naze where I was living with our two children, Michael aged five and Jennifer aged two. He was becoming more and more miserable without his family but now he had been given a licence to build a house in Stony Stratford (this was a necessary formality in 1950 and a licence was not easy to come by).

He had been lucky enough to be granted one and he had found a suitable plot of land, one coveted by many, being the last undeveloped area of the houses built by Mr John Cowley, Senior, in Calverton Road in the 1930s.

Raw materials to build with were in desperately short supply but with the licence we would be able to secure them, and Mr Cowley had some window frames – bay windows of seasoned wood that we could use. The land was to cost £300 and the house would be built for £1,535. The council were willing to give a mortgage at 2½% rate of interest and we had enough money for the purchase of the land.

This was my first chance to see the proposed site and to have a tour of Stony Stratford. If anything was needed to persuade me to move it was the sight of the Ancell Sports Ground in full swing on

Saturday afternoon – tennis, cricket and bowls – white flannels on green grass.

On that first visit it seemed that all our troubles were over and we should soon have a house of our own to begin a new exciting life. But things do not always turn out as planned. We had hoped to have the house finished in six months but delay came upon delay.

To tide us over, Ted's boss, Mr Gunstone, kindly offered us the use of a flat above Lampitts shop in the High Street, Stony Stratford (next door to Green's the pork butcher's). It would be a peppercorn rent – I think we paid six shillings a week for the rooms and there were plenty of them though in a very dilapidated state. The High Street in Stony Stratford was then part of the great A5 road stretching from London to Holyhead.

I was staggered by the volume of traffic which passed through the High Street of Stony Stratford. It never stopped. Even through the night the wheels kept rolling. Our first night nobody slept, the second night we slept better and the third night we were taking no notice and sleeping like tops.

The road seemed to divide Stony into two separate towns. You thought twice before you crossed it. Children who lived on the Wolverton side of the A5 rarely palled up with those on the opposite side. There was a demarcation line almost as great as the Danelaw.

More annoying than the noise of the traffic was the dust and dirt that it brought into the shops and houses which lined the street. You daren't open your windows. Your net curtains in no time at all were black even with closed windows.

For us it was especially difficult to keep clean. We had no bathroom and no running hot water. In fact we had little of anything – the minimum of furniture, just beds and an old trestle table with stools. Cooking arrangements were primitive and sanitary arrangements too. There was a flush toilet in the garden but the 'S' bend was continually becoming blocked. So much for the rules of hygiene! The children flourished and were happy.

Shopkeepers in Stony Stratford were most polite and the shops, after the shortages of wartime on the East Coast, seemed wonderfully well stocked. Everything in Stony seemed to go in pairs. There were two bazaars – Peacocks which mostly went in for cheap oriental blouses and children's clothes, and the bottom bazaar, run by Mr and Mrs Hall, which specialised in children's toys.

There were two ironmongers, Odells and Chipperfields. In Chipperfields two young men, Mr Dennis and Mr Douglas Chipperfield, were most helpful, and in Odells, wonder of wonders, there was not just one smiling face but two – the Odell twin brothers, Lionel and Ron, looking rather like Tweedledum and Tweedledee.

There were two old-fashioned drapers, Meadows at the top of the town and Wickins at the bottom. Anyone who has never seen that marvel of Victorian science, the overhead rail for cash payments, has just never lived! In Wickins shop you were given a bill for the amount of sale, you paid your money, then this would be put into a little container with the bill wrapped round it. This would be sent spinning across the ceiling wire to the cashier who sat in what looked like a little sentry box. She would dispense change with your receipt and send the cylinder reeling back again. I believe a bell rang. It was all very mysterious and exciting.

Then there was a wonderful thing called discount! Syd Wickins would always knock off the odd shilling from your bill and if you wanted to try something "on appro" that was fine. If you wanted something put by for you that was alright too. In the carpet department I noticed a very attractive carpet with an autumn leaf pattern. I asked Mr Graggins, the manager, if this could be saved for me. He kept it for me for over a year for no extra charge.

There were two ladies outfitters – Mrs Brooks and Mrs Clewitts. Side by side they traded amicably next door to the post office.

There were two shoe shops – Allens and Griffiths. A wonderful part of Allens was the shoe mending department. It stretched at the side of the shop down New Street. There seemed to be quite a line of men working on shoes and they would all smile and nod as you passed, rather like those nodding dogs in cars today!

There were two bakers in the High Street, Benbows next to the Public Hall and Haseldines where it is today, but there were two other bakers – Mr Faithful in the Wolverton Road and Mr Cowley on the Market Square. He delivered bread from a horse-drawn cart, and kept his horse in a field by the recreation ground.

There were two clubs – the Working Men's Club and the Conservative Club. Strangely enough, in those days there seemed nothing incongruous in belonging to both of them.

There were even two tennis clubs – the Town club with courts where Cofferidge Close is today, and the Ancell Sports Club which did not allow playing on a Sunday.

There were two excellent cafes for travellers – Lennies the transport cafe served wonderful breakfasts and there was always a meal available at Barnes cafe (except on Sundays).

Then there were the more classy restaurants – the Cross Keys, where Samuel Pepys once dined, and The George where everyone who was anyone would go for morning coffee to be served with iced sponge slices by dear Mrs Beck while Mr Beck hovered in the background wearing his chef's apron.

On a Sunday there were two sets of boarding school children

to be seen out for walks in crocodiles. There were the pupils of York House and then the less socially advantaged, but just as well behaved, children from Fegans Home.

There were several butchers, Canvins and Baxters, Mr Pugh and Mr Higgs. My son says he can remember pigs being killed at the back of Canvins' shop and I can remember Mrs Green turning the handle of the sausage machine as she made the sausages in the back of the shop next door to us.

There were some five grocers – a Greens, an International, a Burtons and there were two fine private grocers – Hall & White and Dudeney & Johnston. There was a W.H. Smith book shop. There were barbers and antiques shops, a gentlemen's outfitter, three radio and television shops, sweet shops – what a wonderful selection of sweets in Donnies! Tobacconists, hairdressers, an undertaker, even a blacksmith's run by Rupe Roberts in Church Street. The children used to love to watch the horses being shod.

The one thing I do not remember is an estate agent. How times have changed!

However, if there were only two of most things there were far more than two pubs! I was told there were once over 30 in the town, but I can only recall the following – The Angel, The White Swan, The White Horse, The Bull, The Cock, The Crown, The Red Lion, The Rising Sun, The Case is Altered, The Foresters, The Plough and The Barley Mow – oh, and The Duke of Edinburgh.'

WENDOVER

'I was brought up in Wendover, firstly in Chiltern Road and later at Sturrick House, a 15th century village house on the Manor Waste, a grassy area in Aylesbury Road planted with beautiful lime trees. At one time the house was a coaching house, later to become the New Inn and then the Tempest Hotel.

My mother was a silversmith with a business in London to which she travelled every day by train. Many a time the stationmaster, Mr Ray, would hold up the train when he saw my mother pounding hurriedly down Station Approach; she'd have missed the train otherwise. After the war her business failed so Sturrick House reverted to its old role as a guest house and did very well. One day an Irishman came offering to do odd jobs and my mother gave him some outside work to do. When he'd completed the work she paid him and then gave him a good, hot dinner which, she told him, he deserved for work well done. As he left the house he said to my mother, "For your kindness, ma'am, you will always prosper and never be in want." The guest house did prosper and we were never in want: I used to wonder if that Irishman had magical powers to see into the future!

Of course there was no central heating in those days at Sturrick House and the bedrooms were very cold in the winter. Each bedroom was furnished with a large floral wash-basin and jug on a stand. Many a time in winter the water in those jugs would be frozen in the morning.

Opposite us lived Mrs Clarke, the church organist, who was a great one for "good works". I was often pressed into service to take beef-tea or broth to a sick parishioner. She would tap on her window as one passed by and woe betide you if you tried to sneak past without noticing. Next door to her was Hill's sweet shop; they had their own pew in church! Manor Farm House, with its yard and buildings, came next. Next door to us was Chiltern House which is very old. It had once been a school for young gentlemen but, in my day, the author Ladbroke Black lived there. On our other side was Archway Cottage where Mrs Philby, a talented local artist, lived. She taught me to paint, sitting on the grass verges to paint the thatched cottages around us.

Mr Grimsdale was a wonderful old character. He used to drive his cart up to Halton each day to collect the swill from the RAF camp. He not only collected the swill but also several village children who would cadge a lift on his cart and, throughout the journey, he led them in hymn singing. One could always hear "Old Grimsdale" coming through the village of Wendover.

I met my husband when he was nine years old. He was the son of the farmer who lived at Bucksbridge. There were always horses in the stables at Bucksbridge: all the farm work was done with horses and the horses for the fire engine were also stabled there. The fire engine itself was housed in the Aylesbury road and, when the alarm sounded, the firemen would leave off work and get into their uniforms and Edgar and one of the men would harness up and ride the horses at full tilt into the village. On fine days two horses would be sufficient to pull the engine but in bad weather it needed three, the third one leading the other two and this one would have to be ridden, either by Edgar or the workman. One snowy evening, the horses were harnessed up to go to a fire up at Peacock Farm, on Aston Hill, but the road was so slippery that the horses made heavy weather of the climb up the hill. Halfway up they met someone coming down who told them that the fire was already put out!

Everyone went to church in those days; either to Matins or Evensong. If it was Evensong, very often the congregation would repair to The Leather Bottle in Scrubwood afterwards. The inn only sold beer or lemonade so there was never any fear of trouble developing.

The village hall was near the Red Rose bus station and was always called the Sweat Box because, being small, low-ceilinged and made of wood, it always got very hot inside. All the local organisations used it; the WI, the Infant Welfare Association and all the young people's clubs. When there was a dance and 50 or more youngsters got in there dancing, it soon got very hot indeed!

In the middle of the village was Carter's garage and taxi service. I'd be taken by taxi before Harvest Festival to all the big houses to collect the fruit and flowers to decorate the church. I was always given a cup of cocoa wherever I went. The harvest fruit and flowers were given to the hospital after the service.

For ten years I drove a pony and trap; we got the pony shod at Mr Birch's at the top of the High Street. I also bred goats as a young woman and heard that the RAF mascot, an elderly animal called Lewis, was due for retirement. I was able to give the RAF a new, young kid, Lewis II and Lewis I went into retirement.

At the Jubilee of George V and Queen Mary in 1935, we decorated a trap, dressed ourselves up as Victorian young ladies and gentlemen and dressed Edgar's father's cowman as our coachman. We joined in the parade of floats and took the first prize at the end. Afterwards Edgar won a medal at the tug-o-war at the sports in Bryant's Acre, which was our playing field. Another grand sight in the village was the arrival, on Boxing Day, of the hunt from Kimble. They used to meet at The Wellhead public house.'

## LITTLE CHALFONT

'We first saw our plot of land at Little Chalfont in 1952. We came out on a steam train from Hampstead (via Finchley Road of course, not directly) and found the country station very unlike the busy, bustling Underground station we had left behind.

Not very many houses were visible from the station and the friendly porter taking our tickets no doubt took us for another pair of "townies" setting off on a walk through the Chilterns. It felt like that for once off the main road we found ourselves on unmade surfaces consisting largely of many-shaped flints making islands between muddy splodge and sizeable puddles, between wild grass verges. The "road" in which we hoped to build our house was lined with big sycamore trees and once we stepped through their line, we were in tall grasses and spikes of tall rosebay willow herb which actually disguised a fair number of young fruit trees about two or three feet high, planted lower down the plot. The land sloped away from the road and there was a marvellous view if you were tall enough to see through the grass etc, across the valley to Latimer House.

29

When we stepped into the jungle to explore I was as lost to view as in a formal garden maze in some stately home! There were only two or three houses dotted along the way, where there are now 40 or 50 and on the other side of the road was a field of corn behind the odd one or two houses. In our early years this corn caught fire as did the section of Forestry Commission young trees nearby. Through the 1950s houses gradually filled in the open spaces and it became more worthwhile for bakers' vans, grocery vans, milkmen and fish deliverers to call.

The baker was a prisoner of war who never returned to his home, Austrian I think. He worked for the Chesham Co-op and came to us for some years until the Co-op ceased to send out roundsmen. The bread was lovely, just as good as the Gloucestershire Co-op bread that had been delivered to my aunt's village before the war. The fish came from Mr Stow's shop in White Lion Road twice a week and our delivery man was also a foreigner, who came here during the war.

Our road remained a quagmire in wet weather and a dust bowl in dry for 14 years, when enough residents clubbed together to have a very thin tarmac surface on a rough surface put down. Of course, within a year or so, a councillor came along visiting friends and the council suddenly decided to make up the road. We, fortunately, were indemnified against these charges but several householders faced quite a bill and another similar one faced us all some years later when we were "put on the mains".

Our trek to the station if we wished to travel, was quite adventurous. We wore wellington boots most of the year and in the early days left them in the booking office and collected them on our return. In later years when more houses were built between us and the station we left them in a friend's porch near the tarmacadamed part of the road! We had a diagonal path across a field and a very muddy bank short cut up the last bit to the station, if we could climb the wooden fence at the top! Sometimes cows were kept in the field and I remember an early treasurer of our WI telling me how she fell over a cow in the dark on her way home one night and frightened the cow as much as herself.

There were only a few shops in the village then, before the new parade was built on the main road, but we had a couple of really good old fashioned stores, the grocer's and the ironmongery general merchant's shop up near the chemist. Mr Lofts of the ironmongery used to tell me tales of carrying pails of water like a milkmaid in his early days and was the first one to tell me of seeing the circus animals walking up the main road to go to the Chipperfield's winter quarters. The elephants used to lumber up tail to tail from the station; it must have been quite a sight.

When the children were young, in the late 1950s, I used to take pram or pushchair in the "fish" van on the steam train to Chesham. The trains were pretty grubby as I recall but the staff were so friendly and helpful both at Chalfont and Chesham. I remember once my daughter dropped a little book of nursery rhymes down between the train and the platform and was most upset. I remember too, her delight when we came back and the porter gave it back to her, having climbed down as soon as the Chesham Chuffer had pulled out.

On the main road there was a large field opposite Statter's Switchgear factory, where Munn and Chapman's petrol pumps etc are now. Lovely old-fashioned iron railings kept the cows away from the road and out of the back gardens of Loudhams Cottages. It really was quite rural right up to the late 1950s and we sometimes cannot believe how built up it now is.'

## NEW BRADWELL

'As a child of the 1930s, born at New Bradwell, my earliest memories are of a settled life in a new three-bedroomed semi in a railway town. My father, like his father and his four brothers, worked for the LMS. The town, together with Wolverton and Stony Stratford, had developed when the railway works were sited there. The first houses fell into two main categories – the very small terraced cottages and the larger, though still terraced, town houses. There were no bathrooms and most houses had black ranges beside the fire grate and outdoor toilets. Wolverton became dubbed the "fish and chips and piano town" since it was thought that many householders were proud of the status symbol of a piano but had to manage on the cheap meal of fish and chips. Certainly many houses had a "front room" grandly furnished which was rarely used – a showpiece.

My maternal grandfather was a lamplighter and as soon as I could toddle I would try to climb up his ladder behind him. He always had chocolate or sweets for me. The lamps, of course, were gas and there was one near our house.'

## QUAINTON

'I came to live in Quainton in November 1933. In those days few of the houses had running water so there were pumps at strategic points in the village. This created a friendly meeting place as we waited to fill our buckets. Only once in that time were the pumps locked up, and this was in the very hot summer in the early 1930s. All pumps were locked, to be opened by Mr Dennis Cannon in the evening when one was allowed two buckets, or in the case of families with young children rather more.

On the subject of liquid refreshment, the village had seven public houses, always well patronised. The friendly atmosphere, created without television or the few wireless sets, was centred on card games, darts and dominoes, and if one could pick out a tune on the piano all the old favourites were sung with gusto.

The village school nearly always had a full complement of children, a total of approximately 150, many walking in from outlying farms and bringing their food to be eaten in the dinner hour with water from the pump. Some children had to walk three or four miles in all weathers.

The places of worship were the parish church, the Baptist chapel and the Primitive chapel, with very active Sunday schools and good congregations as the Sabbath was more strictly observed. No one had any entertainment in the home unless one was very privileged and owned a piano or organ. In those days the church bells were rung morning and evening on Sundays, with the added delight of the chimes which rang out every four hours day and night with the rhyme which went like this.

"There was an old man who lived over Church Hill
He had the gout and can't get out
I hope it will not him kill"

The village had a post office, five grocery shops and one draper's shop. There was no carrying of heavy groceries as deliveries were made. Also there were visiting shops. The International Stores from Aylesbury came on Mondays for orders which were delivered on Wednesdays. There was a travelling Co-op shop, a butcher's cart, and a wet fish man came round the villages from Aylesbury. It was a general thing for some villagers to go to Aylesbury on Saturday nights when the fishmongers on the market knocked down boxes of kippers etc for a few shillings.

The village had three bakers who supplied lovely fresh crusty bread and on Sundays Mr Dunkley and Mr Banham would cook the Sunday joint for a few pence. Folk took their Sunday joint in a baking tin with the Yorkshire pudding in a jug to be put round the meat and also a tin of dripping to have your potatoes roasted in. On Saturdays one could take cakes to be baked at the bakehouse. A favourite thing was to go to the bakehouse and buy a pound of raw dough for about twopence, take it home and mix in fruit, sugar and an egg to make a dough cake and then take it back to the bakehouse to be baked. A treat at Easter was to have fresh baked hot cross buns.

In the early part of the century a carrier cart used to travel to Aylesbury twice a week and the owner would bring back errands asked for by the villagers, a great luxury being cakes and buns from Pages the baker's in town.

The village policeman lived in the police house and was on the streets in the evenings to see that the peace was kept.

Another well known character who visited the village, walking from Waddesdon every Tuesday, was Mr Owen. He came with his handcart selling cottons, elastic and tape. He also brought paraffin, and would give twopence for a rabbit skin.

The favourite sport for most of the village was football and the local team was well supported. There was great pride if the team got through to the Oving Village Cup. The final was played at Oving on Easter Monday and if the Quainton team were in the final, three quarters of the village attended, the main transport being bicycles. If you didn't have one you walked there across the fields.

Another memory is of Mill Farm, which was farmed by Mr Ralph Anstiss. We had really fresh milk brought round to the cottages, not in bottles but in a milk can and with a lovely froth on your jug when the milk had been swirled around. Lots of cottagers kept pigs which were reared for their own consumption and the custom was for those neighbours who had given potato peelings and vegetable waste as food for the pigs to be rewarded with some fresh pig's liver. If you didn't keep hens it was always possible to buy eggs, rich golden brown ones as most folk kept Rhode Island Reds.

Another great delight was Mrs Culley's hog puddings, brought to the door on Saturday mornings in a basket covered with a spotless white cloth. Hog puddings were either black or white and made in the shape of a figure of eight.

Very few villagers owned a motor vehicle, though some of the younger men would perhaps own a motorbike. There was a taxi owned by Mr A. Dymock of the local garage. In the early days it was possible to hire a brougham from Mr Tom Anstiss who kept The White Lion.

A well known custom when a death occurred in the village was that the church sexton would toll the church bell. The bell would toll three times to begin with if it was a man and twice if it was a woman and would then toll for some time.

There was a pond on the village green and it was a scene typical of a Constable painting to see horses and occasionally cows drinking from it. The pond was surrounded by a wall and railings and a favourite sport of children was to run round the wall. If by chance a child fell in, an old lady who lived in the cottages opposite would fish them out with a clothes prop that she kept handy.'

*Village halls, often paid for by the villages themselves, were much used and much valued. This is the hall at Horn Hill in about 1912.*

'I came to Quainton in 1945 to take over the post office with my husband, a native of the village. We sold groceries, oil stoves, all sorts of things. In those days the mail was brought from Aylesbury for us to sort and deliver. One of our post ladies, Eunice, was a noted village character. She was quite choosy and once when asked to deliver a parcel to an inconvenient address said, "Let him fetch it himself", and he did! A time and motion study made no difference to her leisurely pace and she stopped for tea at all her usual places. Approaching the house she could be heard shouting, "Your dog's out", although the dog was quite harmless. She was a prodigious gardener and as she rode or pushed her bicycle around the village could be heard exclaiming, "I dug 20 pole before breakfast".

There was a prisoner of war camp on farmland on the fringe of the village and the Italians worked on the farms. One brought his wife to England after the war and settled in Quainton, he liked it so much.

The post office then, as now, was the hub of the village and people congregated there for advice and meetings. On one occasion a lady put her shopping basket on the counter and out jumped a mouse, causing pandemonium. Another time a lady rushed in saying a neighbour was about to put her head in the gas oven. We calmed her down, though, by pointing out that, "There isn't any gas in the village!"'

SEER GREEN

'The old village of Seer Green, with its church in the centre and a cluster of old cottages surrounding it and lanes bordered by cherry orchards, has ceased to exist. Where Seer Mead now stands it was possible to pick wild daffodils and orchids and mushrooms abounded all over the fields to Jordans. Manor Road and Manor Crescent also yielded their share of hay, wild flowers and mushrooms and made a country walk to Chalfont St Giles.

There was no mains drainage until the early 1950s and one certainly knew when the "smelly lorry" was about if the wind was in the right direction.

The present post office was only a sweet shop and newsagent, the post office then was along the top, opposite the church, and was kept by Mrs Lofty (Flossie) and her daughter Kit. The shop stocked absolutely everything, from a box of matches to a pair of stockings, from rock hard slab toffee to tea, sugar etc. Not many houses were on the telephone at that time, so all urgent messages came by telegram and Kit would deliver them on her bicycle.

Behind the shop and alongside was Flossie's orchard and one could buy the real black cherries from her. On the other side of the road was the pride and joy of Seer Green – the cherry orchard, a wonderful sight in spring when it was just a mass of white blossom.

There was little street lighting, only a few lamps along the main road. None of the side roads were made up and after heavy rain one needed wellingtons to walk along some of them. In the winter one also wore wellington boots to the station and changed into town shoes before the journey, leaving the boots in the capable hands of Charlie or Bill. The woods around the station were the home of the bicycles of the schoolchildren who, along with other travellers, took the steam locomotives to Wycombe, or on into London.

A day at the seaside or Burnham Beeches on the Sunday school outing was the nearest most children got to a holiday away from the village, unless they belonged to the Guides or Scouts. Then they would go away to camp, transported by bike, horse and cart, coal lorry, ballast lorry, furniture van or builder's van! The morning the campers were leaving, most of the village turned out to cheer them on their way, and again to welcome them back.

The slow, trusting way of life when all doors were left open and children were safe to wander alone in the woods is a thing of the past, as is helping with the haymaking and fruit picking. They were pleasures of yesteryear. But picking sprouts in the fields on cold frosty mornings and endless rows of potatoes by hand, or walking behind the horses ploughing in heavy rain were not. It was nothing years ago for children to be away from school simply because they had no winter shoes, and often these children had bread and jam or suet duff as a main meal. Whilst looking at a lost way of life with nostalgia we must be ever mindful of the terrible hardships many villagers suffered but never complained of, and the long working hours, The good old days were good if one had money, if not one made the best of life with cheerful resilience born of necessity.'

# CHURCH AND CHAPEL

**Sunday was a special day, set aside from the rest of the week for worship, Sunday best clothes and relaxation. Church and chapel were at the heart of community life and it was usual for children to attend Sunday school and for the whole family to go to the services, perhaps two or three times in the day. Children looked forward all year to the Sunday school treat, in the days when holidays away from the village were few and far between.**

## THE CHURCH BELLS

'Sometimes we would be out in the fields around Edlesborough when we heard the passing bell. First there would be a sequence of two or three chimes, which indicated whether it was a man or woman who had died. This was followed by single notes according to age. Everyone would then know that old Mr or Mrs So and So had passed over.

A more cheerful use of the bells that I recall is chiming – I think that is the technical term as opposed to proper ringing – the bells for Sunday school. One of us would use the three lighter bells, one with each hand and the third by means of a foot in the bottom of the bell rope. The other two would take a little while to get the heavier bells going but would then join in. It didn't sound half bad either. We took it in turns to ring the "Ting Tang" on the vicar's bell which immediately preceded the service.'

'At High Wycombe in the 1920s we would hear the tolling of St John's church bell every Sunday morning. This was known as "Bogey's Organ" and was sometimes tolled in the week for a special occasion.'

# SUNDAYS

'After Sunday school a good long walk was the rule. My father was free from his work in the afternoons, and took us for walks around Hyde Heath village. One of my favourites was through Brays Wood, down to Little Missenden and through the village, then back across the railway footbridge to Mantles Wood. Spring flowers grew abundantly in the woods and hedgerows. Bluebells carpeted the ground and primroses flourished in the dells. Violets, including the elusive white variety with its lovely scent, could be found in the hedges of Keepers Lane and Chalk Lane. These flowers were picked to decorate many a kitchen windowsill, but the number taken was small compared to their profusion and no harm was done to the plants.

Sunday cricket is normal in many villages today, but then it was unheard of. Our Sunday afternoons were always fully occupied one way or another. Sometimes my father would play the organ which was fitted into the bay window of our house. My mother had a lovely soprano voice, and sometimes our neighbour would bring his violin, so a pleasant afternoon concert resulted. But to go out and play on a Sunday? Never! One just did not do that. It was not regarded as respectable.'

'When I was a child in the 1930s I was always dressed in my best clothes on a Sunday, as was the practice. In my mother's youth the daughters had a new white dress every year for Whitsun and that was their best dress for Sundays until next year. My grandmother, like many women then, was a good needlewoman and made most of her children's clothes. My mother was not happy that I often dressed my children, in the 1950s, in casual clothes on a Sunday. The Victorian standards survived that long.'

## AT THE CENTRE OF VILLAGE LIFE

'Spiritual needs at Drayton Parslow were catered for by the parish church, the Baptist chapel and the Primitive Methodist chapel, and it was around these that most of the social life of the village revolved, particularly the two chapels.

There was the yearly social with its games, laughter and necessary new dress. In the spring both chapels would have their respective Sunday school Anniversaries. These took place on different Sundays and former scholars would return to the village to take part in the special services and renew old friendships. The Sunday school children, of whom there were a great many, and the choir would sing

37

special songs and anthems which they had spent weeks learning. The next day would be a school holiday and after lunch the children and as many of the choir who were not at work would assemble at the chapel and then set off round the village and farms in the parish to sing their songs. When they returned, footsore and weary and no doubt a little hoarse, the children would be given tea in the schoolroom. This tea was provided by the women, many of whom had also walked miles around the parish singing. The weekend's activities were finished off by a service in the chapel when once more the children and choir would render their songs and anthems.

The money given during these weekends was for use by the Sunday schools and some of it was used to finance the Sunday school outing which took place during the summer holiday. The usual destination was Wicksteed Park where the thrills of the swings and roundabouts vied with the delight of shopping in Woolworths. However, as buses gradually developed more speed they actually got to the coast. To many villagers this was their only visit to the seaside and everybody tried to "smell or see the sea first". The day was filled with sand-filled sandwiches, wasps, ice creams, paddles and sunburn and all too soon back to the coach. The pleasure of singing all the way home was yet to come and the effort of staying awake and joining in was almost beyond the capabilities of some of the younger children.

In the autumn came the Harvest Festivals when, once again, former members of the congregations would return to take part in the festivities. A Harvest Sale was held on the Monday evening when the gifts would be auctioned to provide a much needed boost to chapel funds. These auctions were a great source of entertainment as the auctioneers resorted to all sorts of stratagems to bump up the price for each item.

It was in the winter, after Christmas, that one of the highlights of the year occurred – The Methodists' "Gold and Silver Tree". This was a money raising event and people were given a small envelope and asked to put into it a coin and a verse. These were then hung on an old Christmas tree and a local personality was asked to strip the tree and read the verses. Initially these were of a religious and moral nature, but soon humorous homespun verses crept in and eventually outnumbered the others. No one was spared being lampooned and the more skilful "poets" were in great demand to supply verses for those less gifted. Before the tree was stripped the audience was entertained by the men from Stewkley Primitive Methodist chapel. Sadly, this event passed into history in the 1950s when congregations dwindled and television became the main source of entertainment.

In the 1930s the men from the Methodist chapel formed a concert party which was augmented by others from the village. The ages of these performers ranged from twelve to 70. They rendered choruses, solos and recitations, mostly of a religious nature. The main attraction on the programme was the performance by the "orchestra". This was a unique ensemble comprising two violins, two tin whistles, two auto-harps, a saw, an ocarina, two harmonicas and a set of drums. Because it was a novelty it was very popular with both players and audiences, despite the fact that though the instruments were fixed in the key of 'G', unfortunately they were not of the same pitch. The music coming from this strange mixture was such that the choirmaster, a professional musician, declined to be associated with them, saying, "They managed very well on their own." Their fame soon spread beyond the parish boundaries and they were in great demand to give concerts in neighbouring villages. These concerts could not have been very well rehearsed as often the programme was decided upon in the hired coach on the way to the venue.

All organisations were short of money and one year in an effort to boost funds the Methodist men decided to give "A Sausage Supper with Entertainment" – price one shilling. This was to take place in the Carrington Hall, which had no facilities for cooking. The whole affair needed considerable organisation and all went well until the problem of transporting the cooked sausages from the bakehouse at the other end of the village needed to be resolved. One suggestion was that the village hearse could be used. This was a handsome contraption, a smaller version of the horse-drawn and motorised hearses. It was a glass coffin-shaped box decorated with gold and with a gallery round it to accommodate the floral tributes. The whole affair was mounted on four rubber-tyred wheels and was propelled by a "T" bar pushed by four men. Like supermarket trolleys each wheel had a mind of its own and it took a lot of skill and muscle to operate it. Many people thought it would be sacrilege to use it and finally the baker's cart was used instead.'

SUNDAY SCHOOL

'Sunday clothes on, hands and faces scrubbed to a shine, shoes polished, hair combed and tied in a big bow of ribbon that flopped on the side of my head, handkerchief and a penny for collection in my pocket, and I was ready.

The years 1934–1944; the day a Sunday, any Sunday; the time 10 am; the venue Holy Cross Church, Slapton; the event Sunday school. In one hand I clutched a little bag, made by Granny from a scrap of cretonne, just the right size to hold a stamp book.

Sunday school was a big thing to me and the other 20 or so children who attended. If you went, you got a religious stamp with a gummed back that you licked and stuck in the right place in your stamp book. Every six weeks or so, if all your spaces had been filled, you got a large stamp that filled a whole page and for half a book you were rewarded with a decorated text to hang on your bedroom wall. "Thou God Seest Me" or "Repent, for the Kingdom of Heaven is at Hand" they warned. But maybe you were lucky and got "God Is Love" or "Cleanliness is Next to Godliness". If you completed the book and had proof of attendance for a whole year, you went to the Sunday school Christmas party at Bury Farm, the home of Miss Griffin, our Sunday school teacher. Yes! That stamp book was important and certainly warranted its own bag.

At special times of the church's year – Lent, Easter, Advent and Christmas – we had lantern shows in the church given by the rector, Rev Johnson or Rev Brain. In church, at night, in the dark, the flickering magic lantern and its slides transported us to other worlds – the Holy Land, shepherds, deserts, angels, the Garden of Gethsemane, the Sea of Galilee, Golgotha and the Crucifixion, all on a white sheet fixed above the chancel steps. It was pure magic to children who seldom went further than the river Ousel at one end of the village and the canal at the other.

Sunday school was an opening to another life. A life of books, treats, outings, pictures, stories, hymns and carols. I certainly sang "There's a home for little children above the bright blue sky" with great fervour. After all, I *knew* there was. I'd seen it at the magic lantern show!'

'We had glorious Sunday school treats at High Wycombe in the early years of the century. All the coal merchants' lorries were scrubbed out, beautifully cleaned and forms installed and the children rode in them (open to all the elements). They went through the town, with the Sunday school teachers walking in front of the lorries, following a brass band, down to the Rye where we had races. There was throwing of pounds of sweets and it was great fun scrabbling in the grass for them. This was followed by sticky buns and bottles of fizzy lemonade with the pretty marble floating in the necks of the bottles to stem the flow. Rides were available in an open top waggonette drawn by two horses – the Mums in large hats, long skirts and tight silk blouses. When an incline was reached everyone dismounted and walked up the hill, boarding the waggonette again at the top, cheering and laughing at the wonder of the ride.'

'Although I was educated at a church school I was sent to the Methodist Sunday school in Lane End and we had some lovely times. The Sunday school Anniversary was one of the highlights of the year. Parents worked hard to get the girls decked out in new dresses, straw bonnets, white shoes and socks, while the boys had new suits and shirts and shoes. This was the only time we ever had new clothes and had to keep them for Sundays only. On the day, the chapel would be packed full for the three services which were held and people came from far and near to listen to the children's singing and reciting. Because of the war our "treat" took place as a sports day in Beesins meadow in Marlow Road, or if it was wet in the Scout hut. If you won a race you would receive ninepence, the second had sixpence and third threepence. The day always finished with a scramble for sweets. Prizegiving day was in the new year, when tea would be served and any child making 96 attendances out of 102 would receive a book. It was amazing how many did make it.'

'A favourite summer Sunday school outing from Bledlow was to West Wycombe hill where one could hire sledges to skim down the grassy slope. Before the Second World War we used to hold a Whit Monday fete in Reg White's field alongside the railway line, with races for the children, tea in the barn and swingboats. It was great fun to be up in a boat when a train went by and you could wave to the engine driver. After the war we were able to take the children by motor coach to Weymouth or Littlehampton for a great treat, a day by the sea.'

'The Baptist chapel at Speen had a youth club and as we got older our entertainment centred round here with bike rides at Bank Holidays and picnics and, of course, the two highlights of the year – the coach trip to the seaside and the Sunday school Anniversary. For this we all learned recitations and sang especially prepared pieces, with the grown ups singing elaborate anthems to the accompaniment of the cello, violins and various other instruments. A special platform was erected and the chapel was full all day for all three services, people often coming for the day with a picnic.'

'Every Sunday we chapel children at Wycombe Marsh went to Sunday school in the morning and again in the afternoon. There was always a Christmas party for us in the schoolroom and in the summer we always went for a half day outing to Burnham Beeches. Children from the church Sunday school usually went off for a trip in a charabanc but we travelled in open lorries. The very small children had tub chairs to sit on in one lorry, which had to be carried out from the schoolroom. The rest of us just clambered aboard the lorries and either knelt or sat on the floor. We sang all the way there and back, waving to people as we passed by. At the Beeches there were numerous people selling knick-knacks and sweets. We played with our friends among the trees and when we had spent all our pocket money we made our way down to the tea houses. These were like long barns, open to the wind on most sides but with a good roof to keep the rain out. There were long rows of trestle tables and benches to sit on. Here we were given drinks, sandwiches and cakes. When the next sitting arrived we moved on to some nearby fields where we had races, played team games and scrambled in the grass for sweets which were thrown amongst us.

For the Sunday school Anniversary, we girls had new home-made dresses and little straw hats. We always chose the material from a stall in Wycombe market. It was here that I learned that a yard is the distance from the tip of a man's finger on an outstretched arm to the tip of his nose. Nobody used a tape measure. The material usually cost two shillings eleven and three farthings. For the Anniversary we had to learn new choruses to sing and a little poem to recite. We were presented with our prizes for the Scripture exam which we had taken in the spring.'

## REPAIRING THE CHURCH CLOCK

'At the west end of Penn church there is a tablet which states: "The clock in this tower, after 15 years silence, was repaired and set going, Easter 1925 through the unaided efforts of Patricia C. Cuthbert aged 13 years". Unfortunately, the English Language can be rather ambiguous. I did not, in fact, climb the tower with a bag of tools as many visitors think.

I thought it was a pity that the historic, one-handed clock did not work, so decided to do something. I went to the old blind basketmaker in the village and when he had taught me to make baskets, I spent all my spare time working with him in his workshop, making all sorts of baskets and selling them. In this way I raised all the money needed – £35 for the repairs and then £5 for painting the face of the clock. This was quite a lot of money in 1925 and involved making some 200 baskets.

Many people got to hear of my efforts and I received support and orders from strangers and friends, including making a wastepaper basket for Princess Louise, the Duchess of Argyle.

It was a great undertaking but wonderfully satisfying when I heard the clock strike for the first time, and the PCC erected the tablet in recognition.'

42

# GETTING ABOUT

At the beginning of the century, if you wanted to get about you either walked or used horse power, and for most people there was little choice – you walked! Bicycles brought a cheap and easy means of travel which enabled people to work further afield, and the first buses and cars began to appear on the roads. There were always the trains too, of course, and it really did feel like 'our' railway in those days of small branch lines and familiar station staff.

## BY HORSE POWER

'Before the First World War a number of men in Beachampton worked for the railway in Wolverton Works and as there was no transport four men acquired a horse and cart and gave a lift to the others. The fares helped to pay for the horse's keep and the four took turns to feed and care for the horse. At six o'clock in the morning the horse and cart went slowly through the village and passengers jumped on as it went along. Those who did not catch up by the top of the hill out of the village had to walk the five miles to work.'

'I was born in 1918 in Taplow not far from the Thames, and within a few yards of Brunel's famous railway bridge, locally known as "The Sounding Arch" because of the echo beneath it. My father was a fighter pilot in the First World War and one day, to impress his parents, he flew his plane (very small and manoeuvrable in those days) skimming along the river and right under the main span of the bridge.

How calm and peaceful my childhood was. There was hardly any traffic along the main road, that stretch of the ancient Roman highway between Slough and Maidenhead Bridge. I can even remember hopping along with a skipping rope in the centre of the road and passing in all safety under the railway arch in the vicinity of the small Taplow station. My mother told me of the many mornings when my father rode to the station in a horse-drawn hansom cab along the stretch of side road running from the Bath Road parallel to the railway: as often as not, being late, he would be waving frantically whilst still finishing the last of his breakfast, signalling to the stationmaster to hold the train for him. And this he would invariably do, he being an old friend of my father's!

I distinctly remember one occasion when I was about two or three riding along the Bath Road with my parents in a hansom cab. Having been leaning against the door, just before reaching Maidenhead Bridge I fell out of the cab into the road. There must have been occasional traffic along this main road, for on picking myself up I had the presence of mind to run to the grass verge before starting to cry . . having, I suppose, been warned of the danger of being run over by a motorcar.'

## OUR FIRST CAR

'Just after the First World War my father bought a car from the little garage in Little Kingshill. It was a pre-war Humber. It had paraffin lamps and had to be cranked up with a handle. I remember being put in the driver's seat and operating the "spark" and "retard" instrument while my father cranked and told me which one to adjust.'

## EMPTY STREETS

'In the first decades of the century, one of my memories of Wolverton is of empty streets. In the Stratford Road you might see the steam tram ("Puffing Billy") on its way to Stony Stratford or perhaps a horse-drawn dray on its way to or from the printing works, but the rest of the town was traffic free except for a few bicycles or an occasional horse and trap bringing fruit and vegetables from a neighbouring village. Consequently it was perfectly safe for three or four year olds to go to the corner shop or even to school unaccompanied, although it might mean crossing a road. A lamplighter came round at dusk to light the gas lamps and even in the winter children would play outside until their fathers came home to tea at 5.30 pm. The men started work at 6 am, came home to breakfast at 8.15 am, dinner at 1 pm and finished at 5.30 pm – a very long day. Many men walked in six or seven miles from the villages around and were at work, summer and winter, by 6 am.

For those who worked on the railway, quarter fares and one free pass a year meant that Wolverton people travelled far more than working class people usually did in those days. Many managed a week at the seaside. Five thousand went by special train to Blackpool and an equal number to North Wales! These were the two favourite areas as they were on the LNWR and so the free pass took you all the way.'

## THE FIRST BUSES

'When the first buses came to Chalfont St Peter, their route could be changed without warning because the driver would go wherever the majority of passengers wished, stopping at their front gates. Later, when fare stages were introduced, an elderly lady was asked for her excess fare and she gave the driver an apple in lieu. The fare to London was two shillings and sixpence.'

'My father started The Lee & District buses in about 1922. These ran on Wednesdays, Fridays and Saturdays from Kings Ash to Chesham, charging fivepence for the journey. The bus ran every Sunday morning too, picking up passengers in the surrounding villages for the 8 am Communion service at The Lee church.

Some time later another company started, but did not last long. Then London Transport ran some journeys, but when my father wanted to increase his operation, London Transport objected, and I went to London on his behalf to fight the case – and won. This was about 1928, and thereafter The Lee & District buses ran ten return journeys on the route. They are still in existence, though with different management.'

'In pre-war Hyde Heath nearly everyone had a bike of some kind. It was a necessity for getting to and from work outside the village. My first bike was a Hercules costing £12, which was a lot of money then. There was a bus service but the buses never seemed to run at a convenient time for workers. Do they ever? Like many others, I cycled to work in Amersham. Bikes took us everywhere at no cost.

At one time there was no bus service to Amersham at all. If you didn't cycle you walked. There was quite a lot of walking done – and not for pleasure, as it is today. I heard of one farm worker, in the haymaking season, setting off in the early hours and tramping crosscountry to reach Stokenchurch by 7 am.

If you owned a car you were a cut above the rest. In 1928, Hyde Heath probably had less than five cars, other than those used by local tradesmen. In the 1930s more people bought cars, which made the roads more hazardous for cyclists, but nothing like they are today.

Friday was market day in Chesham. The 3.45 bus from the Broadway would be chock-a-block with kids and mums and their shopping. Children were often turned off the bus at the bottom of Fullers Hill because of overloading. It would then chug up the hill and wait for us at the top. The driver usually gave us five minutes to catch up. If we dawdled he would go off without us, leaving us to walk the rest of the way home.'

# OUR RAILWAY

'The railway played a large part in the life of Cheddington village. A lot of the men worked as platelayers on the track and the houses near the station were known as the Fog Cottages. The tenants worked on the railway and had to be available on foggy nights to put detonators on the line. There was a bell outside to call them out.

There was a big staff of about 24 on the station itself, with a stationmaster, porters, signalmen and booking clerks, all working shifts. The fare to Aylesbury was sixpence ha'penny return. There was a branch line to Aylesbury then, axed by that fool Beeching in 1953. The train consisted of two coaches and an engine that always went backwards, and the line made an important connection with the main line and was used by people in Bletchley and Leighton Buzzard to get to Stoke and the Royal Bucks hospitals.

Bert and Froggie, Dick and Georgie, were the drivers and guards and they came along every day to see if all the regular passengers were there. If not, they would go very slowly out of the station in case anyone came dashing up and if they did, they either reversed the train or got down and helped them up into the carriage. As the track went through fields the whole way it was not uncommon to get sheep and cows on the line, and we would stop and the driver had to get down and drive them off.'

'I remember cycling from Tingewick to Water Stratford to catch the train to Buckingham. The cost of a ticket was less than the price of a packet of cigarettes, which was little enough in those days. The train services were better then, with a regular half hourly service from Buckingham to Brackley. One steam engine with just one coach used to go from Water Stratford to Banbury to take people to watch the wrestling at the Winter Gardens. Water Stratford station was built on sleepers on the hill.'

'In the 1920s it was still usual to see horse-drawn carts and vehicles on the streets of Newport Pagnell. Bread, coal and milk were all brought to our doors by these hard working and intelligent creatures; indeed, they were renowned for knowing when to stop at a particular spot, especially if it was outside one of the many pubs in the town.

After a few years cars were increasingly seen on the roads, though not so many that we couldn't sit on a stile by the roadside and take down car numbers. One vehicle no longer on the roads was the charabanc, with a hood that could be let down.

Then there were the trains, and our own dear "Nobby Newport".

This train ran to Wolverton, with two stops in between. It was packed morning and late afternoon with children going to the Wolverton Grammar and the Technical College, and workmen in their hundreds going to the Wolverton railway works. At one of the stations in between the engine had to take in water and we schoolchildren always hoped it would be on the way to school. This train waited for the London train and trains from the North, so we were sometimes late home.

, During the war the trains with their different drivers always waited for any trains due in so you could be sure of getting your connection and arriving home sometime that night or early morning. This reminds me of travelling during the war, returning from leave, when the trains were all blacked out and carrying masses of service people and one had to rely on the helpfulness of fellow travellers to alight at the right station.'

'When the bell rang warning of a train approaching at Marston Gate in the 1940s, whoever was on duty closed the gates, went up into the signalbox to set the signal, came down to the platform to take the tickets, flagged the train on its way, went back to the signalbox to re-set the signal, and came down again to open the gates. Only then could the traffic go.'

'From Wendover it used to take an hour and 20 minutes to get to London by train and my daily fare in the late 1940s was three shillings and sevenpence. If you caught a Marylebone train it was steam all the way but if you caught a Baker Street train it was only steam to Rickmansworth and then the engine was changed because the line was electrified from there. Surprisingly this did not take very long and everyone accepted it without complaint.

With steam engines you sat with your back to the engine if possible, because in summer when the windows were open the smoke stack would blow smuts over your clothes and hair and you could end up looking like a panda if you wore glasses as I did. During the winter of 1947/48 it was extremely cold and the trains were not heated. In the mornings the train froze to the lines, causing us to be late, and the passengers huddled together to keep warm. The carriages were always crowded, with four or five people standing. The Underground was crowded too, with everyone pushing and shoving just as they do today – to get out at Oxford Circus you just had to force your way out.'

# HOUSE & HOME

# THE WAY WE LIVED THEN

**There may have been overcrowding and a general lack of comfort
and amenities, but on the whole we remember the houses we lived
in with some affection. Perhaps it was that we could go out without
locking the door behind us, knowing there was no need to worry.
Times change though, and moving into a new council house with
'mod cons' became the dream of many, while who remembers living
in digs as the only alternative to living at home?**

## TWO UP, TWO DOWN

'I was born in a two up, two down cottage in Farnham Common
in November 1913, being the second eldest of four girls. My mother
also brought up a cousin who was the son of her sister who lived in
London and was in service. My father was invalided out of the army
having been gassed in the First World War.

None of the other families in the row of ten cottages were any
better off than our family and in the cottages there were a total of
32 children (two of the cottages having only one child each!).

At the weekends we would be sent out with our old home-made
truck to collect wood for the fires and for the copper fire for
Monday's washing. Mother took in washing for other people to earn
a little extra. We would also have to collect acorns for Amos Luker's
pigs and leaves for their bedding, for which we got a small amount
of pocket money.

The lady in the cottage at the end of the row had a proper
"laundry" attached to her kitchen and all the water for the
cottages had to be collected in buckets from the well across the
road. The name of the cottage was, appropriately, "Dipping Well".
On Mondays lunch was always bubble and squeak (cold potatoes
and cabbage mashed together and fried) and cold meat and pickles.
The Sunday roast was usually cooked in the local baker's oven for a
small fee together with all the other Sunday joints in the village.'

'In 1943 I came to live, as a boy, with my great grandmother, Granny
Dew, at Wooburn Green. She lived in a small cottage on the green,
in a row to the right of Windsor Hill. She was deaf as a post, and
with an ear trumpet which one had to get close and shout into. She
was quite cantankerous and I recall frequent arguments.

The cottage was two up, two down. The front door on the green side was reached through a small front garden. The door led directly into the front room and from there another door led into the kitchen, which was stone floored. A sink had a water pump adjacent. Water was pumped into a bucket and was so chalky it had to be left to stand for some while, then the clear water drawn·from the top. In the kitchen a narrow, curved and steep staircase took one upstairs to the bedrooms. There was no electricity or gas and lighting was by candles or oil lamps.

The kitchen led to a paved yard, shared by the four cottages in the row. Access could be gained through a small archway between the pairs of cottages, two each side.

Coming from London, the most horrific memory I have is of the lavatories for the cottages. At the end of what I remember as small gardens were the little sheds – a plank across the end, a hole in the plank (the seat) and a bucket under the hole. This bucket was emptied by a neighbour, through the back of the shed, I believe.'

## WE NEVER LOCKED THE DOOR

'I married and moved from London to Frieth in 1948. Just after the war houses were in short supply, so for the first seven years of our married life we lived in my mother in law's house. I had my own kitchen with a new electric cooker but my mother in law still cooked on a kitchen range and did her laundry in a copper heated by a fire lit beneath it. The constant source of heat this old kitchener supplied came in very handy when we had one of the frequent power cuts, and when our first child arrived and Granny put up a clothes line across the kitchen ceiling to air the nappies.

We had a large garden and kept pigs, chickens and bees. All were a great help as there were still some food shortages. What a sad morning it was when we came down to find the fox had visited us in the night and beheaded ten chickens. Then there was the day the pig sticker came to kill our pig – the way Grandma dealt with our side of pork, the head and entrails was an education for a London girl like me. The head was made into pots of brawn to be shared among friends and relations, the pigs fry was cooked for tasty meals and the side of pork was laid down, salted and cured. Have you ever tasted home cured bacon? Believe me, today's shop variety is a poor substitute.

In those days neighbours and relations were always dropping in for a chat and everyone except the rector and the doctor used the back door. Everybody in the village knew everybody else and stopped to pass the time of day when walking up Frieth Hill. We never bothered to lock the back door when we went out, there was no need.

Gone for ever are the velvety black, moonless nights when the stars shone bright and clear. What a joy it was too, to open the bedroom window on a summer evening, smell the warm dampness of the earth and enjoy the deep stillness. Now the silence is broken by the distant rumble of traffic and yellow from the glow of the sodium lamps on the M40.'

## LIFE ON THE FARM

'Our farmhouse at Marsh Gibbon was jerry-built Victorian, stone with a slated roof which let in the driving snow, and was cold, damp and inconvenient. Electricity didn't come to the village until 1939 and then we could only afford to have it put in downstairs. Until then lighting was by oil lamps, usually only in one room at a time, and we struggled with our homework by the light of the Aladdin lamp standing in the middle of the dining room table. As the room had three doors, all of them badly fitting, the draughts often caused the lamp to flare up and burn the mantle. It then had to be turned right down until the mantle burned clean again, and we sat in semi-darkness. Dad loved his wireless and we competed against the news and music hall and all the comedy programmes, trying to think what to write.

Things were not so bad in the summer, when we could use the kitchen, but the fire was allowed to go out after the midday meal was cooked, to save coal, and only the living room was heated. There was no heating upstairs of any sort, and we went to bed by candlelight. There was a bathroom, but all hot water had to be carried up in buckets from the farm copper across the courtyard – bathnight was quite an undertaking for my mother who was usually on transport. Sanitation was in a shed in the corner of the courtyard, and was a two-seater bucket job, one hole for adults and one smaller and lower for children. We used the usual chamber pots under the bed. Dad buried the contents of the buckets in holes dug in the garden, just like everyone else, and the garden grew lovely vegetables.'

'My mother would never forget the autumn of 1936, the year my family moved from the village community of East Claydon with all its activities, to a county council smallholding at Thornborough – a farmhouse and buildings with about 60 acres. Mother missed her kind neighbours in the village we had left, but most of all she missed her electric iron and had to find the old flat irons again to use. She also had to buy oil lamps and candles. It proved an improvement in the working arrangements for my father because he had the fields close to home now; before the move he rented a few acres two miles away from home where he had built shelter for store, stock and a cowhouse. The new farm stood two miles from a village, half a mile from the nearest neighbour, and a few hundred yards off the road. For three weeks that same autumn, thick fog blanketed every sight and sound.

I was eight and a half years old at the time, and walked the two miles to the village school. My elder brother and sister attended schools for older children, where I also went when I got older, catching the school bus or cycling there. There was a lot of work for all that first year and as children we didn't have time to miss the playmates we left behind. The animals took our time now, feeding the fowl, collecting the eggs and learning new skills of milking the gentle cows and teaching the calves to drink from a bucket when they were taken away from their mothers.

The overgrown hedges were cut and laid over the years to make them stockproof and to provide fuel for the house. One of the hardest jobs was stone-picking on the ploughing. These were picked up by the bucketful, carted home by the cartload, and used to fill up the ruts in the field roadway. This job also proved one of the most rewarding, as the roadway could once more be used by the tradespeople. No longer would the coal be left at the roadside, no longer would Mother have to wait there in the cold to catch the butcher on his rounds to buy the weekend joint, and for the grocer and others who had risked the axles wearing out being bumped and jolted across the field it was a comfortable ride after that to deliver the goods.

The farmhouse formed one side of the farmyard, and was bounded on two more sides with the farm buildings. The stable was joined to the farmhouse, with an extra bedroom in the stable loft with access through a door off the main bedroom of the house. The occupant was woken up by the horses arriving for their breakfast down below. The stable, a large barn and low pigsties were on the north side. The third side consisted of the cowshed and open cart shed. The fourth side of the yard had gates leading to three fields. A duck pond was situated in one corner where ducks and pigs enjoyed hot sunny days. The toilet was an outside lavatory up the garden path – tacked on to the stable wall. We got used to walking to and fro in the dark winter nights without torchlight during the war to save the batteries which were in short supply.

Much of the water on the farm was supplied by a pump and well, and near it, in a corner of the house and stable, was the corrugated lean-to cooling shed where the milk was strained and poured into churns, one from evening milking (by hand in those days) and one from the early morning. These were taken to the road gate in the milk float to wait collection by the lorry. The milk float was a small cart with pneumatic tyres and a moveable bench seat and was used for all light work on the farm – carting forage to sheep and young stock in the fields, taking animals to market and bringing the shopping home. The main means of transport was the bicycle. We used them for visits and attending meetings of Guides, youth clubs and village "hops". Most of the necessities were delivered to the farm, including coal, groceries and meat. The postman left the mail in a box fixed to the road gate post. Loaves of bread were left in the box as well until the horse found a way to lift the lid and have a nibble of bread – then it had to be fastened down securely!

In the kitchen were strong nails in the walls to support sides of home cured bacon and hams, covered with muslin to keep the flies away. Slices were cut off these and popped into the frying pan for breakfast along with fresh eggs and mushrooms too when in season, all cooked in home-made lard. Two pigs were killed for home use during the year and nearly every part of the animal was made use of. Joints of pork and helpings of offal were given to neighbours who, in return, would give some to us when they had a pig "down". The sides of bacon and hams were cured in a "lead" – a large shallow container in the pantry.'

VISITING CARDS

'We lived for over 50 years in a pre-Elizabethan cottage in Horsenden, a hamlet based on the manor house, manor farm, a few farm cottages and a tiny church. Our cottage had at one time been the rectory although it showed evidence of having been two cottages, with twin staircases winding round an enormous core of two chimneys out of proportion to the size of the rooms.

It was a romantic setting with water drawn from the well, though I was none too pleased when my husband invited guests to have a bath. Once a frog startled me when I was putting the butter in a china dish to cool on a ledge in the well. It must still be at the bottom. It was not so romantic once the first baby was born and the burden of laundering all those towelling and gauze nappies tried even the resources of the well. We could afford a live-in cook cum parlourmaid cum nanny who slept in the tiny guest room, barely big enough for a bed.

I boasted of receiving over 200 visiting cards, the custom being to call on the new couple leaving three cards and staying only 15 minutes. The call was politely returned. After this appraisal, if no friendship emerged, no offence was felt and in fact there was a certain measure of relief. Loneliness was a problem for a while as I found nobody on my wavelength.

Living in a hamlet unchanged since feudal times caused difficulties socially. Meeting the domestic staff during walks along the only lane from the manor house one would hear, willy nilly, gossip from the house. One had to remain deaf to the gossip, only to have it repeated at a higher level in the evening, and do a "volte face" about the trials with the staff.

The daughter at the "big house" was presented at the last Presentation Court in England. Later, she received us in her presentation gown made by her devoted nanny, with Prince of Wales feathers in her hair. The local dance band, led by George Jacobs, the Princes Risborough garage owner, played till morning. Horsenden was aglow with lights among the trees. Unforgettable.'

## THROUGH THE WAR

'I lived with my in-laws in a terraced cottage at Wingrave during the war. It had no running water, only a pump, and we collected rainwater in tanks and butts. Toilets were buckets situated up the garden in sheds with a wooden seating arrangement. We used rainwater for bathing, which we did in front of the fire, and we re-used the water for laundry and saved a pailful for cleaning the floor, so not a drop was wasted.

I had three children while living there. Evenings were spent making the children's clothing. I had an old treadle machine, which was useful, and I knitted socks, jumpers and cardigans. I used to go to jumble sales and get items I could unpick and remake into garments; this helped out with the clothing coupons. The scraps we made into aprons, peg bags, iron holders and rugs, hooked or pegged.

We managed with paraffin lamps and candles for lighting – I wonder now how I could see to work. No television or radio, either. My first oven was made out of a biscuit tin. We placed this on top of an oil stove and the lid was the oven door, with holes punched in one side of it.

Eventually, in 1955, I was given a council house. To have running water, cold *and* hot, plus a bathroom, electric copper and electric lighting, not to mention a flush toilet – sheer heaven!'

## LIVING IN DIGS

'Before I could start my first job on leaving university, at the Forest

Products Research Laboratory at Princes Risborough, I had to find accommodation. The only option for me in the 1950s was to find "digs".

My first home was in a very old black and white thatched cottage in Bell Street. I had my own bedroom and I was expected to make my own bed but a weekly cleaning lady used to clean and dust the room. Some foods were still rationed but my landlady, a maiden lady, was a superb cook and prepared delicious meals with vegetables she had grown in her garden.

We shared the dining room with a large floor-standing loom at which she wove lengths of tweed for sale to supplement the income from her paying guests.

I lived as a member of her family and I remember having Sunday afternoon tea with her and her friends around a large open fire piled high with logs and a black kettle boiling away to top up the pot. We had to sit close to the fire to keep warm as the draughts in the old cottage were chilling.

Then I moved to a bed-sitter in a modern house. My landlady, another excellent cook, brought my meals to my room. I even had breakfast in bed! She cleaned the room whilst I was at work and lit the fire before I returned, but I did my own laundry at the weekends. For all this luxury I paid £3 a week – and that included electricity and coal.

After two years I had the chance to live in some rooms in Bledlow in an old house which had originally been The Queen public house. I had to shop for my own food but that was quite easy as I phoned the grocer with the order and the box of groceries was delivered on a Thursday. On a Saturday morning the butcher delivered meat. For other shopping I could cycle in the lunch hour or after work to a cluster of shops near the laboratory in Summerleys and Station Roads – a chemist, ironmonger, stationer, grocer, butcher, shoe shop and newspaper stall – now all gone.

The water for washing and bathing was heated by a solid fuel boiler in the kitchen and it had to be stoked twice a day by removing the dead ashes at the base with a poker and pushing them through the bars underneath, to be topped up with anthracite from the hod by the grate. This procedure always produced clouds of dust which settled everywhere and had to be wiped up. Alas, the fire often went out and my elderly landlady and I struggled to relight it with paper, wood chopped by her gardener and anthracite – a dirty job! As there was no central heating we heated the rooms with coal fires. I had to light mine when I got home but never remember the house feeling too cold as it had very thick walls.

My own daughters and their contemporaries can, and do, opt to share flats and houses, cooking and eating communally. They take on the full responsibility of sharing expenses, rents and mortgages. What a contrast in lifestyle from one generation to the next!'

# LIGHT, WATER AND WASHDAY

**It was the lack of amenities that made simple things as bathnight so time consuming and such hard work. Electricity came to many places only after the Second World War, sometimes a considerable time after, and piped water was equally rare. Perhaps the hardest chore of all was washday, which did indeed take a day, sometimes two with the ironing as well. Were they really the good old days?**

## NO ELECTRICITY IN THOSE DAYS

'We came to Little Kingshill when I was four in 1918. There was no electricity in those days and we cooked on an old fashioned range in the kitchen. The ashes had to be raked out every morning but the food was delicious. There was no thermometer and my mother would open the oven door and quickly put her hand in to feel the heat. She could tell the right moment to put the food in. We had to heat the irons on top, one in use and one getting hot, and we had to be sure to clean the iron well before use. There was a built-in copper in the corner of the scullery which had to be filled with water and a fire lighted underneath on washing day.

Lamps and candles gave light and open fires heated the rooms, with oil stoves for the bedrooms. Then electricity was connected and made life so much easier. Though we still had real fires, and a wonderful built-in stove replaced the old range – it used coal and was called a Triplex and it heated the water, cooked the food and was also an open fire, much the most economical and pleasant looking stove with tiled ovens and hearth. It lasted until the house was finally vacated and pulled down in 1971.'

'In 1908 my father had a house built in Knotty Green, Penn. He had electric wiring installed anticipating the arrival of mains current. Until this connection was available, the electricity was "delivered"

*A promotion for Omo washing powder at Bonner's General Store, Stoke Hammond, in 1961. New detergents were beginning to ease the burden of washday.*

once a week by horse and waggon from Uxbridge (eight miles away) in the form of rechargeable batteries placed in a brick construction – rather like a large cold frame – in the yard. These were similar to present day batteries but there were several all connected together.'

'Only a few houses in Bledlow had electricity even in the 1930s, and Mother's first job of the day used to be to trim and refill the ceiling-hung oil lamps. Eventually electricity was connected to our house so that we had four lights.'

'Our living room was lit by an oil lamp placed on the table in the centre of the room. It was quite a large room and the light from the lamp was really quite inadequate. Later we progressed to an Aladdin oil lamp which had a delicate mantle over the wick and gave out a much clearer, brighter light. Candles were taken upstairs for use in the bedrooms. "Blow the candle out as soon as you get into bed, and *don't* read in bed!" was our parents' cry.'

# DRAWING THE WATER

'I was born into a farming family in 1920, high up in the Chilterns. My earliest recollection of those days was getting water from a well nearly 100 ft deep. There were two 16 gallon buckets, one up and one down. To operate it one turned a wheel sited on a platform nearby. The water was delicious, clear, sparkling and very cold even on the hottest day.

Friday night was bath night, in a tin bath in front of the fire in winter. We used soft soap to wash our hair and Euthymol toothpaste to clean our teeth.

Many of the cottages in the village of Great Hampden had only rainwater which was collected from the roof into an underground tank. The housewife was quite adept at drawing water in a pail using either a pole or a rope to let the bucket down into the tank. Quite often the pail was lost in the tank and a neighbour with a pole with a hook on would help to retrieve it.

During hot weather a bar was placed across the opening of the tank and a bucket on a rope attached to it. Meat and butter were placed in the bucket and it was hung down in the tank, which was always cool. We had no fridges in those days.'

'In 1920 we moved to a small house in Penn village. There were candles and lamps for light but no mains water supply. A boy came in every day on his way from school and pumped rainwater from a well in the backyard to a tank in the roof. He then took two large jugs to a fresh water spring about five minutes walk away in a private park and returned with our supply of drinking water for the next 24 hours.'

'Askett was a wonderful place to be brought up in before the Second World War, even though I lived in an old cottage two up and two down with no sanitation and no piped water. Our toilet was a shed in the garden and was just a wooden seat with a bucket. Later we had an Elsan, the contents of which had to be buried in the garden about once a week. Father grew wonderful flowers and vegetables so it obviously did the ground a great deal of good. Our drinking water was drawn from a well which we shared with the families in the cottages next to ours. The well was very deep and we used to clip the pail on to the end of a long pole and drop it down into the well and scoop up the water. If there had been a lot of rain it wasn't always necessary to use the pole, it could just be scooped out by kneeling at the well head. Thinking back, it is a wonder no one ever fell in.

We had a tin bath which we used to stand in front of the kitchen fire and fill with water which came from our two rainwater butts. This water we heated in a large boiler. One night my mother got the rainwater in after dark, popped the lid on the boiler and when it was piping hot went to pour it into the bath, only to find we'd boiled up a frog and the poor thing had boiled white. We just couldn't face a bath that night.'

'Our water at Bledlow was drawn from a well that served five cottages. Some households had a bucket on a rope, ours was on a pole. When a bucket fell in there would be a shout, "Fetch the snitchers". This was a four-clawed device on a rope which would hook up the bucket.'

'When we moved to Quainton in 1940 we had no mains water laid on to our bungalow at first. After a day or so, a boy of about ten years old came to us and said, "Can I be your water boy?" When we asked him what he meant, he said, "I will fetch you a bucket of water in the morning and another in the afternoon from the standpipe down the road, and that will be sixpence a week." We gave him the job, and I think paid him a shilling and he was delighted. We had a tank of rainwater outside with a tap to our kitchen sink, so always had a supply of lovely soft rainwater for washing etc.'

INTO THE PIT

'The lavatory at our cottage at Buckland Common in the 1920s was about 60 ft up the garden, and was of the wooden seat and bucket variety, which had to be emptied into the "Guzzle Hole" – a big hole dug in the garden into which all the waste matter was placed. Toilet paper was squares of newspaper with a hole in the corner, threaded with a piece of string and hung on a nail. Keeping the candle alight and running up the garden on a cold, windy or rainy evening was not very easy, especially when you were terrified of the dark.'

'My father employed an elderly man in the village at West Wycombe to empty our lavatory bucket into a pit on the common. This, of course, would have been done during the hours of darkness. He once fell over with the filled bucket and never did this job again. Who could blame him!

My grandmother steadfastly refused to buy toilet paper, considering it a sinful waste of money to, as she put it, "buy paper to wipe your bottom on". Squares were cut from her weekly magazine, *The Sunday Companion*, and were threaded at the corner with string. This paper she considered to have the appropriate qualities of strength and (comparative) softness. We were never short of reading matter in *our* lavatory.

Many villagers used the contents of the lavatory bucket to enrich their gardens. It was considered particularly good to put in the celery trenches, and the finest celery was produced. I have never liked celery.'

'In 1955, when we were first married, we were moved by my husband's firm from Hampshire to Buckinghamshire. Being young and impoverished, our first home was a delightful thatched cottage in the village of Ford near Aylesbury which we rented for ten shillings a week. This cottage had no mod cons apart from electricity. Water had to be drawn from a standpipe in the front garden of the cottage two doors away. Washday was a nightmare, made even more difficult when this pipe was frozen. Sanitation was in the form of a bucket in a wooden shed at the end of the garden, the only means of ventilation and light being a knot hole in the wood, about waist high. Once a week this bucket was emptied by men wearing huge cover-up overalls who came in a special lorry. We never enquired from whence they came but only assumed that it was an admirable service laid on by the council.

In 1956 we moved to another rented cottage in Meadle. This one cost us £1 per week. Here, as before, the plumbing was somewhat primitive. We did have cold running water in the kitchen but the bathroom taps were fed by a tank in the loft into which the rainwater from the roof had been collected. Not only did it smell most unpleasant, but there were no means by which the water could be heated and the tank in the loft tended to overflow during heavy rain, so we had to keep the one and only bath tap on during a thunderstorm. Sanitation was an Elsan in a cubicle outside the back door. There was no light in this cubicle and the only ventilator, bucket high, faced due north. No one ever took their library book into this toilet! There were no nice men from the council to empty this bucket and we had to dispose of the contents by burying them in the garden, which, fortunately, was very large. Frosted ground presented huge problems and on many an occasion I had to do this during broad daylight because the ground would be too hard by the time my husband got home. I used to hope that no one would look through the hedge or that the local hunt would not use the public footpath which ran through our garden. Although this cottage was very isolated and petrol was unobtainable owing to the Suez Crisis, shopping presented few problems as the grocer, baker, butcher and fishmonger called twice a week. I still have a copy of my grocery list

61

and this came to 19 shillings and sixpence. For other shopping we had to walk over a mile to a bus stop or walk the whole three and a half miles each way to the shops.

Oh, the joy when we purchased our first home, a little terraced cottage in Aylesbury, which had a brand new bathroom with hot running water and the ultimate in flush toilets.'

## WASHDAY

'No washing machines, spindriers, tumble driers, electric irons etc in those days! Not even detergents. Washday was a twelve hour job and really hard work.

It had to be Monday and Mother was up early, lighting the copper fire. The washing was done by scrubbing brush and a washboard and with yellow soap. Then followed a session in the dolly-tub before all but the woollens and coloureds were put in the copper to boil. After starching the cottons, everything had to be mangled before hanging out in the garden if fine, or on a clothes horse round the fire on wet days.

Dinner was easy to prepare – only the vegetables to cook, as there was cold meat left from the Sunday joint. Then came a fruit pie (cooked the previous day). Enough fruit was bottled during the summer to last all year.

When all the clothes were almost dry, they were again mangled. The kitchen floor and table were scrubbed and then the ironing finished, if possible before bedtime. Irons had to be heated at the fire, frills and lace goffered and then everything thoroughly aired before putting away.

A real hard day's work.'

'I lived with my grandmother for a while in the 1920s when my parents moved from Aylesbury to Buckland. She taught me how to do the washing. This was done by using a coal copper, a dolly tub, a rubbing board, a posher and a tool called Peggy Legs. The latter looked like a milking stool with a long handle which one turned around and around in the dolly tub. The next step was to rub the washing on the rubbing board. Whites were boiled in the copper, then taken out and put into "Reckitts Blue" bag water and finally put through a large wooden roller mangle. The whites always looked as white as driven snow. The ironing was done using flat irons that were heated on the oil stove.'

'I was born in a newly built house in Edlesborough in 1929. The kitchen was a large concrete floored room with a big black copper in one corner.

On Mondays, washday, Father would light the copper before he went to work. This was done by laying a fire in the space beneath the copper, which held the water. He also filled the copper with buckets of water – we had taps but the water had to be pumped up from the well to a tank in the roof first. The water took some time to heat through.

Then the "washing lady" would arrive. She just came in on the Monday to help, and had been one of the village strawplaiters. Collars and cuffs were soaped with White Windsor in the sink, then the hot water was transferred by bucket to our "washing machine". This was a vast wooden square object with a large round wooden cage inside. The clothes were put in the latter, it was fastened up and the cover put over the whole machine. Then by means of a lever at the side the cage was rotated in the hot water.

One end of the machine sported a large mangle so sheets could be put straight from the drum through it into a basket.

If it was a fine day then the washing was dried outside, otherwise it meant housing as much as possible on the wooden rails which could be lowered from the ceiling. At least there was a tap to empty the machine, and the suds were used to scrub the kitchen floor.'

'Being the youngest of five children, they all said I was spoilt, but I didn't think so on washday, as it was my job to keep the fire going under the copper, and make the starch.

It was alright when it was Robin starch but not so good when it was Reckitt's as that was all nobbly and a job to mix. Just making the starch wasn't the end. The little blue bag was stirred into it for just a minute and I can remember sometimes I left it in a little too long and made it too blue, and my mother wasn't too pleased.'

'In our bungalow at Wycombe Marsh in the 1920s all the cooking was done on a blackleaded kitchen range. Next to the range was a built-in copper for heating bath water and boiling clothes. A large white enamelled cast iron bath was by the wall and hot water had to be ladled into it. Bath night was once a week and we children all used the same water. When the bath was not in use it was covered with a large wooden lid with a small trapdoor. All dirty clothes were popped through it. These were handwashed in the kitchen sink or put to soak in a large galvanised bath which was kept hanging in the shed. Once washed and rinsed the clothes were put through a heavy wooden mangle and then hung out to dry. As our family grew in size the copper, bath and mangle were moved out into a purpose-built shed. The shed had a sloping concrete floor so we had great fun splashing each other. The heat from the copper kept the shed very warm in winter.

Our near neighbour was the proud owner of a washing machine. She could sit and read a book while moving a handle in the lid, back and forth. This moved a paddle which swished the clothes backwards and forwards in the soapsuds. A small rubber wringer was attached to the machine so that, when she had finished her chapter, she could put the clothes through it and they would drop into a bath of rinsing water.

All the heating in the house was from open fires or portable oil stoves. These needed careful handling or they often left a sooty deposit and a dreadful smell in the room. Several irons were kept in the oven so it didn't take long to get them hot on the fire. To test whether or not the iron was hot enough to use, you spat on the base. If the spittle bounced off, the iron was hot. If it just sizzled then you put the iron back on the fire. As one iron cooled off there was another heating up.'

# PIGS AND CHERRY TREES

**Keeping a pig at the bottom of the garden was common in the country before the Second World War, ensuring a supply of bacon and pork for the family. Food tended to be plain and simple fare, but no less appetising for that – though perhaps rook pie and lambs tails would not be to everyone's taste. A mouthwatering cherry pie certainly would, and what a tragedy that we have lost this great traditional fare.**

## MOST PEOPLE HAD A PIG

'Most people in the 1930s had a few fowls and perhaps a pig. Ours were at the top of the garden of our house in Tingewick, quite a large chicken run and two pigsties about 60 ft away from the house. When a pig was killed, Grandfather salted quite a lot of the meat. He had converted his old stable into a salting room. The remainder of the meat was smoked, bacon for breakfast being cut from the smoked joints which hung in the large pantry. My maternal grandfather was a gardener and one of his hobbies was beekeeping, producing quite a lot of honey which kept the family well supplied.'

'All the houses in Speen had large vegetable gardens and rabbits and chickens were kept in most of them. Most families also kept a pig in the garden for their own use. When a pig was killed, quite a lot of the children congregated to watch. First the poor pig was killed, then bled and finally put on a pole and hung over the fire and turned to burn off all the bristles. It was then put upright, still on the pole, and was scraped to take off the burned bristles that were left. A lucky child was given the pig's bladder, which was blown up to use as a football.'

'Money was always tight. Living on a farm at Marsh Gibbon in the 1920s we had enough plain food to eat, but only the cracked or misshapen eggs – the good ones were to sell. Our only vegetables were from the garden, with occasional tinned or dried peas. Breakfast was either a boiled egg or cold home-cured bacon, with sometimes porridge in the winter or cornflakes in the summer. Dad sometimes brought a bag of little oranges home from market, and sometimes a stick of celery. We had lots of apples, plums and pears from the orchard trees, and jam was made from the blackberries. After the age of eleven school dinners were a nasty shock, and I was often hungry in the afternoon, though I usually ate whatever was put in front of me – if not you went without.

Pig killing day meant a lot of hard work for everyone but resulted in an abundance of luscious food for several days. I once begged to stay home from school to watch but the squeals of the poor pig, and the sight of the blood from its slit throat being caught in a big jug to be made into hog-puddings, was too much and ever afterwards I kept my distance. The pig was hung until quite cold and firm, then cut into sides and hams by the butcher who killed it. These were cured by the salt brine method, in big lead troughs, and had to be turned over and anointed every day. Woe betide the female who touched the bacon while she was menstruating – there was a firm belief that this sent the meat bad! True or false, it was a good excuse for passing the job over to someone else for a few days. Hog-puddings were made from the thoroughly cleaned and turned small intestines, the large intestine became chitterlings and the fresh liver fried with chunks of fat was mouthwatering. Much of this had to be given away – no fridges and freezers, but you *hoped* that friends and relatives would be equally generous when they killed their pigs.'

65

# ROOK PIE AND NURSE'S PUDDING

'At the farm at Great Hampden there was bacon hanging every-where, wrapped in muslin. Every cottage kept two pigs, one to keep for themselves and one to sell. Every part of the pig was used and the mainstay of the farm workers' meals was the bacon badger. This was a suet crust rolled into an oblong, covered with bacon, potato and onion, rolled up like a roly-poly pudding in a cloth and cooked in boiling water for several hours.

One of my favourite meals was lambs tail pudding or pie, when the tails were cut off in the spring. They were skinned and jointed. Nothing was wasted. We had rook pie in May as this was the time when the young rooks were shot. Only the breasts were used.'

'I was born in 1927 at Bellingdon Farm, three miles north of Chesham. It was a large farmhouse which we shared with my father's parents. In our back kitchen, where we spent most time, was an open fire over which kettles and pots were hung where my mother cooked. Bacon dumplings, steak and kidney pudding and fruit puddings were regulars along with rabbit stew and boiled fowl (an elderly chicken). We had fresh vegetables from the garden, and apples, pears, plums and cherries from the orchard. Blackberries grew along the hedgerows and some meadows had mushrooms in their season. We did not sell milk, but always had one or two cows to rear calves and provide us with milk. I remember my grandfather coming to our door after he had been milking, telling me to fetch my cup (chipped orange enamel) into which he poured some milk straight from the cow.

In another room there was a range fuelled by coal which had an oven where my mother baked. We had roast joints, various pies and milk puddings. Some years a pig would be killed and the sides of bacon would be put into large shallow troughs and salted. I liked the fresh liver and fresh pork, some of which would be made into pork pies in the shape of large pasties, but I did not like the brawn which my mother also made. The fat of the pig would be boiled down, strained into a bucket and became lard which seemed to keep for a long time, in spite of no refrigeration.'

'Home between the wars was a cosy flint cottage in Chapel Lane, Bledlow where my brothers and I lived with my mother. Father died a few years after, and as a result of, the Great War. The District Nurse who visited him gave Mother a recipe we have always called Nurse's Pudding and it was a great favourite of mine. A layer of chopped apple and sugar was put in the bottom of a deep pie dish and topped with a mixture of 6oz self raising flour, 3oz suet, more chopped apple and sugar. Milk was stirred in to make a stiff batter and it was baked in the oven (no egg, that would have been an extravagance).

Potatoes in a muslin bag tied with tape were always cooked in with the cabbage to save a saucepan. There was usually plenty of tape about the house, never string, bought from Tommy Heybourn who regularly pushed his handcart, stocked with haberdashery, round the village.

We had plenty of apples, as relations in the village had large orchards, and we made dandelion wine in the summer and blackberry wine in the autumn. I used to walk over the fields to Ilmer to pick blackberries which I remember selling, I think for the dyeing industry, and with the pocket money earned would go to Thame Fair in September on the train. My mother would go into Thame on Tuesdays, market day, and bring back fish and lardy cake.'

'On Sunday in 1940 at Thornborough, the roast went to the bakery for cooking. There would be a roast joint, roast potatoes and a Yorkshire pudding, as well as an apple pie and the weekly fruit cake – all cooked by the baker. Sunday tea would be sandwiches and sometimes a fruit salad or jelly, and the fruit cake from the bakehouse. The rest of the week I managed with two double burner Beatrice stoves (paraffin) and an open fire with a very small oven at the side, which was really rather useless. We had stews, chops, beef puddings and Buckinghamshire Clanger, which was a suet pudding filled with bacon and onions (some people called them bacon badgers).'


HELPING THE COUNTRYWOMAN

'There was not much money around in the 1920s and for many women in country areas, the WI provided the only means of entertainment and instruction. The Institutes aimed to bring useful ideas to the countrywoman – in our case at Lane End mostly farmers' wives and the wives of men who worked in the local furniture factories. The yearly programme provided talks on cooking, preserving, sewing and other useful tips for the home. I remember watching demonstrations on cake, bread and pastry making as well as bottling fruit, jam, pickle and wine making. Later there was canning and the members were able to hire from the County Office a canning machine. For sewing we were shown how to make our own clothes and to convert adult clothes into children's garments. Rummage sales were popular as the villagers were not very well off.'

## WHATEVER HAPPENED TO THE CHERRY TREES?

'In 1932, when I was eight years old, my maternal grandfather died and we moved house to live with my grandmother in Hazlemere. My grandfather had been an active member of the village chapel, and after his death the family carried on with his interests. My brother, sisters and I attended the Sunday school with our friends. It was the highlight of the week, to wear, and be seen in, our Sunday best. We often joined the adults for the evening service as well. There were bible classes, fetes, harvest suppers and numerous activities planned to entertain and bring the village community together . . . but to me the most memorable was the annual Cherry Pie Supper.

The locality boasted the best cherry orchards in the county, and at least one tree grew in every back yard. Our garden was large and rambling and the cherry tree was situated by the garage, with a swing tied to one of its branches.

It was the sweet little black cherries, known as "Little Blacks", which were used to fill the pies, and as they ripened the date was fixed for the supper. The whole village was a hive of activity as posters advertising the date were posted in the village shop and on the noticeboard by the chapel door. Long ladders were placed against the old gnarled branches of the trees and the cherries carefully picked so as not to bruise the delicate skins. Stalks were taken off and the fruit washed.

Meanwhile, the ladies were busy looking for their pastry recipes, as everyone had their favourite. Now, for the ideal cherry pie the pastry must be firm enough not to break when filled with the cherries, but short enough to melt in the mouth when eaten. My grandmother's recipe called for a proportion of a quarter fat to plain flour, mixed with warm water to make a pliable dough. The pastry should not crack or have breaks which would let the juices out. My grandmother always used lard as the fat – she kept at least one pig, which was eventually slaughtered and the fat rendered down to make the lard.

A saucer was used to guide the shape of the pies, which resembled Cornish pasties, and as many cherries piled in as possible with sugar and a spoonful of water to make the juice. The edges were pinched together and pleated with the finger and thumb to give the traditional look. Cherry stones were always left in as the children would space them round the plate to play "He loves me, he loves me not".

We waited impatiently for the day. During the afternoon the Sunday school room was transformed. Rows of chairs were placed facing the small stage, and at the other end of the room long trestle tables were covered with clean white cloths. As opening time drew near, a crowd gathered outside, mostly children hoping to get the best seats.

The evening started with a concert organised by the choir master. The Minister was MC and heartily welcomed everyone. The choir sang lustily, brave members sang solos, and children who had spent hours learning new pieces, hesitantly recited small poems and extracts from the Bible. Sometimes the ladies would put on a play, and despite the forgotten lines and all the odd things that go wrong with such a production, the audience, unaccustomed to the sophistication of modern entertainment, applauded enthusiastically.

It all ended far too soon, and the moment came that everyone had worked for . . . refreshments with cherry pies, tea and lemonade for the children.

There were mountains of cherry pies, and the large plates normally used to hold the Sunday roast were piled high. The pies quickly disappeared as teeth sank into the luscious, warm pastry and wonderful cherries. The juice dripped everywhere, though we always tried to bite off a corner so that we could collect the juice before it ran away. To a child the evening was magical.

We ate pies at home too, of course. Bearing in mind the short cherry season and the abundance of fruit, my grandmother would make about four dozen pies for the family to eat over a weekend. One could usually eat three pies at a time!

Recently as I was driving along Watchet Lane towards Sawpit Hill, I looked to my left at the road junction and saw the estate of box-like houses and thought to myself, so that's what happened to the cherry trees.'

'The road between Hazlemere and Penn was lined with cherry orchards in the late 1940s, and in the springtime we would take a bus ride just to sit on the top deck and marvel at the sea of white and pink blossom on either side. The distinctive cherry pickers' ladders, broad at the base and tapering to only a few inches at the top, yards and yards long, were lying ready to be used. Sadly, there were accidents to pickers and I understand that insurance premiums, together with the high labour cost, meant that our local cherry crops could not compete in price with cheaper products and no more cherries ("Naps" mostly) were picked. The ladders rotted in the orchards and now the road to Hazlemere is lined with housing estates.

Lacey Green, about eight miles away, had a pub called The Pink and Lily, and at cherrytime "Cherry Pie Sunday" was celebrated when one could buy individual pies with one's pint.'

'Before the war, children at Beacons Bottom school were often kept at home to help with seasonal tasks at harvest, haymaking and cherry picking time. There were several orchards in the area. Most of the cherries were beautiful big White Harts, but the little sweet black ones Mum made into cherry turnovers were best. Children set out the stones around the plate and said this rhyme: "Who would you marry? Tinker, tailor, soldier, sailor, rich man, poor man, beggar man, thief. This year, next year, sometime, never. How would you get there? Coach, carriage, wheelbarrow, dung cart. What would you wear? Silk, satin, muslin, rags."'

## PLUMS AT CHEDDINGTON

'Plums and apples grew at Cheddington in great profusion before the war, the majority of the orchards being prunes and damsons, Victorias, greengages, Ponds Seedlings and Black Diamond varieties.

The prunes which my mother said were used for dyes in the First World War are a plum shaped like a Victoria but not as large, with a blue stone. They were not ripe until September and they would hang on the trees until all the leaves were gone. They made good jam and wine but were not a plum you could eat raw unless very ripe. Most people had a tree in their garden and the fruit from the orchards was sent to the fruit markets in Spitalfields, Covent Garden and Birmingham.

In my time I have packed a ton of prunes in a day. At fruit picking time all hands to the wheel! The plums were put in round willow baskets (skips) each holding 24 lbs, covered with paper and with a string across – and always with a few leaves at the top to indicate freshness. Every day Tommy Lambourne, who worked for the local coal merchant, would come with his cart and the plums would be sent by LMS to London. Sometimes they fetched a good price but the last lot we sent were not so lucky and we had nothing to show for our labour.'

# SHOPPING AND CALLERS
# TO THE DOOR

**The butcher, the baker, the grocer, the milkman – not only were they at the heart of the village itself, but they also delivered direct to your door, welcome and familiar figures in homes throughout the county.**

## THE CARRIER SERVICE

'From the 1930s to the 1950s A. J. Woods and son Peter provided a general carrier service for Marsh Gibbon. Unlike today most people had no motor vehicles and so rarely travelled out of the village, thus making this service invaluable.

The carrier's original transport was a horse and van. In frosty and snowy weather the horse would have had screws put in its shoes, to stop it from slipping. The deliveries were made from Marsh Gibbon to Bicester via Launton. On the outgoing trip accumulators were taken to be recharged, to be used with a six volt battery to work the wireless as there was no electricity. Harnesses were sent for repair, empty medicine bottles to be refilled and money to be deposited in the bank.

They made the deliveries twice a week, Tuesday and Friday. The customers would take orders to the Woods' home or place an envelope in their own window so it could be seen en route indicating that they required the service. The needs were different according to the season. In the spring seeds and garden tools were required. In summer straw hats to wear for haymaking and harvest and in the winter Christmas trees and holly wreaths. Normally the service provided anything, including lavatory buckets and underwear. Once in Bicester the orders were given in at the grocer's, draper's, cobbler, dry cleaner's, chemist's, corn merchant's and ironmonger's, and the traders then wrapped, labelled and priced the orders. The Woods paid for the items then added a charge of twopence, threepence or sixpence according to the size of the order. They delivered the orders to the customers on the return journey and collected the money in the process.'

71

## THE TRADESMEN WHO CALLED

'When I first came to Hughenden over 50 years ago, so much depended on a splendid postal service and on goods being delivered to the door as there were not many cars about (though there were more buses then). There was a good corner shop and in addition the baker came two or three times a week with baskets of cakes and buns as well as bread. Then there was the butcher who, when he came, took orders and delivered for the weekend. Coal, papers and milk were delivered as well, as they are still. All garden requirements could be ordered from Wycombe and delivered and there were no delivery charges for anything. In fact the Co-op gave trading stamps as well.

The oil van was a necessity. Paraffin stoves were much in use and besides oil there was hardware of all kinds – pails, polishes, brooms and brushes, soaps (Sunlight and Lifebuoy were the favourites on the van), washing powders like Rinso and Oxydol (no detergents then) and soap flakes, Robin Starch and Reckitts Blue, pegs and clothes lines . . in fact, all kinds of domestic requirements. There was more time then, somehow, and one could go out to the van and have a good look. I still have the excellent aluminium pastry tins bought then – the oil man said they would last forever. Eggs, including duck and goose eggs, were sold privately, as well as poultry and rabbits. All kinds of fruit in season were sold privately, as they were much in demand for jam making and bottling. A lady on her own could go blackberrying, mushrooming or wood gathering (no central heating then) without fear. Those were the days. Or were they?'

'I was born in Chalfont St Peter in 1902 and remember well the conditions before the First World War. The milk was delivered to my home by a man who carried a heavy can, with half pint and pint measures suspended inside the can. We came to the door with a jug for twice-daily deliveries and once on Sunday. If we needed milk on Sunday afternoon, we collected it from the farm.

Mr Keys was the postmaster and he also ran a grocery business on the same premises. Mr Mills had a bakery and sold both bread and groceries in his shop. Mr Brown sold groceries, hardware and paraffin oil (no oil to be sold after dark!). Mr Bonsey kept The George and he also had a butcher's shop, now the saloon bar. At the rear of The George was a slaughterhouse where cattle were brought on foot, controlled by a dog and a man (or often a boy), from Watford cattle market (ten miles away) and Slough (six miles). Mr Stone also had a bakery and confectioner's shop. Mr Dell was the carrier "to and from London twice per week", and Mr Bastin "to and from Uxbridge daily".'

'The lady who lived opposite us in Quainton in 1940 had five children, so they used to go up to the local milkman's farm before they went to school in the morning to get their milk. They went with galvanised cans, because if you fetched the milk it was a halfpenny cheaper than being delivered. They also had to go after school in the afternoon. I believe the cost was about a penny – cheap by today's standards, but of course we did not have so much money in those days.'

'The early morning round of the village milkman in Taplow in the 1920s was heralded by the clip-clop of his pony-drawn purpose-built cart. He would alight and supply the householders with milk from a metal container, using a measuring jug. In the summer a weighted net covered the container.

Another tradesman to the village was the baker, bringing his bread basket to the door, offering freshly baked rolls and loaves. He was from a nearby town and arrived in a motor driven van.

Once weekly the oil man came offering a variety of household goods. Most of his wares were announced from his van in a nasal sing-song voice.

Another sound of the times was the ice cream man's bell when he trundled all the way from Maidenhead on his tricycle. The days when it was hot and sunny we would try to make a one penny "Snowfruit" last as long as possible.

There were four little shops in the village in those days – the grocer/post office, a butcher's, a dairy shop and a tuck shop. Gradually, after the war, one by one they closed and now there are none.'

'Great Brickhill was well catered for with one shop selling groceries while another sold clothing in the middle of the shop and carried out shoe repairs at one end and bicycle repairs at the other – a most valuable service in the 1930s as, apart from the farms and the dairy which provided employment for men as lorry drivers and for women in the bottling plant, work was only available in the nearby towns and a bicycle was the only means of transport.

The bakery produced mouthwatering crusty bread and, even into their seventies, the baker and his wife were still starting up the ovens at 3 am, baking the bread and delivering it that same morning. Walter the milkman was an engaging character whose deliveries were somewhat erratic. Some mornings milk was on the doorstep at 8 am, other days at 2 pm, and sometimes not at all!

The greengrocer and the butcher would come to the village from Bletchley to collect orders for delivery the next day. There was even a village barber, who attended to his clients' needs in their own homes. He did one style only, short back and sides – and this went for girls as well.'

## AND THE GIPSIES

'Gipsies regularly came to the village of Ley Hill in the 1930s. Ley Hill Common was a good camping place because of the availability of water. There was an outside tap for use by the occupants of a row of cottages, from which the gipsies were able to fill their water containers. The hazel bushes in the hedge beside the common were a good source of the raw materials for the making of clothes pegs, which were then sold by the gipsies to local inhabitants.

We were also about halfway between the workhouse at Hemel Hempstead and that at Old Amersham (now the general hospital). Regularly, a tramp called in Ley Hill on his way from one workhouse to the other, for a billycan of hot water to make his tea. Occasionally the tea leaves were also needed!'

## THE BUTCHER'S SHOP

'When I was a girl, and starting work in the butcher's shop at Princes Risborough in 1945, obviously everything was so very different. I would go as far as to say the only thing that has stayed the same is the sawdust, which is still allowed. I presume people know it is put down to absorb fat spillage and it appears no one has been able to find a non-slip surface which acts with such efficiency.

The display window itself was a huge marble slab and the only means apart from the coldness of the marble, to keep things cool, was a gap of an inch and a half to two inches where the plate glass window ended, before the marble. If the wind was in a westerly direction, it blew in the gap with great vigour, and of course, dust came in also. This was not, at that time, suggested to be a health hazard.

Everything in the shop was wooden, not the easy stainless steel wipe-down of today. In order to keep the woodwork clean every inch was scrubbed hard with hot soda water – no bleach or fat eating detergents in the 1940s. Even the means of supply for hot water was different; it was a gas-run copper and that was considered modern!

When a customer purchased meat it was laid upon the smallest piece of white paper, not greaseproof but just a mock-type paper. It was then wrapped in newspaper. Some people, I recall, used to bring a plate in a wiping-up cloth to cover it with. The size of the plate did not have to be very large. The rationing, as we all have heard, was very small.

We became very popular indeed as the boss owned a farm. Fair to say, he must have been a good shot, because we sold rabbits (loads of them) and they went far quicker than the hours it took for shooting them. Word would travel around the village at no uncertain speed and if the greengrocer down the road was able to produce a few bananas at the same time, it was an invasion on the High Street.

The scales were weight controlled. The weights were brass and great pride was taken in polishing them well. The vim and vigour of that meant that they had to be tested by the Weights and Measures Inspectors and sometimes we had to add small amounts of lead to counteract the abrasion of polishing with, say Brasso.

A delivery service was maintained in the war years, just once a week. Gone are the days when a customer could ring at 10 am and give the order for lunch. To help eke out the petrol allowance, we had two Saturday boys on bikes with wicker baskets. They did work hard – they used to have very heavy loads. Everyone used to ask for bones with their orders to make nourishing soup etc and the customers always lived in hope that the butcher's knife was not too sharp and extra meat was left on the bone.'

THE BAKER

'My father was the village baker at Edlesborough, and from the time I left school in 1939 I used to work for him. I had a pony and trap to deliver the bread and later a tradesman's cycle, then at 17 when I was old enough to drive, we had a Standard Nine car, which was much better as I could keep the bread dry when it rained.

I remember my father making the dough for the next day's bread. In the winter months it could be made in the evening, but came the warmer weather, if it was made too early it would have proved too much and risen out of the trough. It was really hard work in those days. The dough had to be kneaded by hand, which we called punching the dough, and later on my father was able to purchase a dough machine and that helped a lot.'

'The baker at Wingrave got up and made the dough, then serviced accumulators, mended push bikes or motor bikes, and would often go on his racing bike, with spare wheels on his back, up to 30 miles to a race meeting. Having won a race, he cycled back, wheels still on his back, with his prize. He would then knead the dough, make the loaves, bake them and deliver them on his trike to Rowsham and

Wingrave, often up to midnight. He was known as "The Midnight Baker". He said it was a good loaf if, when you cut it, the crust flew and hit the wall on the other side of the kitchen, and his nearly did.'

## THE GROCER

'How keeping shop has changed. Although it is 25 years since my husband and I left the grocery and provision trade in Long Crendon, my memory takes me back much further.

The cheese came in crates, each containing two round 56 lb cheeses. English Cheddar, once uncrated, was put on a slab and kept for about six months to mature, being turned once a week. By then the muslin top and bottom was ever so difficult to remove but that on the side more easily peeled off. New Zealand cheese was packed similarly but was not stored. Stilton cheese was only available for Christmas and there were no fancy cheeses at all.

Sides of bacon were delivered twice weekly and looked splendid hanging in the storeroom. They had to be boned and cut, and this was quite an art. Customers could ask for their rashers to be thickly or thinly sliced on the bacon machine. Even earlier, when I was employed as a book-keeper in a large grocer's, the bacon was delivered uncured and green, and was then smoked over burning oak sawdust in a warehouse behind the premises.

Salt came in blocks from three to 14 lbs. Primrose soap was in 3 lb bars so soft when sold that it had to be left in a cupboard to harden off before use.

Biscuit tins had glass-topped display areas showing a sample of the contents below, which were loose and not packeted.

Everything came in bulk and had to be weighed and bagged – including flour, and sugar which was always put into bags of stiff blue paper. Tea and dried fruit, and how sticky that was too, were flat wrapped, heaped onto paper, wrapped like a parcel with the ends tucked in, each variety of tea and each type of fruit in its particular coloured stiff paper.

Small tins of pineapple cost fourpence ha'penny and tins of Del Monte yellow cling peaches tenpence. Gin and whisky cost seven shillings and sixpence. Our shops were open until 10 pm on Fridays and Saturdays. Nearly all goods bought from the shop were delivered. A boy with a white apron, one corner tucked into his belt, used to take the local orders round by carrier bike. These orders had been collected by the town and country travellers employed by the shop.

My husband remembered from his earlier days how customers

used to bring jars for the thick dark treacle, which came in large barrels. In cold weather this ran very slowly. One Saturday night the tap of the barrel, which was up two steps in the storeroom, was left open by mistake. The first person to work on Monday morning went paddling in treacle, which had trickled down the steps and all over the shop floor. He couldn't remember just what happened to the culprit!'

## THE MILK ROUND

'My father was a dairy farmer in Kingswood, two miles from Grendon Underwood. He sold his milk direct to Nestle in Aylesbury. In 1931 he received notice that Nestle were cutting back on supplies, one lorry was being withdrawn and no more milk would be bought from him after the following Saturday.

The closure of the Nestle contract forced a family conference and I was asked to try to set up a milk round in Kingswood and Grendon Underwood. I spent two evenings going from door to door to see whether there would be enough demand. Many villagers were encouraging because it saved them the daily walk to collect their milk from the neighbouring farm. By the Saturday deadline, I had bought my equipment – a milk float, a bucket, a pint and a half pint measure. The farm already had a pony.

I built up a good milk round. Leaving at 8 am I was on the road till noon selling milk at twopence a pint or a penny a half pint, poured into the jug or can at the door.

Many and varied were the other services I rendered my customers. Once I was called in to repair the damage after a young wife had tried to "bob" her own hair. Another time I was asked to take a bowl of bread and milk to a caged magpie and to be sure to remember to pick some parsley on the way back through the garden. Whether it was wringing out sheets, turning a mattress or wringing a hen's neck, I took it in my stride.

Perhaps the most unusual task was one day when an old lady asked me to remove one of her two last remaining teeth which had grown long and unsightly. Behind closed doors, "in case she hollered", I gave a fast yank and away the tooth went. A few moments later the other was out too. "That looks and feels better," declared the patient and I was able to continue on my round. Perhaps this was one of the many days when the pony cleared off and made for home, only to be turned round by some helpful villager to go back to meet his milk maid.'

# IN SICKNESS AND IN HEALTH

**In the past you were more than likely to be born, be ill and die in your own home. Most people saw the doctor only rarely, if at all, in the days when every visit had to be paid for, and home cures were sworn by for everything from colds to whooping cough. Sadly, many children died young from preventable diseases such as diphtheria until immunisation gradually became widespread.**

## HOME CURES

'"We were poor but we did not know we were poor." This quote seems to sum up the general situation of many of us villagers in my childhood of more than 60 years ago. One aspect of making-do in those long-ago times was managing without a doctor or a chemist in times of illness. The NHS was far into the future. A doctor's visit cost half a crown and so only in serious circumstances was he called to the house. The local midwife dealt with births, neighbours rallying round to lend a hand with illness, birth and death. Raspberry leaf tea helped childbirth pains.

Straw strewn on the road to deaden traffic noise told us that someone was dangerously ill, and the local "layer-out" dealt with death. We always drew our curtains as a mark of respect for a departed neighbour. People were ill at home, were nursed at home and died at home.

Winter, of course, brought extra problems. Many were the home-made cures with which Mother treated the ailments of her family. Warm olive oil on cotton wool was the treatment for earache and a brown paper poultice soaked in vinegar and liberally sprinkled with pepper was applied to toothache. It was a case of one pain counteracting the other. A loose tooth would be extracted by tying a cotton from it to the door handle and suddenly slamming the door! Coughs and colds got a blackcurrant or lemon and honey drink, hot bread and milk and some eucalyptus on a hanky. Mother's woolly stocking was wrapped around a sore throat and a spoonful of butter and sugar soothed inwardly. Chests were rubbed with camphorated oil and wrapped in flannel, while a brick heated in the oven brought comfort in a cold bed. Not even in severe weather was the bedroom window closed. We had a vague idea that warm bedrooms, like carpets, were unhealthy.

When measles struck, the bedroom curtains were kept closed because "the light could damage your eyes". Children with whooping cough were taken for walks round the gasworks because "the fumes are good for your chest". And oh, those painful chilblains! A cut onion dipped in salt was one relief and another was to put the affected foot in a half-filled chamber pot! Every child knew that nettle stings could be eased with a dockleaf, a wasp sting with the bluebag, a bleeding cut with a cobweb, a burn with butter or soap, an abcess with a bread poultice and a cold key down your back stopped a nosebleed. Hiccups? Drink some water while pinching your nose, dear. Hair nits were killed with paraffin. Constipation called for those dreadful senna pods, liquorice powder or castor oil, followed quickly and thankfully by a spoonful of jam. And many a harassed mother would dose her fretful baby to sleep with a little poppy tea.

Grandmas would bathe their tired eyes with cold tea and grandpas carried a nutmeg in their pockets for the "screws". Nearly every village had an old woman who could charm away warts. False teeth were badly fitting and often kept in a drawer, while spectacles could be bought from a market stall.

The good old days? Well, it was life before aspirin and certainly different!'

## SO MUCH FOR X-RAYS

'When I was six years old in 1919 I broke my arm very badly after having a lift on a friend's bicycle. The nearest doctor was almost four miles away, so as there was no transport my uncle, who worked at the local vicarage, had to harness the pony and trap and take me to him. I had to wait until the following morning to be taken to the hospital at Aylesbury, five miles away. I was in hospital for three months and my mother and family had to walk to visit me. My arm was x-rayed. I was laid on a table and covered with a black cloth, but with the damaged arm exposed. It was like a big lantern coming through the wall. So much for x-rays in those days.'

## TAKING OUT INSURANCE

'Many villagers couldn't afford to pay for a doctor in the 1920s. Women had their babies at home with just a midwife in attendance. Soon after their baby was registered, mothers took out a tuppenny death policy for it. Many children died in the early years from infectious diseases. My youngest sister died from diphtheria at the age of three.

Our isolation hospital was at Booker. I well remember visiting my brother there when he had diphtheria. Nobody was allowed inside the building. Those children who were well enough were brought to the windows of the ward. Visitors stood outside and shouted to them through the glass. Families who could afford it paid into a Friendly Society each month. If a doctor was needed the Society paid part of the fees. Working men were alright. Their National Insurance contributions covered them for doctor's visits, but not their wives and children.

Men working in the chair factories didn't have a regular wage. They were paid for what they completed. If they were off sick they had no income. Many of them joined a Slate Club every January, paying about a shilling every week. If they were sick during the year the Club paid out a regular amount for about six weeks. At the end of the year each member got a share of the money left in the bank.'

## COMBATING DISEASE

'Mrs Angela Jones, who lived at Fingest Grove for many years and then later at Cutlers, started the first baby welfare clinic in Lane End in the 1930s. Mothers could take their children, have them weighed and see the doctor.

The Hon Mrs Jones went to America and saw the way they were combating the terrible diseases of scarlet fever and diphtheria by immunisation. She kept on to the government of the day, badgering them to do something like that in this country as so many young lives were being claimed. Often the ambulance would come hurrying through the village with its bell ringing, taking another victim of the disease to Booker isolation hospital. Then one day we were given a day off school. Doctors and nurses came and so did coachloads of children from the schools in the area, to be immunised. I wasn't done on that day but it later became compulsory for all children to be immunised so we had to go down to the Baby Welfare where a doctor was waiting. Thanks to the determination of that great lady those diseases have become almost extinct.'

## THE FUNERAL CORTEGE

'When I was about ten years old my grandmother, who had always lived with us, died. As was the custom then, her body was in her bedroom until the funeral. I found the whole time simply terrifying – the coming and going of weeping relatives and the undertakers and the gloominess of the house, as the blinds had to be kept down until after the funeral.

At least my brother and I were not asked to see her in her coffin but we had to attend the funeral service. Had I been asked what I wanted to do I would have said, "Please let me stay at home", but in those days children were seldom given choices, or expected to have an opinion of their own.

My brother and I travelled in a horse-drawn carriage, with other adult members of the family. In the mid 1930s this really was an outdated sight in a funeral cortege but my father had decided to have one or two horse-drawn carriages as well as the usual large black saloons in deference to my grandmother who, I'm sure, never came to terms with motor vehicles. After all, she was born in the mid 1800s.

Each time I caught my brother's eye, I'm ashamed to say we giggled. We were really rather embarrassed at riding in this old-fashioned carriage. As a sign of mourning a black diamond-shaped patch was sewn onto the upper part of my coat sleeve.'

## A BLACK AND WHITE CAREER

'Living in the 1940s in Lacey Green I called on a neighbour and found her choking in her smoke-filled living room. She needed her chimney sweeping, badly. So we went off to borrow a set of brushes and I swept her chimney; obviously so well that my fame soon spread. The new lady chimney sweep was soon getting bookings, people coming to the house to arrange a visit. I would set off on my bicycle in dark overalls and head scarf with a new set of brushes strapped across the handlebars – downhill to Hughenden, Princes Risborough and as far as Chinnor. After sweeping chimneys at Chequers Lodge I was once asked to sweep in the lovely sitting room at Chequers itself. I swept chimneys at the HQ of Bomber Command in the house where Bomber Harris lived during the war. I charged a shilling a chimney and later that went up to five shillings.

At this time a relation of my husband was the "layer out" in Lacey Green, getting older and wanting to give up the job. I helped her out on one occasion and must have coped well enough because she persuaded me to take over from her. The local doctor would call me out at any time of day or night. For this I was paid £5. One day when I had four chimneys booked to sweep, the doctor called me and I had to do a quick change from my dirty black to a clean white outfit.'

# CHILDHOOD &
# SCHOOLDAYS

SLEDGING ON CHAIRBACKS, WEST WYCOMBE HILL, 1930's.

# A COUNTRY CHILDHOOD

Most children in Buckinghamshire in the first half of the century experienced a country childhood, even those brought up in areas now covered with houses and roads. There may have been few luxuries, and children may have had to help on the farm or in the house at an early age, but they also had a freedom and a delight in simple pleasures which today's children, sadly, may never discover.

## GROWING UP BEFORE THE FIRST WORLD WAR

'I was born in 1907 and brought up in the lovely old village of Cuddington. At school I was taught reading, writing and arithmetic. We girls were also taught sewing and the boys were taught gardening.

We were a very large family, and lived in a small cottage where the village hall now stands. My parents slept in one of our two bedrooms, and all the brothers and sisters slept in the second bedroom, four or five in one bed, some at the top and some at the bottom of the bed. By the morning some of us would be under the bed.

We had one living room and a small scullery. There was no sink and water had to be drawn from the well which was halfway up the garden. The old earth closet was up the other side of the garden. Cooking was done on an open fire. There was no electric light; we used candles and an oil lamp.

We had a large garden planted with vegetables, and Father had an allotment where he grew potatoes and greens which kept us going through the winter.

Father worked on a farm, and in the summer we had to take him his tea when he was haymaking and harvesting, sometimes having to walk a few miles across the fields. Mother was a very busy woman, and she would be called out any time of the day or night to deliver somebody's baby; she was a sort of local midwife, and when she had a little one of her own, she had to take it with her. She was also called out if someone died, to perform the necessary duties.

In the school holidays, we used to play down at the mill and paddle in the mill pond, and play in the meadows and make daisy chains. We found all kinds of wild flowers – cowslips, ladysmocks, ragged robins, orchids (which we used to call King Fingers) and lovely quaking grasses.

We didn't have any luxuries; no Easter eggs, or toys at Christmas, no birthday cards, but we were quite happy and contented. There were always a lot of gipsies around and on Sunday mornings one would come with his barrel organ and monkey and play in the street.

We had a brass band in the village, and they paraded around the village at holiday time. We had a Village Feast once a year in May, with swings, roundabouts, coconut shy and stalls – in all a great occasion.

Our village had a post office, a grocer's and a butcher, and when we came out of school we would watch the butcher kill the pigs in the yard, and burn them on straw. The butcher would then throw the pigs' toenails across the road, and we would all scramble to get one to chew. They tasted delicious.

I left school when I was 13 years old, and stayed at home for a time to help Mother. Then I went into service in Aylesbury, my first job. On my half day I would walk home and back (six miles each way) as there were no buses and I didn't have a bicycle. Then I got married and settled down in my village of Cuddington, and I have been here ever since.'

'Born in High Wycombe before the First World War, my childhood was spent in a quiet period of time – no aeroplanes, no motor cars, wireless or television. Our enjoyment of music came from an Edison Bell gramophone with 60 cylinders, a present from an uncle. Apart from the occasional horse and cart, the roads were free for games of hopscotch and hoop-bowling.

Close to home were beechwoods, Oakridge and Castlefield, where many happy days were spent playing tag around the trees in the fallen leaves.

Mother would say, "Don't forget to put your hats on!" We were never allowed to go out without one: tam-o'shanters for weekdays, straw hats decorated with ribbons and flowers for Sundays, worn with a lovely shantung dress, black woollen stockings and high buttoned boots. How smart we looked.

The most exciting day of the year was the Sunday school treat. We were transported by horse and cart from the church hall of St John's, Desborough Road, to a local park, Daw's Hill or the Rye. Each child was given a penny and an orange and there were cakes and lemonade for tea. We took part in racing games, and, if tired of that, the long grass was inviting.

85

Sometimes in summer, Mother would take my sister and me to Tom Birt's Hill (on which is now built the hospital) with a basket of tea and cakes. We also had our sledges. What fun speeding down the grass slopes and bumping into each other.

When I was about 15 in the mid 1920s, I joined the local High Wycombe Operatic Society and after being called upon to sing solo on the stage I thought I was destined for the West End at the very least. I joined the Optimists Concert Party and we put on many concerts in surrounding towns such as Amersham and Marlow as well as in High Wycombe. Alas, the call to the West End never came and when I left school I found a job in the office of a local factory.'

'I was born in Winchmore Hill in 1903 and always lived there. As a child, I recall, after walking home from Penn Street school, I would be met at the door by my mother with a piece of bread and jam in one hand and a milk can in the other, and off I would go again walking to Woodrow to get a pennyworth of skimmed milk.

The annual chapel outing was usually to Burnham Beeches. Mr Hatch from Fagnall Farm was Superintendent of the chapel and his horses and carts transported the villagers. The carts may have been the dung carts the day before, but the men stayed until they were scrubbed clean for the outing.

My grandfather lived at the Lord Nelson public house and made chair legs for the other chair factories in the village. A cul de sac of houses called Nelsons Close now stands on the site of The Lord Nelson. In those days Winchmore Hill had three shops and two chapels, but neither of the latter had a licence to perform marriages. It was said Winchmore Hill people were looked down upon because they had to go to Penn Street to be married.'

## LIVING WITH MY GRANDPARENTS

'I was born in 1915 in Hyde Heath. My mother married in 1914 and my father died eight months after they were wed. By this time I was "on the way" and my mother had to come home to my grandmother until I was born. She was packed off very soon afterwards into service leaving me to be brought up by my grandparents. As they had had 14 children of their own I'm sure my Gran could have done without me; only two of her own were left at home unmarried. She was very stern and strict and always had a cane on the table at mealtimes; manners and good behaviour at mealtimes were very important in our house.

My Gramp was an old softie and I soon learnt to ask for things only when he was there. The earliest thing I can remember is the

Saturday morning trips in the donkey cart into Chesham. After a few bits of shopping for Gran, the rest of the morning I spent sitting in the cart in the Red Lion yard until my grandfather staggered out at closing time. The donkey knew his way home, so we always arrived back safely.

My Gramp was always happy in his cups, so we had few problems. My Gran was a very good-living woman. She was the village midwife and layer out after deaths, and up to school age I always went with her to the after care of mothers and babies. Many of the "children" now in the 70 year age group I nursed on my knee while my Gran prepared their baths.

I went to the village school which consisted of one room for the infants and one room for the older children, one teacher and one headmistress. When the headmistress was sick (which was often) the infants teacher had to teach in the big room and one of the older girls had to teach the infants. The cane was very widely used and I must say the thought of it kept us in order. We left school at 14, though some of the boys left much earlier to work on the farms.

Sunday was the Sabbath day and was kept as such, with Sunday school morning and afternoons and an evening service for adults, after which most of my Gran's family came "home" for supper, quite a gathering. Although my grandparents were poor we were all well fed. A large boiler hung over the open fire, filled with nets of vegetables and "swimmers" (dumplings in cloths) and *always* steak and sausage for Sunday breakfast. The drinking water had to be fetched from a communal tap in the village; for everything else water was used from the well in the garden. The closet or WC was at the bottom of the garden, no water toilets in those days. All the villagers kept chickens and many kept a pig in the garden. When it was killed it was hung up in the wood shed with a net curtain round it to keep the flies off, and it was eventually salted down in a barrel; not too much thought given to hygiene in those days. Butter and milk etc was lowered in a bucket down into the well to keep it cool.

The ladies of the village met in the hall once a week for sewing parties and gossip and exchanging recipes. This was before the WI and was known as "Mothers Meeting". A travelling concert party visited the village once a year and some of the families in the village boarded them for a small fee. They put on a different performance every night for a week, such as *Maria Marten in the Red Barn* etc, very melodramatic but entertaining for the villagers.

Each season brought jobs for the children: picking raspberries, blackberries, mushrooms, elderberries for wine and dropped acorns for the pigs and sometimes potato picking for the farmer. Some

Saturday mornings were spent grinding swedes for the farmers' animals.

The winters seemed to be much harder. With no central heating and no gas or electricity (oil lamps and candlesticks), the water by my bed often froze over in the night. The village pond was frozen over for long periods and as children we had great fun; the older boys would tie a rope round their waist and all the smaller children would hang on and be pulled around the ice. Lanterns were hung on poles around the pond. I remember it well, great fun.

Our yearly Sunday school outing was a very exciting day. Picnics were packed and we were taken by charabanc to Coombe Hill or Whiteleaf Cross. The school always had an open air concert on May Day on the common, with the "Crowning of the Queen of the May". My one regret was that I was never chosen as Queen but I was a good dancer so I always got the dancing parts. I was once invited with my partner by the Squire of the village to dance Harlequin and Columbine to a house party in his drawing room (a great honour).

Guy Fawkes night was celebrated with a huge bonfire. The children worked hard for weeks before collecting anything that would burn and a charabanc brought people from other villages to join in the fun with singing and dancing round the fire, while hot soup was provided by the ladies.

Saturday night was bath night, with hair washed, plaited and crimped ready for Sunday, in a long tin bath in front of the fire (what a job this must have been with 14 children). My hair was waist length and every morning before I went to school my Gran brushed my hair with either paraffin or vinegar to keep any nits away. It was a great disgrace to be given a note from the "Head Nurse" to take home to your parents.'

## HELPING ON THE FARM

'I was born on a farm in Wendover in 1922. As my mother died when I was four, life was not quite as normal as in most families. My two brothers and I had to help on the farm, especially on school holidays.

I remember walking up and down the fields leading a horse which was putting a hoe between rows of turnips and mangolds etc, and how my father used to shout at me when I let the horse put its foot on the plants. Then, in the summer, we used to drive the horses and carts to the harvest fields, taking empty carts out and bringing full ones home with sheaves for ricks and barns. Sometimes I would drive a horse round and round to work an elevator which took hay etc to the top of a rick in the field. I must have walked miles in a day on all these jobs! Some of the fields I used to tramp up and down as a child are now covered in houses.

My father kept ferrets and I learned how to handle them quite well; I would much rather do that than risk a very vicious peck trying to take an egg from under a broody hen.

I attended the village school when it was near the clock tower. We were so near we could wait until we heard the bell start to ring and then just had time to get there if we ran. When I was in Miss Smith's class (a teacher who was very interested in wild flowers) she told us about a very rare flower called a Lizard Orchid, which smelled like goats. Apparently no one had seen one for a long time. One day, while walking in one of our fields I found an unusual looking flower which smelled strongly of goats, and in my ignorance, picked it and took it straight to her house. I can remember how excited she was – it really was a Lizard Orchid. After that we had people from Oxford University and various biologists visiting us and I had to show them where I had found it. Unfortunately, because I had picked it, no more grew the next year. However, I did get invited to go with some of them on a botanical expedition and I have been very interested in wild flowers ever since. I used to know where all the best violets, cowslips and blackberries were growing.

Miss Smith was a friend of Lady Nora Barlow and every summer she invited her class up to Boswells for an afternoon. I remember the lovely gardens and woods she let us play in and the wonderful strawberry and cream tea laid on before we returned home.

Sometimes we would hear a bell ringing – it was the muffin man walking up the road with a large tray on his head, covered with a black cloth. I can still remember the delicious muffins we used to toast in front of the fire for tea.

On Sundays it was Sunday school followed by the Congregational chapel in the morning and Sunday school in the afternoon. Every summer we had an outing to places like Wicksteed Park or even to the seaside in a charabanc. This outing was a real treat for me because my father took us everywhere in a pony and trap.

Occasionally the fire warning would sound and, if we were quick, we reached the fire station soon enough to see the firemen wearing their shining brass helmets turning out with the fire engine. We used to peer through the window where the helmets were hanging in rows in the station.

When I grew older the highlight of the week used to be dances in the village hall, commonly called the "Sweatbox". We had plenty of partners, having the RAF station just up the road.'

'My first recollection of Lower Winchenden (now known as Nether

Winchenden) in the 1920s was living next door to the old watermill and hearing the rumbling of the grindstones, grinding the corn for flour and animal feedstuffs. The water that drove the mill was emptied into what was known as the mill tail, which became a great paddling pool for the children from all around during the summer. It was the nearest they got to the seaside until the coming of buses.

I well remember the day a charabanc, one with a roof that could be let down, came to take the schoolchildren to the sea. What a day! We thought we would never get there, then there was a shout, "There's the sea!" and we had arrived.

Transport in my early days was on foot, horseback or horse and cart, then came bicycles and later cars and buses. Some children had a long walk to school, then at twelve years of age we had to go to Cuddington school which meant a mile and a half walk for some of us. In summer we used to walk home for dinner but in winter took sandwiches and ate them around the stove in the schoolroom. There were no hot drinks.

During the summer the older children had to carry tea to the hay and harvest fields, and woe betide if you were late or spilt the tea. We could then stay and watch, hoping we would get a ride home in the haywaggon at night or on a horse.

The hay and sheaves of corn had to be pitched up into waggons by hand fork. There is an art in pitching hay, otherwise it falls back over your head.

As time progressed a machine called a pitcher was used behind the waggons to take the hay up, then came the sweep, drawn by two horses, which was much quicker if the ricks were being built in the field. It was quite a sight at the end of summer to see rows of hay and corn ricks, neatly thatched, the corn ricks to stand till winter when the steam threshing machine arrived.'

'I had a very happy childhood in Longwick in the 1920s. I remember wandering the fields picking wild flowers, fishing for tiddlers with a bent pin in the stream, and seeing "Hobble Gobbles" (kingcups), "Fraw Cups" (fritillaries) and many, many purple orchids. Ragged robin grew in the damp ditches and violets and primroses at Foxhill Farm. Cowslips grew on the railway banks in abundance. These we picked to make a garland for May Day, together with a Crown Imperial, many of which grew in Longwick, mostly in Mrs Kingham's garden.

Summers were spent helping with the haymaking and harvesting the corn and picking the fruit from my parents' and grandparents' orchards. The orchard at Kingsey was quite dangerous as the pigs were allowed to roam in it and the boar was a bit ferocious. I remember the double-seated privy at Foxhill, covered in ivy. We helped feed the ducks, de-tailed the lambs, watched the pig being slaughtered and helped grandmother with the chitlings etc and to salt the bacon on the slab in the large dairy. In August we all went to Bournemouth in the open Sunbeam Tourer. It was full of us – children plus nanny. I was usually sick; it seemed a long journey in those days.'

'Childhood in the 1930s in Horn Hill was fully of happy long days. The Epilepsy Colony played a large part in village life; we put on plays and concerts and competed in all sports together. We could all deal with their disability when needed.

I remember collecting mushrooms from the fields on early damp and dewy mornings. This was for my pocket money. And there was picking blackberries, cherry plums and crabapples from the hedgerows, helping prepare fruit and vegetables for jam, pickles and preserves, packing runner beans and beetroot in layers of salt and bottling fruit in kilner jars – all for winter use.

The mother hen would sit on eggs impatiently waiting for them to hatch. Oh, the wonder of the first chip of the shell, then a wet little face appearing, and the sadness when at Christmas the now large chickens became festive dinners!

Summer days were spent in the hayfields. We would help to load the hay onto horse-drawn carts, for the enjoyment of a ride through the lanes to the farmyard. A lonely horse worked the elevator by walking in a circle attached to an arm on the central axle. After many teabreaks the hayricks continued to rise.

Milking time was fun; calling the cows in from the fields, each with its own name and stall, and doing the milking by hand. I didn't like that part very much so I helped fill the churns ready for the early morning milkround. Tom was a clever horse. We always said he could have served the customers himself, stopping at all the usual houses!'

'At Speen some of the men used to cycle into High Wycombe to work in the chair factories, but the village is in the middle of the beechwoods and many men made their living there. There were a lot of small chair bodgers shops in the village; one in particular I recall was William's. He always made us children very welcome and sometimes we stacked the chair legs or staves which had been made or we sat on the side of the bench and chatted to the men as they worked their lathes.

William was the Sunday school superintendent and he was a very kind man. We used to go with him and his little donkey cart to collect dried ferns for the donkey's bedding for the winter, riding there and walking back.

We had no means of transport save the horse and cart, or "Shanks's pony" as my parents used to call walking. I remember being taken to Saunderton in a pushchair to meet relatives at what was our nearest railway station. When one of the local builders bought a lorry we were able to book one of the seats he put along the sides in the back to take us into High Wycombe and back. That was quite an occasion.

I used to help on a small farm with the buttermaking. The milk was put into large flat pans and left overnight. The cream was then skimmed off and put into a wooden churn on an iron stand. I used to sit and turn this. It took quite a long time and it was always a relief when I heard the butter plop around in the milk that was left. The skimmed milk was sold for a penny a pint or given to the calves.

There was time for us to play when we came out of school, but unlike the children of today, we always played in large groups. Tiles was a favourite and of course we had our metal hoops which we ran along with, keeping them going by hitting them with sticks. All this was long before television, but we listened to the wireless through earphones, often sharing one pair, with each child having one earpiece.'

## WE DIDN'T HAVE A LOT OF MONEY

'I was born in the 1920s at Centre Cottages, Grendon Underwood, which is a village ten miles from Aylesbury. We were a large family; I had five brothers and one sister older than me, and a younger sister and brother.

We had oil lamps downstairs and candles upstairs. There was no convenience in any of the houses and all cooking had to be done over the fire; washing was boiled in a big boiler over the fire too. Taps in the village supplied the water for the houses. After afternoon school, it was left to my sister and me to take pails to go and fetch the water, the older ones being out at work or having left home. Sometimes the water would run quite fast and on other occasions, especially in the summertime, it would just trickle. When that occurred some of the children who lived nearby would come out and we would practise the country dancing which we had learned at school.

Whoever was old enough had to fetch the milk twice a day from the farm up in the village, ours and a neighbour's. We carried three cans in each hand. When the farmer was busy hay-making we often had to wait in the evening for the cows to be milked and watch the milk being cooled before bringing it home. We had a big horse-chestnut tree in the front of the house under which we played when we could. At the bottom of the garden was a big quince tree; the fruit smelled lovely and was delicious, mixed with apples, in pies and puddings.

My father cycled three and a half miles each morning to the brickworks at Calvert where he worked. My brothers worked away and some lived away at work. My elder sister and I spent the greater part of each evening washing up as the men seemed to come home one after the other. We were always in the school concerts etc, so we practised all those whilst washing up. I am sure our mother knew the words off by heart long before the actual concerts.

My younger sister used to cry at the least little thing. One afternoon we were coming home from school when it began to rain heavily. We went to shelter in the garage at the bakehouse (of course, she was crying!) and the lady came out with some little tarts thinking she would stop. Unfortunately, they were marmalade tarts, so she cried all the more because she didn't like marmalade!

After some years the council built some houses so we left Centre Cottages and moved into No 2, Crescent Cottages. We didn't have a lot of money but we never went hungry or dirty: our mother was very clean and particular.

We were all brought up to go to church and Sunday school. Our father rang the bells and wound the church clock for over 25 years. As each one of us became old enough we went into the church choir. We went to choir practice, Band of Hope and anything else that was on. There were no pavements or lights in the road so we had to watch out coming home in the dark. When we did have any free time during the summer holidays we would go up into the fields with another family and we would play Mothers and Fathers. Gaps in the hedges were our houses, tins and lids were our cooking utensils, willow leaves we used for bacon and acorns for eggs. We were all happy in our way because we had never had much so did not miss anything.

On Saturdays we all had jobs to do; one to clean the knives, one the spoons and forks and another the saucepan lids. We three girls were always much better dressed than the other girls in the village because our aunt worked at the Manor House, where Colonel and Mrs Piggott lived. The Colonel's brother, his wife and three daughters visited them two or three times a year. The girls were about our age and size and their clothes, which were all very good, were given to my aunt for us. We thought we were the cat's whiskers!

Sometimes on a Saturday evening, my younger sister and I, the elder sister having now gone away to work, had a penny to spend.

We went over to the little shop to buy toffees; she always had the "ten-a-penny" sort and I had the "five-a-penny" sort. I used to say to her, "It's the quality that counts, not the quantity!" She remembers me saying it to this day, she tells me.

When I was 14 years old I left school at the beginning of April and, by the end of April, I, too, had left home. Our mother had a sister who was not very well and she had no children so our mother lent me to her. There was no public transport in Grendon Underwood so on the day I went away one of my brothers, who was at home on holiday, put my case on his bicycle and we had to walk together about two miles to the place where the Black & White coach came through for Birmingham. I had never before been away from home and had never seen my aunt or uncle, nor they me.

I had one and a half hours to wait at the Bull Ring before getting on a Midland Red bus for Great Malvern. My uncle met me, my mother having written and told him the colour of the hat and coat I would be wearing. I was very frightened (but did not cry!). It was quite an ordeal for a 14 year old. It was 18 months before I went home again for a holiday. I stayed in Malvern for five years but my childhood was over the day I left Grendon Underwood.'

'I started at St Leonard's Church of England school before my fourth birthday in the mid 1920s, a walk of about a mile and a half each way from our home at Buckland Common and, for a time, used a slate on which to write. My teeth are still on edge when I recall the noise of the "pencil" on the slate. We always went to the nearby church on St George's Day.

I well remember learning how to knit the heels of socks, not the whole sock, just the heel and these made ideal dolls' hats for the rag dolls we made from mother's old black stockings. There were no organised leisure activities. We wandered the fields and woods, played with hoops, tops and skipping ropes. Another pastime was plaiting reeds found in local ponds.

The highlights of our year were the Sunday school outing and the Christmas party. The summer outing was to the seaside and at the Christmas party we all had a present, probably a doll or doll's tea set. Riches indeed. My older brother recalled, when he was young, that the Rothschild family used to visit the villages at Christmas in a waggon, bringing parcels for the children. At Cholesbury village hall they sometimes had magic lantern shows and, to us, they *were* magic.'

# THROUGH THE WEEK

'This was a week in my life when I was young, in High Wycombe in the 1920s:

*Sunday* – Mother was up early so that the household could go to church and Sunday school. We were home about 11.30 to have a roast dinner that had been prepared the day before. Sunday school again in the afternoon until three o'clock when most of the boys and girls went for a long walk, arriving back about half past four in time to have a wash ready for high tea, then off to church for the Eventide service. When the family came home about half past seven they had a sing song round the piano. Then to bed ready for school the next day.

*Monday* – Older members of the family had their chores to do and young ones went to school at nine o'clock. The very young ones went to Westbourne Street school, no longer there. Being only three years old I was not entitled to go but was allowed to sit in class with the older ones, for the morning only. After the family had sat down to the evening meal, the table was cleared and we sat round it either doing homework or playing games. In the lighter evenings we played outside with the tops that we painted pretty colours, and a string whip to make the tops spin. The young ones went to bed by 6.30, the older ones later. Sometimes they would go to the pictures.

*Tuesday* – Same as Monday except in the evening we went to church for Christian Endeavour.

*Wednesday* – Only morning school. In the afternoon the family visited relatives, mainly grandparents.

*Thursday* – All day school. Evening social in the church hall and piano lessons.

*Friday* – Market day. The evening meal was always fish of some sort. I hated boiled fish but when we had fried fish from Prowtons in Desborough Road the whole family thoroughly enjoyed it. Fish was threepence a piece and chips a penny a large bag.

*Saturday* – This was our day to do much as we liked. The older ones went to the morning pictures. There were at that time four picture houses in the town: the Palace Theatre, the Majestic, the Electric Scope and Desborough Road. An adult had to chaperone them. Being the youngest of a large family I was taken to the Saturday market where there was a "spinner". People paid for tickets and won a prize if lucky on the spin. This was situated under the Guildhall, and I loved to watch. The spinner was run by local people to make money for the poor and needy. The evening was again a sing-along when people came to the house to sing or tell stories. Mother would make cake and home-made lemonade. These were very jolly days, and I enjoyed watching the other boys and girls.

My eldest sister married when I was two and a half years old. Over the next few years restrictions at home were relaxed little by little, though when I was 17 I still had to be chaperoned.'

## WHAT WE WORE

'During my childhood in the 1920s we mainly wore hand knitted jerseys with brown pleated skirts hung from a cotton bodice, with heavyweight woollen vests and liberty bodice underneath, plus elastic-legged dark knickers. The number of buttons on the liberty bodice bore a direct relation to the quality of "help" Mum had with the laundry, as the washing was boiled in the copper and then put through the big iron mangle. Buttons could pop off in all directions if carelessly mangled. In summer we were allowed cotton vests and pants and short simple sleeveless cotton dresses. One summer a friend of the family who was a dressmaker made matching dresses for us all, in graduated sizes. They were duck egg blue net over a silky fabric, trimmed with net flounces and rosebuds, and must have been devils to iron. Poor Mildred as the youngest wore the dresses as Sunday best for most of her childhood and hated them, as we all did. Strong brown lace-up shoes were winter wear, with crepe-soled sandals in summer with knee length socks. How I longed for black patent ankle strap shoes and ankle socks, but was never allowed to have them. Once into grammar school we wore the regulation school gymslips and blazers most of the time, with whatever Mum could make-over from relatives' cast-offs in the skirt line, and home-made cotton frocks in the summer for weekends.'

## SUMMER WALKS AND PARTIES

'I grew up in the 1920s at Cholesbury, near Tring, leading a peaceful existence with my parents and two sisters, with just one village store between our village and Hawridge.

We all knew one another, walked everywhere and grew our own fruit and vegetables. My mother bottled or salted the vegetables and made her own wine (though she was teetotal), jam, bread and cakes. We kept chickens that were able to run free on the common outside.

At night bats flew overhead and we could hear owls hooting in the trees and foxes howling up on the hill, nightingales and nightjars. There were cuckoos in spring and summer, not drowned by today's noise, and the most beautiful butterflies. Walking over the common we found a wonderful collection of wild flowers and grasses for which we won prizes at our local Flower Show. My father would call me early to collect mushrooms with him. We loved going "wooding" – plenty to be had in the local wood. In summer there were raspberries and blackberries to be picked and dandelions for wine, and in the autumn elderberries and nuts for Christmas.

Come Christmas we went carol singing – a lovely sight to see the lanterns in the darkness. My father started us off with his mouth organ and we really sang. Money was scarce in those days but our parents managed and we were very happy.'

'A favourite summer family walk in the 1930s was to the Cherry Orchard on the hills above Bledlow, beyond the Cross. We bought White Hart cherries, putting a pair of them on our ears for earrings and trying very hard not to be tempted to eat them before we arrived back down the hill at The Red Lion. I believe the lady who sold lemonade there was Ada Gomme.

Another walk was to Lodge Hill, coming home via The Piggeries and along the "white road", white because of the chalk soil, down to The Red Lion again.

When we walked across the fields via Saunderton and on to Horsenden my sisters and I always hoped we'd stop at The Warrens public house. We were disappointed if we didn't, so dragged our feet and sat down on the verges and then had to run to catch up.

At Hinton crossing, on the Oxford line through Bledlow, Mr Percy Smith, when he was there, always gave our parents a glass of home-made wine.

Playing in the Lyde, the steep-sided ravine by the church was creepy but exciting. The game I liked was using a torch in the undergrowth and under the trees, rather like Hide and Seek, and shouting, "Jack, Jack show a light". And Tipney Tailing over the Lyde railings until you got giddy.

Watching cricket at the moor you always had the chance to show off if Mr Palin asked you to take the wooden box round to take up the collection from the onlookers in the rough grass round the edge. These would be mainly villagers but you would also know many of the visiting team's supporters.

Messrs Witneys and Strathdee and George Seymour took part in shows in the village hall and would also go to other villages in Mr Witney's grocery van, in which they put wooden planks on wooden boxes to sit on. (I wonder what it was like when they went round corners – they laughed a lot, I bet.) Two songs I remember were "Widecombe Fair" and "A kipper, a haddock, a bloater."

I loved to go out on a Saturday, catching the afternoon Watlington

Donkey (one-coach steam train) on our other railway line to Princes Risborough. We had tea, toast and cakes at the tea shop in Summerleys Road, then it was on to the Carlton Cinema to see the first performance, catching the 8pm train home. The guard would wait to put out the halt light till you had all got to the bottom of the steps. Mrs Croxford from Chinnor was often on the train having been to High Wycombe to buy fish and chips for Chinnor people. She would very often open them up and sell chips there and then if she knew you.'

'Most of our leisure time in the 1930s was spent playing in the fields between Askett and Monks Risborough. There were streams to paddle in, hollow willow trees where we played "house" and tadpoles to be caught in the spring. In the summer we picnicked in the woods behind The Plough at Cadsdean. We paid a small amount, about a shilling a year, and we were allowed to gather firewood from the woods. Our neighbour had an old wickerwork bath chair with a steering handle on the front and we would take it up to the woods and pile it high with firewood. In Whiteleaf village there was a library in a converted barn which opened every Sunday.'

'I was born and brought up in Princes Risborough. I remember the house where I was born, as it was then, with an outside lavatory, a bath in the kitchen and a pump for the water. Later we did graduate to a cold tap, but there was a good old-fashioned copper for washdays and, of course, a coal fire in the living-room, the coal delivered by horse and cart.

In my early years I attended the council school, which was about a mile from my home. No school dinners then, so I walked home each lunch time. Walking to school was sometimes a bit of a torment as I had to pass the rector's geese, which were on the grass opposite the rectory. I'm not sure that they actually attacked me, but they certainly used to come after me making hissing noises.

An uncle was a builder, so I spent a lot of time in his yard and was often in the carpenter's shop, watching coffins being made, as he was also an undertaker. I grew up with it and it seemed perfectly normal to me.

I loved animals and as this uncle had two horses, two dogs, at least one cat, plus chickens and ducks in his meadow, I was usually to be found in the vicinity of at least one animal. There was also a pig during the war, though this was kept elsewhere so I never got to know it well! There was a blacksmith nearby and I loved to watch the horses being shod, though I never ventured inside the forge.

Those were the days of country walks with my dog, without any fear for my safety, haystacks in the fields and the local dairy farmer's cows meandering down the High Street to the milking parlour.'

'Unlike today's children we played in the road, as well as in the fields and woods. We played a game called Tiles and turned a large skipping rope the width of the road – we were annoyed when the occasional car wanted to pass. During the summer holidays we spent time clearing out the stream through the woods and collected wild flowers, wild strawberries and blackberries. Then, of course, there were the picnics at haymaking time.

My father belonged to the British Legion at Wooburn and each year a grand party was given for the children, with food, entertainment and a really super present for each child to take home. In the summer the Sunday school had an annual outing to such places as Bricket Wood and California (in England!). There was usually a church fete and various other tea parties. Mrs Finch-Smith and Miss Gilbey lived at the Manor House then and various local organisations held events in the grounds there.

We went to Burnham Beeches sometimes, especially on Bank Holidays. As well as the open space where we could play rounders, cricket etc, there used to be a small funfair and later a swimming pool.

In retrospect life seems to have been better but perhaps one tends to forget the hard times and the disappointments; money was not so plentiful in the 1930s but things were less expensive. Four different sweets could be bought for a penny, and for a little more sherbet dabs, liquorice sticks and small slabs of chocolate could be bought. There was a very good fish and chip shop about half a mile up the road and chips were threepence or fourpence a bag. The Walls ice cream man came round on his tricycle (the "Stop Me and Buy One" man) and for a few coppers a fruit ice cream could be purchased in a three-cornered cardboard container.

We could walk down to the river Thames on a summer evening or a Sunday afternoon and see the steamers or other boats go by, or take a trip across the river on the ferry. Saturday morning children's picture shows cost about fourpence and the bus fare to get there was quite cheap.

I used to cycle quite a lot as I became older and went on trips with friends or with the local youth club. For some years a youth club run by the churches met in St Mary's church hall each week and was quite successful. I belonged to the Brownies and then the Guides and we used to have camp fires and cook our supper out of doors.

Children of today think it must have been like the Dark Ages with no television or computer games, but during the winter evenings or wet afternoons we played cards, ludo, snakes and ladders and other board games. I liked reading, jigsaw puzzles and listening to the wireless (steam radio). At Christmas time we played different games. On Boxing Day we usually had a party and afterwards played Consequences, Charades, The Parson's Cat, Mrs Brown Packed Her Bag, Tip-it and others.

Looking back the summers of childhood seem mostly to have been long and sunny and the winters cold and snowy but that is probably an illusion.'


## THROUGH THE WAR YEARS

'Growing up in Stony Stratford in the 1940s was a far cry from the lifestyle children now have, since the town was enveloped within Milton Keynes' boundaries.

Some of my childhood memories are of the pleasures that the rural area offered us, such as taking Sunday evening walks with my parents across the Mill fields, sometimes having to wait to use the footbridge over the river Ouse whilst the cows crossed it on their way to the milking sheds at Old Wolverton Mill Farm. Once over the footbridge we then crossed two more fields, clambering over stiles, heading towards the Grand Union Canal.

My sisters and I eagerly chased each other through to the viaduct leading towards the local pub, which had garden tables with seats around and we were grateful to rest upon them. We were refreshed with a glass of lemonade and a packet of Smith's crisps with the little blue packet of salt invariably at the bottom!

We ventured home following the towpath along the canal, hoping we would see the barges using the locks. Sometimes we would wave to the bargee's children who always seemed to have grubby faces. Further along we walked over the "Iron Bridge"; this was a nostalgic place for my parents, where they first met when they were in their twenties. They watched people skating on the frozen river below. It was the only time many elderly people recall anyone being able to skate on the frozen ice.

We continued along the towpath towards Old Wolverton, up the side of the bridge, then along the road towards Stony Stratford. We gladly got into bed, tired out!

Each week we went to Sunday school. We were given a stamp which we then stuck onto a postcard; when the card was full it formed a biblical picture. We also had prize-giving at Christmas time followed by sardine sandwiches, egg and cress sandwiches and a jelly in a little wax dish and a fairy cake. Great excitement filled the parish hall of St Mary's when Father Christmas arrived.

The countryside provided us with its bounty. We collected rosehips from the hedgerow and took them to school the next day in a large jam jar and they were sent away to make rosehip syrup. My mother collected blackberries and made jam. Sometimes we went out in the early morning to gather mushrooms. We enjoyed them for our breakfast. The taste was so different from those we get today.

We always looked forward to Christmas as all children still do. The thrill of hanging up our stocking and being excited as we anxiously felt with our young hands exploring its contents. We were content with an apple, orange and some nuts, and one year I had a set of skittles!

These were war years and everything was in short supply. Many of our friends were not as lucky as we were. My family kept chickens and we luckily had a cockerel for our Christmas dinner, got ready by my mother.'

'I grew up in Loudwater, in a house next to the post office and general stores. In the 1940s with less traffic on the roads and petrol rationing, it was possible for me to stand on the other side of the road and shout to my mother to come out and cross me over. The river Wye ran past the bottom of our garden and my father kept foreign birds in an aviary. Across the stream was an area of land where Charlie Lilley kept large white Aylesbury ducks and beyond this stretched three fields. I can just remember these fields being dotted with concrete posts, I think to prevent enemy aircraft landing. In the first field which was used as the village football ground, was an enormous elm tree which was a splendid sight from our bathroom window. It was from this same window that my parents could look eastwards and see the night sky ablaze with the reflection of all the fires during the blitz on London.

One of my favourite pastimes each spring was to go off in search of wild flowers. The far side of the third field seemed to grow more cowslips than grass and even now I can smell the delicious scent of their perfume. Just over the level crossing at the bottom of Treadaway Hill was a curving flight of steps with an iron handrail which led up into the woods. In the lower part of the wood were clumps of delicate white wood anemones. Another foray took me along the London Road past Burleighfield House, the council tip and The Beech Tree public house to Knaves Beech – the haunt of a former highwayman. Just beyond Little Farm the chalk bank at the side of the road rose steeply, and along the top of this bank grew strongly scented purple violets. One field further back was the entrance to Whitehouse Tunnel and also a crossing where the sloping ground levelled out. I was always afraid of this place and never went there alone; the trains seemed to appear from nowhere, and I wanted to run when crossing the track. On the same side of the village, up steeply rising Dereham's Lane between banked hedges I once found viper's bugloss growing; before this I had only seen it in picture books. At the top of Dereham's Lane, across a flat field was a wood carpeted with bluebells and fringed with green curling bracken. This was another fairytale place where I half expected Flower Fairies to appear from behind the trees dressed in blue skirts and with bluebell caps on their heads.'

INTO THE 1950s

'We lived at the Westlington end of Dinton village from 1946, right by the village green, and so my journey to school was quite a long walk for a five year old, and because I didn't stay for a school dinner, I did it twice a day. In the summer we took the short cut across the fields known as the school fields, but in the winter or on wet days, we went round the road. This necessitated passing Mr Gregory's farmyard in which lived a flock of geese, and I can still remember being terrified of them as they came squawking and flapping at this little group of children wending their way to school.

Dinton was very much a "village" where everyone knew everyone else (and most of the time all their business too!). When I was very young the bread was delivered in a hand-cart by Mr Hitchcock, but when he retired we had to fetch the bread from the bakehouse. I can vividly remember the wonderful smell of baking bread that greeted one, and the feel of a lovely warm loaf (the taste too. I'm afraid the bread frequently had little holes in it before it arrived home – nothing to do with mice, just a naughty little girl). In the early days after the war the milk was delivered in churns, and the milkman filled the jugs at the door with his pint measure.

Although we had mains water, the main sewers did not arrive until much later, probably the mid 1950s, but I can't be sure of the exact date, and so once a week the cesspit had to be emptied, which was a very smelly business, but not as unpleasant as the bucket lavatories that some people, including the school, had to endure. Because our cesspit was not very big, bath water had to be rationed, and so my brother and I shared our weekly bath.

As children we were taught to have respect for our elders, and once a week I used to do some shopping in the village shop for an elderly housebound lady, Mrs Blanc. Our parents were not afraid to let us wander round the village to visit people, and one of our favourite haunts was the home of "Aunt Ginny", who seemed to have a constant supply of kittens. Goodness knows how many cats she had to produce all those youngsters, but we children loved to pop in to cuddle the kittens.

It probably sounds trite to say that our pleasures were simple, but they were, and as my parents didn't possess a car, summer Sunday afternoons were spent enjoying a nice long walk, my grandmother in her wheelchair, and a simple picnic in the basket, to be eaten somewhere down the Cuddington road. My father, being a country man, taught my brother and I to appreciate the countryside, pointing out the wild flowers, butterflies and birds as we walked.

Our only means of transport to Aylesbury was the bus, which didn't come down into the village. When I started work I didn't get home until six o'clock, and so every day I had a long walk home, in the dark in the winter, as there were no street lights. When I started courting, my boyfriend had no car either, and so my caring father was always up at the bus stop to meet the bus and walk down the road with me. However, this did mean that I had to catch the nine o'clock bus home, but my long suffering boyfriend didn't complain, and he is in fact now my husband. I wonder how today's youngsters would have accepted such limitations!'

'My memories are of Pann Mill and the Rye during the fifties. I spent a large part of my early life living in the mill house and the Rye was my playground.

My grandfather had bought the mill in 1921 and my father had taken over after the war. In 1947, my parents bought the little cafe on the edge of the Rye, close to the mill. My mother ran the cafe from March to October. At that time, housing was scarce and many women who had married at the end of the war and were living with relations, spent part of their time on the Rye with their young children so playmates were never a problem.

There were characters who came to the cafe, like Uncle Tom, who supervised the children's playground and my "uncle" Percy who ran the rowing boats on the Dyke. He was great fun and I spent hours watching him paint and repair the boats. On summer evenings, while my parents tidied up at the cafe, I would go with Percy along the Dyke to get all the abandoned rowing boats and bring them back to the boathouse.

During the holidays I would go out with my father on the lorry delivering to farms and smallholdings around Wycombe. Everywhere we were met with hospitality and although we were not able to stay long at all places, there was always time for a chat and a look at the animals. One of my favourites was Hall Barn, Beaconsfield where the head groom would show me the beautiful horses in the stables, particularly in winter months. Another favourite was Winchmore Hill, where my father often bought a lorry load of hay or straw straight from the field and that was great fun riding on top back to the farmyard.

Living in the mill house would have been unbearable today as the road had been built close to it but then it was just the occasional car. I would be awakened in the mornings by the Tate and Lyle lorries rumbling by, then the road sweeper came swishing up and down. Then the occasional car passed but it was mainly buses and bicycles. Collecting car numbers was a favourite pastime but it took ages to get a dozen or more.

The Rye itself was almost the same as now but the swings and roundabouts were not so modern. The favourite thing was the model steam railway that ran at the far end of the Rye. For a few pence you could have a ride on the miniature train. Inside the track there was a putting green for all budding golfers.

Looking back, I think it was the freedom we children had in those days to roam the Rye or later, when we moved to Totteridge, to go into the woods and build camps and play cowboys and indians that I remember. Freedom to be children and to use our imagination in our games. We had few purpose-built toys, but we had days packed with enjoyment.'

'When I was a child in the late 1940s my brother, sister and I would spend many special times visiting our grandparents at Dorneywood, Burnham, the then home of Lord Courtauld Thomson. My grandfather was the cowman and groundsman and my grandmother helped in the big house and in the kitchen when there were large gatherings to cater for. My grandparents lived in one of the cottages on the estate.

Early in the morning we would cycle from Farnham Common, through Burnham Beeches to Dorneywood and enter the estate through a gate in "the top field" just off Green Lane. We would cycle through the field, down the hill and through the five-barred gate, through the next field and there at the top gate would be Granny in her cross-over pinny and her hairnet keeping her very thin, wispy hair in place. "Com'on me dears, I have just put a bacon badger on to boil for your dinners." (This was suetcrust pastry rolled into an oblong, sprinkled with sliced onions and rashers of streaky bacon layered across, herbs and seasoning. This was then rolled up like a swiss roll, placed in a floured cloth which was stitched along with a large darning needle, the ends tied with string. It was placed

104

*Farm horses such as Tommy, seen here at Verney near the Claydons in 1934, often did duty as entertainment for the children.*

in a large saucepan of boiling water and boiled for about three hours. Delicious when you are really hungry having run around in the fields all morning.)

We would then go and find Grandad in the cowsheds milking the cows, with his flat cap back-to-front and his head pressed into the warm side of the cow, drawing the milk into a shining pail. I can still remember the taste of that warm milk (not sterilised, of course), having an enamel mug full straight from the pail. When he had finished we would help him take the milk to the big house kitchen where Mrs Bridger would be waiting to make some of it into butter for the table.

Another memory is of the feel and smell of the old barn where Grandad would do his "inside work" if the weather was bad. There was a large chopping block where the wood for the house fires was split. The barn would smell of a mixture of creosote, pine, damp and warm wood and we would sit in there with Grandad and share his can of tea and bread and cheese for mid-morning break; this always tasted much better than eating it indoors off a plate!

Sometimes Granny would ask us to take his mid-morning break out to him where he was working hedging and ditching. "He's probably in the leg-of-mutton-field by now," Granny would say and off we would go to the field at the end of Park Road and again share the food while sitting on the bank with our feet in the ditch. For clearing the ditches Grandad always had a forked stick and a sickle.

105

If we had stayed overnight we would get up early on a misty morning and go mushrooming and come back and cook them with bacon for our breakfast.

At lunch time we would go into Granny's kitchen with its black-leaded kitchen range and large table in the middle of the room, which we all sat round for our bacon badger and veg. Sometimes Grandad would come home during the day for his lunch and on asking whether he would like some he would say, "Ah, I'll have a small decoption." Very often he would say to we children, "You go and wash your hands before you eat, they're as black as Newgate's knocker" – it was a long time before I knew what he meant by that saying!

Very often Lord Courtauld Thomson would come over to the cottage when he knew we were there. We would go with him to the three-sided barn to play table tennis and his dog Buster would have to retrieve the ball when it went under the table and was lodged in the brick parquet-flooring. This barn had stained-glass windows in it, one being the badge of the St John's Ambulance Brigade.

In the garden there was a sunken garden with a bank all round and a lawn in the middle. In the centre of the lawn was an old apple tree with honeysuckle growing up it. My sister and I buried an empty walnut shell with a note in it; that was our secret. I wonder if it is still there!

Now, of course, Dorneywood belongs to the country, ie the Government, having been left by Lord Courtauld Thomson in his will. It is the country home of the Chancellor of the Exchequer. Because of security we are not even allowed to enter the gates, except by payment on the one open day a year, let alone glide up the drive on our bicycles, play table tennis or football on the lawns. Just shows you should never take anything for granted!'

'Bred in Bucks, I missed being born here by a few months. My parents moved to Prestwood in 1950, and I had been born in that January. My sister is a true Bucks lady – she was born in June 1953 and my mother tells a wonderful tale of the Coronation celebrations on Prestwood Common which she and my father attended. My London-born Mum sallied forth in all her nine-month glory to participate, only to be frowned upon by the local dowagers and ostracised for "flaunting herself in *that* condition".

In the 1950s Prestwood was a village very different to the sprawling modern development it is today. Famous for "Prestwood Black" cherries and "Prestwood Red" bricks, for a child it held wonderful secret places in the woods and fields, and the derelict Prestwood Lodge, out of whose haunted cellars some brave local

106

lads had run screaming one All Hallows Eve. It isn't so long ago, but the Prestwood of my lovely childhood has vanished forever.

It was a very self-contained place then. As well as the grocers and butchers, there were the intriguing mysteries of Mrs Langley's bra and corset shop, whose window was for some reason shrouded in a sort of yellow cling film; Mr Fowler's "Electrics" where I saw my first television; the wood yard which gave me sawdust for my guinea pigs; Mr Rae the chemist who (unbelievably now) chain smoked over the prescriptions; and the delights of "Joyce's" sweet shop, where I went every Saturday to spend my half-crown pocket money.

Frequent buses (which ran on time) at a penny ha'penny fare "down the hill" meant I could go, alone, to Great Missenden where my dance classes were and my best friend lived. I did this from the age of six, and if I missed the bus, I walked the mile through the woods. I also walked alone the half mile to Brownies – in the dark in wintertime, but we were never frightened because there was nothing to be frightened of. Now I worry if my eleven year old is late returning from his friend's house 100 yards away. My childhood was so carefree. When I remember how I camped in the fields and went on long, all day bike rides, I feel very resentful that the world has become so frighteningly dangerous for our children, and in such a short space of time.'

# FUN AND GAMES

**Children's games were often highly organised, with intricate rules which seem to have been understood intuitively by all participants! Toys themselves had to be fairly cheap and long-lasting, but were none the less exciting for that. Don't you rather like the idea of toboganning down Wycombe hill on a chair back?**

OUT OF SCHOOL

'Out of school, we really came to life. Some of the games we played then at Hyde Heath are still played today, such as hopscotch, skipping and rounders. But I have not seen any child of today bowling a hoop or whipping a spinning top in the road. These hoops were made of wood or steel, the boys loving the steel ones for the noise they made. Whips and tops were bought from Murrells, one penny for the top and a halfpenny for the whip. Plain wood tops we coloured with chalks, and very pretty they looked when spinning. I earned my pennies for these by picking up stones in the Wick garden, a penny a bucketful. Another way of earning pennies was running errands, and delivering notes to so-called posh houses with invitations to bridge parties. All our gang had an eye for the main chance.

Playing on the common was sheer heaven. Except for some frontage of bare heathland it was a wild refuge where we could hide from angry parents, among the ferns and gorse. The trees you see today were young saplings then and very few trees were climbable. We could tread among primroses and violets, harebells and broom. Here we could build a camp among the bracken. We might find a rabbit warren, or newts, grass snakes or stoats.

When the Tarzan films were first shown at the old Astoria Cinema in Chesham, time off was spent in Brays Wood, the boys swinging from the trees with bloodcurdling cries showing off to us girls. We would ignore them by carrying on picking primroses or making daisy chains from the dog daisies in the nearby field.

Lots of time was spent in the summer by the river at Little Missenden, and scrumping apples from Mantles Farm on the way home. If any real mischief was done our parents were sure to hear of it before we arrived home. Then it was a good hiding and no going out to play for a week.'

'It was lovely when the spring came and the evenings were light enough for us to play outside with our tops – some were "window breakers", the long ones were "carrots" and the short dumpy ones, "cabbages". We played sevens with our balls against a flat wall and in the autumn helped in the cornfields, "shocking", which meant stacking the dried sheaves in four pairs to create a tunnel to speed the drying – but they were fun to crawl through too. We gleaned for corn for our two hens.'

'The village of Marsh Gibbon was mainly owned, and still is, by the Ewelme Trustees, based in the Oxfordshire village of Ewelme. So we had no "big house" personalities to tug our forelocks to, and as most of the farms were only tenanted, we were all nearly as good as each other.

The village was surrounded by mature elm and chestnut trees, all waiting for us to climb. In spite of many warnings – "You'll fall out and break your legs!", we never did, and I spent many

108

happy hours aloft. One elm tree had a branch which overhung the main street, and I enjoyed lying along that branch, waiting quietly for an unsuspecting cyclist, and dropping little twigs on his head. Inevitably someone told on me, and Dad took his rusty old saw and hacked off the offending branch.

One year many of the mature elms were cut down by the Trustees and I still remember the sound of those lovely trees groaning before crashing to the ground. The tops of the trees were fun to swing and bounce in before they were cleared away and burnt, and the big trunks were carted away to the outskirts of the village and there sawn into planks. These were stacked up and left to mature, and we were told they were to be used to make coffins. The buzz of the saw seemed to go on for weeks and the village seemed sadly bare and denuded without its trees. The great pile of sawdust gradually consolidated and then we children dug channels in it and made "houses".

One day the schoolmaster's son Kenneth and Guy from the Manor Farm came "slumming" to our end of the village and began to tease us. I lashed out at Kenneth with my knitted hat, forgetting the "diamante" ornament pinned to it, which opened up a cut in his head. I dashed for home in fear and trembling, and hid myself in the farm buildings with my latest *School Girls Own* to read, expecting Mr Elias to come to the farm and complain. But nothing was ever said, so perhaps Kenneth kept quiet.

My *School Girls Own* weekly magazine was a great joy, and I regarded Betty Barton, Polly Linton and Pam Willoughby as my friends. I wonder if anyone else still remembers their fictitious boarding school – no silly cartoon drawings in that comic, with balloons coming out of people's mouths, but good solid stories which kept me reading for days. Books were not so easily available them. One dreadful morning I came home to dinner from school to find my mother in the throes of spring cleaning and all my carefully hoarded copies on the bonfire.'

GRASS TOBOGGANING

'During the 1920s and 1930s children could hire chair backs complete with the back legs only, from cottagers living in West Wycombe village. These they smeared with paraffin-soaked rags and used them to grass-toboggan down West Wycombe Hill. Many came off into the road and some girls were not allowed to join in as their parents considered it unladylike.'

'I would walk from the centre of High Wycombe with my two sisters to West Wycombe Hill carrying a very heavy wooden sledge. We would also have a bottle of water, or lemonade if lucky, and doorstep sandwiches, and would be gone all day. We bought a bottle of paraffin for a penny to rub on the skis, climbed to the top of the hill and sped down. Wonderful! We would come home for tea tired but happy, with lots of grazes.

Another treat was the old open air swimming pool in Desborough Road Recreation Ground. There, for a penny, you could swim all day alongside flies, spiders, tadpoles etc. No such thing as chlorine. Then on to the Rec for a game of ball and perhaps a collection to see if we could afford a bag of chips.'

## AYE ACKEE

'Aye Ackee was a game played in Chesham in the past. You needed a home base (usually a manhole cover), a large stone and a number of children. One person remained at the base and counted to an agreed number while the rest hid. The catcher called "Coming" and if they could see anyone they called "Aye Ackee one, two, three" (banging three times on the manhole cover with the stone), "I spy Mary" (or Tom, or whatever the child's name was). Then whoever had been caught had to stand at the base.

The catcher went on looking for the others until all were found but if one of them could get to the stone without being caught they called "Aye Ackee", knocking three times again, and those already caught were freed.

If any were not released at the end of the game, they became catcher; if not the original catcher carried on.'

## THROW TIN AND SEVEN TILES

'These two games were played in the road at Great Hampden, which was quite safe and free from traffic 70 years ago.

For Seven Tiles two sides were chosen. The seven tiles, mostly broken pieces, were piled on top of each other. The first player threw the ball at the tiles, knocking them down, and called the name of one of the players on the opposing side who then ran for the ball, threw it and tried to hit the player who was piling up the tiles again. If he succeeded, it counted one for his side. Each player had a turn and successful hits were counted. Then the other side played. The side with the most hits was the winner. If, when the ball was thrown and knocked down the tiles, the opposing player caught it, then the other side was out and lost the game!

With Throw Tin, one of the players was chosen to throw the tin as far as he could, calling out the name of the one he had chosen to fetch it. While he was fetching it, all the others hid in sheds etc, anywhere they could find a place. When the player got back to the starting place, he then had to search for the hidden players, and also prevent any of them creeping unnoticed to the tin. If they succeeded in reaching the tin unnoticed, they were the winners. However, if the finder found all the hidden players, he was the winner. If the finder failed to find all the players he would shout, "Ooper oller, opperay, if you don't oller I don't play" (Bucks dialect). Whereupon the hidden person would make a small noise to give a clue.'

# SCHOOLDAYS: THE BEST YEARS OF OUR LIVES?

**Small village schools, tortoise stoves in the winter, slates to write on, a slap or the cane if you were naughty – memories that span a half century or more. By the age of 14, children were expected to be earning their living and had left school, thankfully or otherwise, but many had cause to be grateful for a firm grounding in education given by hard working, if strict, teachers.**

BASIC BUT THOROUGH

'Schooling in the Claydons in the old days was basic but thorough. Most pupils finished education at 14 when they left the village school; only one of Claydons pupils per year was awarded a place at the Latin School in Buckingham, with likely candidates getting two chances to sit the exams at eleven to twelve years old. However, some parents thought it was "not worth educating a girl" so didn't allow them to sit the exams anyway.

In the very early days pre 1900 the village boys over seven years attended the Park School in Middle Claydon, which meant a walk of two to three miles for the majority of pupils who lived in East and Botolph Claydon. Girls apparently were not catered for at all. If a recalcitrant pupil could not be thrashed by the headmaster the

111

village policeman was sent for! When the East Claydon school was built (1900) the Park School closed and the building was put to use as a library.

The East Claydon school was a traditional Victorian village school which taught up to Standard Seven. Classes were defined by age range, and the same teacher taught that class all subjects. The only relief from this was the month long spell during which older pupils were sent to special classroom facilities in Quainton to do Domestic Science or Woodwork.

The village school was much busier than today, with around 70 pupils in the 1920s. Several teachers made a lasting impression. Miss Manton suffered from asthma, so kept the windows open and everyone froze. She wore half-moon glasses and an old overcoat, and would "thump your hand" for minor transgressions. However, "if she couldn't get it over to you, no one could". Miss Steele ("by name and by nature") terrified one pupil so much that she remembers frantically practising her figure 3 in her custard at home so as to be able to get it right at school that afternoon. Another pupil vividly recalled needlework and knitting – the latter done by both sexes. When told by Miss Bradley that she had dropped a stitch she nervously blurted out, "I'll go back and see if I can find it."

School dinners did not exist. If you lived in the village you walked home for lunch; those from further afield sat in the schoolyard and ate food brought from home. The bell was rung first thing in the morning and after lunch. Later memories include halfpenny cocoa in the winter, and tins of biscuits sold at three plain or one chocolate for a penny. The building was heated by coke stoves in the winter. The cast iron fence round the stove provided somewhere to dry off damp clothes – so the classrooms often smelled of steaming clothes. The boiler needed to be replenished two to three times a day, usually by the children.

School was also the route by which medical inspections and dentistry were brought to village children. The School Dentist took over the infants classroom (the Little Room). One member who grew up in a village in the north of the county was required, as the tallest pupil in the school, to work the dentist's treadle for the drill and to dispose of the extracted teeth. This went on as recently as 1952.

For medicals the girls had to line up in their navy bloomers, and the boys in their underpants. At one time one of the male school governors used to sit in on the medicals, until protests from the parents of some of the older girls put a stop to it.'

## INFANTS SCHOOLS TO GRAMMAR SCHOOLS

'As children before the First World War, we had to walk from our home in Horn Hill to the infants school in Chalfont St Peter, and take our sandwiches for lunch. We often got our feet wet – there were no such things as wellingtons then, and I remember my mother writing to the headmistress asking if we could bring slippers to wear in school. The answer was "no" – it would make too much complication in the cloakroom! There were no flush lavatories, of course, but we had at the side of the school a row of buckets and wooden seats and a row of racks in which were newspapers, and the caretaker used to empty the buckets – perhaps in the adjoining allotments, from which we often pinched the peas.

As a family we weren't brainy and none of us won scholarships, but our parents at great sacrifice sent we three girls to Wycombe High School, and our brother cycled to Amersham Grammar School. It meant we all had to have bicycles to get to Gerrards Cross station, four miles away. During the winter we came home in the dark so lamps were necessary. I remember the old oil lamps, with wicks that needed trimming, and then there were lamps using "carbide" – they were a task to keep alight and we had a lot of trouble trying to avoid the policeman when the lamps were out. He had a habit, when he came along and found us struggling in the dark, of feeling the wretched lamp to see if it was warm and had just gone out.

Often we had punctures and tyres and tubes would become beyond repair. It might be weeks before our parents had money enough to renew them, so we just had to walk to the station. I don't remember we made any fuss, it was just part of life. When my youngest sister got to the grammar school, she being ten years my junior, she used the first bus. It was called "The Fever Bus" as it was full to bursting with passengers (no control of numbers then) and the windows got so steamed up you couldn't see out! Even then she had to walk a mile to catch it.

During those early years we were really poor and I well remember that we had hands covered with chilblains and, until we learned to knit and could make wool cuffs, and later knit gloves, our hands were never warm. No one outside the family knew the hard struggle our parents had with clothing, fares, buying school books etc, but we all ended up having respectable jobs and I hope have been able to repay their sacrifices.'

'Just after the First World War I was ten and working for a scholarship to the grammar school. To everyone's surprise three of us got in. If you didn't get in, you stayed at the village school at Quainton until you were 14 and went to work. I started at the grammar school when I was eleven and while we were there Mrs Ashley taught needlework – everybody hated her, when she laughed she had to hold her teeth in, which we loathed. She had five girls in her family who all wore black stockings and we had to darn them. I was good at sewing so I got a lot of it, on one of those funny mushrooms. Then we used to turn her sheets sides to middle, oversewed one end to the other and then hemmed the sides, all by hand.'

'My first memory is going to the church school which was just outside the village of Hambleden, and we could safely spin our tops along the road on the way. Most children had a few miles walk so would bring food for the day. One family came in their father's mule cart from up on the hills. At that time there were about 100 children and four teachers. Since then the school has closed and what few children there are join in with Frieth school in the next village. We first wrote in sand trays with our fingers in the infants class, later with pencils, then dipping our pen nibs into inkwells in our desks. The boys and girls had separate playgrounds, with outside bucket lavatories.

The dentist visited the school to give treatment and the District Nurse would examine our heads to see if we were clean! The headmaster would use the cane on either sex when necessary. Girls were taken to Marlow once a week for Cookery. Those pupils who won a scholarship went to Henley grammar school, boys to Sir William Borlase in Marlow. Of those who left school at 14, the girls mostly went to work in the large houses, later moving to London or elsewhere to better themselves, while boys would work in shops, gardening or on the farms.'

SCHOOLS IN THE 1920s

'Children walked to Asheridge school through woods and across fields from the villages of Chartridge, Bellingdon and Asheridge itself. Most children walked or ran home to lunch, for which an hour and a half was allowed in the summer and an hour and a quarter in winter. The children who stayed at school took potatoes which the schoolmistress, Mrs Ogborn baked for them, after each child had carved their initials in their own potato. The children had cocoa for their mid-morning break and those who stayed at school for lunch were given another cup then.

Mrs Ogborn and her husband lived in the schoolhouse next to the school and they were both very good to the children, taking them on frequent outings. One fondly remembered was to Southend, and they also went to the Empire Exhibition at Wembley in 1924.

Games were played according to the season; hopscotch, conkers, spinning tops, marbles, hoops, skipping and sliding on the ice and snowballing in winter. Festival days were celebrated with much rejoicing; the children still had to attend school but instead of lessons the activity would be appropriate to the day – maypole dancing on May Day, making their own Union Jack on Empire Day, making pancakes on Shrove Tuesday and waving ash twigs on Ash Wednesday. The school was used for village activities in the evening such as whist drives and occasional concerts.'

'We were three boys and one girl in the family and I started at Padbury school in the 1920s when I was five years old. My brothers too, went to Padbury school.

The outside of the school looked just as it does now except that there were railings along the front adjoining the road. The inside of the school had two rooms, one of which was very large and had a portable screen across so that it could be divided into two. The other was always referred to as the "little room". There were two teachers and about 60 children aged from five to 14 years.

When you started school you went into the little room. The teacher was called Miss Lidgett. She was a very good kind teacher but was very strict. If children were naughty she would smack them on their hands with a ruler and remember, you didn't talk when you were working, and had to sit in little desks; no wandering round or sitting on mats for stories as children do today.

Just after I started school and not knowing any better, when Miss Lidgett smacked one little boy, unfairly as I thought, I told her that she shouldn't have done it. I had to go and stand outside in the cloakroom as a punishment and can still remember the feeling of shame, not helped by other children passing by and saying, "What are you here for?"

At the same time there were wet playtimes when we crowded around a cheerful fire with Miss Lidgett (there was an iron guard) and listened to stories. The larger room had two tall tortoise stoves. These were not nearly so cosy and had to be stoked with coke and often smoked.

Miss Lidgett loved flowers and we all vied in taking her little bunches which she put in her collection of pretty vases. They brightened up the classroom.

We didn't have all the lovely materials and paints that children have today. We first used slates and slate pencils. We did try to make circular scarves on mahogany frames with pegs in, using a blacksmith's nail to pop the stitches over. We used a great deal of plasticine (always a dingy colour). Miss Lidgett was very helpful with handwork and finding new ideas.

Going to the toilet was always an adventure, an escape from lessons for a little while as you had to go outside the cloakroom door onto the road and round the school to a row of toilets in the playground. Of course they were not flush toilets but bucket toilets which had to be emptied each week.

The playground was very rough and gravelly. We didn't have any grass playing fields so couldn't play cricket or football, and the little ones had just the small playground. However, we still managed to enjoy playtimes and played all kinds of games like Sheep, Sheep Come Home.

You felt very grown up when you left the little room and Miss Lidgett and it took quite a lot of getting used to being in the "big room". For one thing the desks were much bigger. Here, our teacher was called Miss Steel and she was very kind and helpful.

Very few children had sandwiches in school at dinner time, only one or two who lived in places like the Coombs, a good distance away. Everybody else went home for dinner and that meant walking and being back when the bell went.

We had "prayers" every morning and sang a hymn, the infants joining us for this, and we always sang a hymn before home. Every year we had a special scripture examination by a visiting vicar for what was called the "Bishops Prize". I think most local schools had that.

In those days we only had oranges as a treat at Christmas time and very few bananas so we were all pleased in the autumn when a gentleman called Mr Gore Langton who lived in the big house in the village, Padbury Lodge, came to school with a large basket of lovely red apples from his orchard and gave us all one.

We all had a little garden to look after in front of the school. Some grew flowers and some vegetables and there was a prize for the best one each year. We had very few books and no library. A lot of the girls wore white starched frilled overalls, especially when they were in the "little room". Boys and girls wore buttoned boots.

Outside school it was possible to play games in the main road, difficult to imagine in these days of heavy traffic. We used to play spinning tops with a whip. There were two kinds of tops, one thicker than the other. Then there was playing with hoops, the boys using metal ones and the girls wooden ones, seeing how far you could keep them bowling along with a stick.

The present butcher's shop was then a grocer's shop but at Christmas one window was devoted to toys and as one very seldom went to Buckingham (no cars etc), Christmas presents were bought from there and many children spent happy hours deciding which present they hoped to have.'

'The school at Fawley Green consisted of two rooms, one for the infants and a larger room for the eight to 14 year olds. It was heated by a coke-burning stove which was surrounded by a guard rail and socks were put on this to dry. Some of the children had walked long distances and none of us had wellingtons then. The school lavatory was very primitive, a pit with a box seat with a hole in it – a good crop of nettles grew in the hole so it could be a bit hazardous!'

'8.45 am. The school bell has just rung, so we get ready for school which begins at 9 am. First we all stand for prayers, and then as it is Friday the rector comes in for an hour and reads out a text from the Bible. One was 2 Corinthians 13–14; for some reason we all remembered that.
   There were around 50 children at Adstock school and two teachers. One of my brothers used to get in two buckets of water for the headmaster who lived next door to the school. There was a fence of iron railings down the middle of the playground, boys one side, girls and infants the other. There was a big open fire in each room and water in the cloakroom if anyone needed a drink. We sat two to a desk with an inkwell sunk in it, one each. On Monday mornings one of the bigger boys filled them up out of a brown stone jar. We had drawing and painting some days, but always started with arithmetic and tables for the younger ones. On two afternoons we girls had sewing; learning to gather the garment, setting it into a band and sewing buttonholes in the top piece, so that not a bit was wasted. While we did this the boys were drawing – plants and leaves mostly. Children walked from Addington and Adstock Fields. During the winter it was very bad, but they were not often absent.'

'One of my earliest memories of school in Speen was taking a mug each day for milk, which was delivered by Mr Parslow in a large churn which he brought up the hill from his farm in the valley.
   On cold snowy days the tortoise stove in the big school room only seemed to puff out smoke, and little heat could be felt, so our wet gloves and hats never dried while we stayed cold. As spring arrived we began to practise maypole dancing in the playground day after day, with the boys sitting on the middle platform to keep it steady while the girls tried to dance. Every Thursday afternoon (if it was dry) we all walked to the playing field to play rounders, which was the highlight of the week.

117

When we at last had school dinners, which were delivered in a van with heatproof containers from Green Street school in High Wycombe, we would eat our meal as quickly as we could, then run as fast as possible down to Parslow's Bank and the last to arrive would be "it". We would then play Tin Can Tommy until we heard the whistle blow to mark the end of lunchtime.

Another happy lunchtime would be when Mr Dean the local chair bodger would arrive at the school with his horse and cart loaded with sacks of wood chips for the stoves. After unloading we would have a ride out of the village, then run back as fast as we could to avoid being late for afternoon class.'

'I first saw Hyde Heath in the late 1920s. Our family were early settlers from London. My first sight of Hyde Heath school was terrifying. I'd already had two months' rather horrible schooling in London, and this didn't look much better. Feeling hesitant and shy, I was ushered into the cloakroom with my sister and allotted a peg for my hat and coat.

All the children stared at us as we entered the huge classroom. Word had got around that we were foreigners twice over: our parents were Flemish, and we two girls had been born in London. Hyde Heath then was a very "closed" village, and we were worthy of a good gawp.

We were led into a smaller classroom and given small rounded-back chairs, then a slate and a slate pencil. Miss Reynolds the infants teacher must have had a vague hope that these would prompt us to produce something for her to assess, but I just burst into tears and wanted to go home.

Somehow I eventually settled into school life. Learning was a hard process. I was made to feel as thick as two planks. But I made friends easily with the other children, and remain friends to this day with those few who are still left in Hyde Heath.

At 8.50 am the school bell would be heard in the village, summoning us to hurry and get to school on time. We stampeded up Brays Lane, and even most of the dawdlers managed to make it. Those who didn't were lined up in the cloakroom for a swipe of the cane. This practice was carried on by the headmistress – Miss Fassam then and Mrs Donaldson in the 1930s.

Fear of the cane was a great persuader, and learning was pushed and beaten into pupils aged from five to eleven. After rollcall, our morning began with mumbled prayers. The first lesson was nearly always "sums".

We would recite our tables up to twelve-times until we knew them by heart. Then there were add-ups and take-aways, advancing (painfully for me) to other forms of mathematics. Calculators hadn't been invented! All that we could cram into our little brains, of history, geography, English and general knowledge, was reinforced by prolific use of the cane.

One day Joan Coutts and I sneaked the cane out of the classroom when Mrs Donaldson was in the schoolhouse. We threw it over the school wall into a thick hedge. That was one afternoon at least when it couldn't be used.

Winters at the school were very cold. Heating came from coal-stoves, one at each end of the big room. We pupils didn't benefit much, as Mrs Donaldson used to stand in front of one of them, rubbing her hands on the back of her skirt until it rose to reveal the legs of her brown directoire knickers. This sent the nearest pupils into fits of the giggles, for which we were rapped across the knuckles with the edge of a ruler. Our schooldays were very hard compared with today's – and we learned the hard way.

During summer playtimes we were allowed on the common. It was a pleasure to sit around the dewpond opposite the schoolhouse and catch tiddlers and frogs, plait rushes, make daisy-chains and play to our hearts' content until the school bell rang calling us back. I feel I learned more about the countryside than about the three Rs.

The toilets or "lavvies" were a sight not to behold – the last word in the hygiene of the day. There were three galvanised buckets under wooden seats with holes just big enough not to fall through. But there were at least partitions for privacy. No such luxury as toilet rolls those days – we had newspapers torn into squares, perforated at one corner and hung on string from a nail. The buckets were emptied daily by a man whose name I withhold from kindness. Goodness knows where he tipped the contents, but his family won prizes for the best veg and flowers at the annual Produce Show.'


INTO THE 1930s

'Walking to school in Tylers Green twice a day (home for dinner) was fun. What a lot children today miss with their constant transportation.

There were, of course, no pavements – but then, there were very few cars. Quite a lot of horse-drawn vehicles were still in use in the mid 1930s. I recall being picked up by the butcher one rainy day. There was no protection on his gig so I am sure I got even wetter.

Wet days were particular fun as the steep sides of the roads ran with gullies of water, down which we floated matches and twigs. The same roads in summer were a delightful hazard of wet tar on one's boots or shoes. I nostalgically recall the smell of newly-laid tar mingling with the aroma of newly-cut hay. A not-so-enticing smell was that of the cesspool emptier. We called this machine "Dirty Dennis".

We dawdled to school, sometimes playing with marbles, yoyos, skipping ropes, conkers (there was an unwritten "season" for such activities) or, failing these accessories, leap-frogging each other until we heard the tone of the school bell change. It pealed for about five minutes but the last half minute, it tolled. Then we ran the last few yards as it was a punishable offence to be late. A "big boy" in the school had the somewhat doubtful privilege of ringing the bell.

About twice a year, the ragman would be found waiting outside the school gate. This engendered great excitement. We raced home to beg old cast-off clothing and were then the recipients of a balloon or some such trifle from this quaint though crafty character.

Autumn brought the fruits of the earth – pear-scrumping time. A large pear tree, sadly no longer in the village, overhung a wall, and armed with sticks and stones we knocked the fruit to the ground till chased away by the irate owner. Great fun!'

'I attended Chalfont St Peter Church of England school from 1930 to 1936. We used to chalk on small blackboards until we were allowed paper and pencil in the top class. After that in the girls school adjoining, we sat in double desks, always in rows, which had a hole for the inkwell.

Every day started with prayers and a hymn, then Scripture and Arithmetic. After playtime came English. Reading aloud, reciting poetry and chanting tables were important activities and slow readers were helped in groups by the more advanced in the class. The playground was a stony slope draining into a slippery gutter of mud by the boys school.

The boys had a two-valve radio set and used water colours whereas the girls had only pastels. There was not much equipment, only coloured sashes for team games and bean bags, but we enjoyed school and progressed and were given an orange each to take home at Christmas. The "nit nurse" was a regular visitor.

Heavy rain washed gravel from the roads downhill so the High Street looked like a river of milky tea, but Mr Tomlin soon came with a barrow and shovel to clear the drains. At dusk Mr Dolby the lamplighter used his long pole to pull down the chains which turned the gas taps on top of the few street lights, which lit with a pop from the pilot flame.'

'My earliest recollection is of greeting my mother as I came out of Wendover school on my first afternoon with, "Mummy, I have learned *There is a happy land far, far away"*, then adding quickly, "My teacher says she taught Dad." Dad denied it.

Wendover school, along the Heron Path, was solidly built but without any modern conveniences. At lunchtime I rushed home for the loo; never was I going to use the one in the corner of the playground. The classrooms had high ceilings and windows from which no inattentive child could gaze out. We sat in rows in double desks, scarce daring to spill ink on the top. All was so orderly and well disciplined.

We were a Church of England school and began every morning with Scripture. We possessed no hall for our morning assemblies, the folding doors between the two classrooms were simply opened and all the "big" children crowded in. A large piano stood in the corner of one classroom on which "Tiger" Eldridge, as we irreverently called her, noisily accompanied our hymns. On Ascension Day morning we walked in crocodile with our bunches of flowers to the local church. I can't recall the service, but as soon as it was over the rest of the day was a holiday. Some nonconformist parents sent their children to Halton council school, but we met up later at Aylesbury grammar school, for competition was keen between Wendover and Halton schools as to which one could gain the most scholarship places.

In those pre-war days concentration was on the three Rs – we read regularly, often the Bible, were taught to write legibly and creatively and the importance of grammar (back to "Tiger" Eldridge – "Ain't fell in a pot of paint"), and mental arithmetic was an important ingredient in our education.

Physical education was simply "drill" in the playground. Alas, I was a well built clumsy child and looked longingly up at those high windows, thrilled if I saw rain. There was no grass for games, the playground was painted out in squares so we could play a modified form of netball, and we were so close to the main road that all passers-by could watch us.

A special treat every year for the pupils in Standard Five, Miss Smith's class, followed a sedate walk along the Heron Path, by the church into Barlow's Lane, to the home of Lord and Lady Barlow. Here we were each given a dish of strawberries and cream, then allowed to wander into the large garden to pick twelve sweetpeas to take home.'

'Monks Risborough Church School in the 1930s was just three rooms, one for the infants, one for the juniors and the largest room for the seniors. At eleven years old you sat the exam for the grammar or the high school and if you didn't pass you stayed at the village school until you left at the age of 14. I remember the infants class

121

very clearly. We played with plasticine, sewed stitches onto sheets of paper and painted pictures, copying leaves or flowers which we had picked from the hedgerows. Because it was a church school we used to sing a lot of hymns and always sang "Be present at our table, Lord" before we went home to dinner. Many of the children who came from Meadle had to walk two or three miles to school every day and they were allowed to bring their sandwiches for midday. There were very few cars about and certainly no one was brought to school in one, so on wet days we must have all arrived soaking wet. We had an open fire in the infants room with a guard around it and we would sit round the fire in the afternoon and Miss Williams, who had also taught my father, would read us a story – bliss! I could read fluently by the time I was six years old and remember going home one afternoon to tell my mother that I knew how to spell a word with 15 letters in it. "Insubordination," I said. "Ah," she replied, "but do you know what it means?" Regrettably I didn't.'

## BOARDING AT LITTLE MISSENDEN ABBEY

'Between 1936 and 1939 I was at boarding school in Little Missenden Abbey, very much nearer Great than Little Missenden! The 17th century abbey house, the gatehouse and stables are all now a mere pimple beside the huge, pink carbuncle of the Chiltern Hospital. In those days the river Misbourne flowed through the grounds and was sufficiently broad and deep at its Deep Mill end to sustain watercress beds and, in the school grounds, was large and deep enough for swimming and the use of a punt.

From time to time young intellectuals, fresh from university or from guerrilla fighting with the International Brigade in Spain, would take short teaching jobs at the school before embarking on their careers. Among them were artists and poets later to become quite well known, Douglas Glass being one such. Sir Michael Tippett taught at the school for a year before settling down to musical composition.

In the great hall stood an elegant grand piano belonging to the young composer, Edmund Rubbra, on which, amazingly, we were permitted to tinkle away at *Shepherd's Hey* or *Annie Laurie*. Rubbra visited the school quite frequently to see friends, walking over the hills from Piggot's, near Speen, the home of Eric Gill, the sculptor. On one occasion he arrived during the afternoon with a friend. A stocky figure, his hair was abundant and coppery-brown as was his beard; he wore brown corduroy trousers and a brown cloak with a scarlet lining. His friend, a dark saturnine figure, wore black cords and a black cloak with a splendid crimson lining. Rubbra sat down

122

at the piano, threw the cloak away from his shoulders (the better to reveal its lining?) and dashed through the first movement of his newest piano concerto. Having finished his recital, he stood up to replace the piano lid whereat a very young pupil, who had listened raptly to the music, remarked, "That wasn't too bad for a tramp!"

The headmistress drove a large and noisy Bugatti in which she would sometimes take three or four of us out driving, perhaps to Wendover to swim in the deep reservoir where we couldn't touch the bottom or perhaps to the Hampdens or the Kingshills. She drove with verve and great aplomb. When she had reason to apply the brakes over-fiercely, there were occasions when the child sitting on the car's tail, feet on the back seat, would fall off. No one was ever badly hurt!

In Great Missenden High Street a charming 18th century house was used as a guesthouse and tea-room by a Miss Chalker. On our half-days we would take it in turns to walk into Missenden to help "Chalker" for the afternoon, waiting at table, setting up the delicious cream teas and stuffing ourselves full of Chalker's superb home-made cakes before going back to school for supper, tired, but often the wealthier by two shillings and sixpence as a result of the tips which we were allowed to keep. Sadly Chalker's lovely house no longer graces Great Missenden High Street.'

## THE WAR YEARS AND AFTER

'Until the early years of the Second World War, children attending Wing village school were, once a year, offered boots, shirts or dresses by the Rothschild family. The shirts were grey flannel and the dresses navy blue with a peter pan collar and a row of buttons down the front. The boys' boots were ordinary ankle boots, but the girls' were calf length. I remember having a dress, but would dearly have loved a pair of black calf length boots.

The school grew at the outbreak of war with evacuees from London. Classes were big and presumably materials short, but we didn't notice this too much. With a strict headmaster, who always wore plus fours, waistcoat and jacket even in summer, we had a good all-round education. We all learned prayers and psalms, poetry, civics and Shakespeare, in addition to the more usual subjects. We were encouraged to write to sailors on the ship we adopted, and to knit balaclava helmets, scarfs, seaboot stockings, socks etc. We collected salvage which had to be sorted and tied up, the store being the reading room. In the summer we collected herbs and blackberries for bottling, and also went gleaning after the harvest was completed. School sports day until the mid 1950s was held on the cricket ground at Ascott. It always seemed to be fine and warm and a wonderful time was had by all, ending with an ice cream for each child and with Mrs Anthony de Rothschild presenting the cups and shields and declaring a half day holiday for the school.

Mrs de Rothschild was a regular visitor to the school and knew all the village families – their joys, sorrows and .problems. During the war she used to come into the school in a very small Red Cross Commandant's uniform. We later learned that this was just a front for her real work, which was a courier/aide at the Cypher Centre at Bletchley.'

'When five, just as the war was ending, I attended Beacons Bottom school at Stokenchurch. I remember particularly the times the school dentist would come, and for examination and treatment you had to sit in front of the window of the smallest classroom. Some of the children in the playground would peep in through the window. After treatment, you had to lie down on the floor on your coat to rest by the tortoise stove if it was cold weather.

During the war and just after, the school received parcels from Canada and Australia. They consisted of sugar, cocoa and raisins and were divided amongst the children. For the Victory Day celebrations in 1946 the children had a fancy dress competition and a tea party.

During the winter of 1947 there was a heavy snowfall and flooding followed in Beacons Bottom. The teacher took us along to the bottom of Brick Lane to see the water rushing across the road from the fields and through the gardens. In some cases houses were also flooded. I was so fascinated by this that I didn't arrive back at school at the same time as the others.'

'At Speen the school was run by a headmistress, Miss Hopton and one other teacher, Miss Smith. There was the "big room" and the "little room", the latter for the infants. During the war years the big room was divided and an extra teacher employed to cope with the evacuees. We had no central heating in those days, just a tortoise stove surrounded by a guard on which we hung our wet gloves – usually after we had been snowballing, and also on which a large steamer was placed to heat our dinners. This was a Church of England school and the vicar from Lacey Green would come once a week to take our Scripture lesson.

The playground had a clinker covered surface and I seemed to have permanent scars on my knees from falling over. We also had an air raid shelter which stood for many years after the war and was used to store sports equipment and of course the maypole which was brought into use every spring for the May Day celebrations. Many a romance was started after the passing of secret notes in class, with the meeting place "round the back of the air raid shelter".

After school and during the holidays we spent a lot of our time in Hampden Woods, where we would "help" the chair bodgers, fetching and carrying things for them and sitting round their fire at lunchtime. Then we would perhaps spend the afternoon making "moss castles". We each had a tree stump which we covered in moss, using mirrors for ponds, gravel for paths etc, and linked them up into little villages.'

'At West Wycombe school after the war the infants room was decorated with the one to twelve times table made up of the paper gollies from the Robertsons jam jars. We had miniature blackboards to work on which as monitor I had to collect up each night. All the lessons were taught in the one room for your year. The room had high windows, wooden furniture and was heated by a tortoise stove.

During the summer months I remember going on walks to pick blackberries to help with school dinners. Nature walks were fun, when we were allowed to pick wild flowers. On warm days the girls did their hand sewing under the large yew trees on the face of the hill and I lost a needle down between the gnarled roots that were above ground. We had sports day on the hill and did maypole dancing at the fete in the grounds of the dower house each year. My last positive memory at this school is in 1952, of hearing of the death of George VI while standing in the top playground at dinnertime.'


AYLESBURY'S FIRST SECONDARY MODERN

'One June morning in 1947 at about half past ten, I was standing outside Woolworth's (now Smith's) in Aylesbury High Street, having travelled there from Leamington Spa for an interview at two o'clock. I had applied for a post on the staff of the first non-selective mixed secondary school in Aylesbury. In response to the 1944 Education Act, it was to be established in what had been a boys elementary school and is now the Arts Centre and Limelight Theatre in Queen's Park.

What to do until two o'clock? I asked a passing policeman the whereabouts of the library and reading room, only to be told by that much amused officer that Aylesbury had no such facility. I found out two months later that he was in error, and there was in fact a library in a very old redundant school in Pebble Lane. I had been told by my uncle, who had been stationed at Hartwell House with army recruits during the war, that there were 16 pubs in the Market Square, but felt these were not for me, so I walked down to the Vale Gardens, where I watched a game of lawn bowls until it was time for my interview.

I was offered the post and in September came to Aylesbury to teach Biology and Needlework in its first secondary modern school for boys and girls of eleven to 14 years. From 300 pupils at Queen's Park, we expanded into temporary hut classrooms in Beaconsfield Road. In 1954 a fire at Aylesbury grammar school caused a shortage of accommodation there, so we vacated our school and huts for them to use and moved into those parts of a new school being built for us in Wendover Way which were habitable. There we made the best of things while the builders finished the rest – the laboratories, the assembly hall, the canteen, the gymnasium, woodwork and metalwork rooms and five more classrooms. We used one of the cookery rooms for biology lessons and there were two classes in the large library room – as yet bare of books, but there were nine classrooms fitted with desks and chairs and, most important of all, there were two blocks of toilets already in working order – and inside, if you please. Such luxury!

Thus was born the Grange School. Its aim then, as now, was to offer its pupils the facilities to fulfil their academic potential and to give them the chance to find a sport or other leisure activity which they could pursue with enthusiasm and confidence, and so become "whole men and women".'

# THE WORLD OF WORK

# ON THE FARM

**Farming has for centuries been the backbone of Buckinghamshire's working life. We tend now to look back at the days of horse power with nostalgia, and there was certainly great satisfaction and comradeship to be found in the slow turn of the farming year, but it is as well also to recall that the life of the labourer was hard and poorly paid – and that the sun didn't always shine!**

## LIFE ON THE FARM

'I was five years old when the war broke out in 1914. We farmed on the Bucks/Oxfordshire border, near Thame and our herd of 40 dairy cows was hand-milked twice daily by our cowman, Benjamin, and the milk was cooled by water from a nearby spring. The churns were taken by horse and cart to the station for the journey to London, and sometimes as a small child I was given a lift to school up behind Old Tom, the big black horse.

Benjamin brought his lunch every day, which consisted of the top of a cottage loaf, a large raw onion, a large piece of home-cured fat bacon and very often an apple dumpling. He cut all the food very deftly with a pocket knife, and washed it down with a bottle of cold tea.

Ploughing was done with a single furrow plough drawn by two horses in tandem, a slow and steady occupation. Later the corn was sown by a seed drill drawn by one horse. We had five horses in the stables.

There were sheep on the farm, and in those days all the disinfecting was done by hand. Hens scratched around in the yards and we children used to love collecting eggs from the mangers and the cowhouse.

At harvest time two horses abreast drew a binder which cut and bound the corn into sheaves, and we children helped stack the sheaves into stooks. These were pitchforked on to the waggons and we looked forward to the ride up on top back to the rickyard. The sheaves were hoisted on to the rick by means of a pony-driven elevator. The ricks were all beautifully thatched, corn ricks round and hay ricks square. Later we hired a steam engine and threshing machine and the bagged corn was then put up into the granary. All our dogs watched out for rats running from the ricks.

On one occasion during the First World War five soldiers were sent to help us with the haymaking, and we also entertained several convalescent soldiers from the local hospital at times. To help regain their health they used to skate and slide on our big pond during the hard winters.'

'In 1932 my father started farming at Strawberry Hill Farm, part of The Lee estate, owned by the Liberty family. The farm had been empty for the previous year, so the first year was rent free. The land was very poor, with thousands of rabbits eating whatever grew. Dad's first job was to get rid of them.

My father was a wheelwright and carpenter by trade, so that came in useful, as not only was he able to make and mend his own carts, but at busy times he was able to go back to help his old boss at Stoke Mandeville. This supplemented Dad's income, which at the time was a very meagre one.

My mother was a good manager, she seemed to be able to make a meal out of almost nothing – in fact in the early days at the farm, we practically lived on rabbits and rice puddings. Mum's rabbit pies were delicious. My brother and I were clothed in hand-me-downs, we never had anything new.

As all the farm work was done with horses, work was done at a more leisurely pace, and at haymaking and harvest time lots of people came to give a hand and to shoot rabbits. Food and drink was taken out to the helpers in the fields. It was a very happy time, but with the outbreak of war in 1939 things changed – the

*The master in his trap oversees the ploughing, done with a single furrow plough on this farm on the Bucks/Oxon border.*

young men who had worked in the manor gardens had to go to war and the farms began to use the new fertilizers and became more mechanised.'

'In the 1950s Singleborough had four dairy herds, where there are now only sheep and beef cattle. You could tell the size of the herd by the number of churns standing outside the farm gate, waiting for the milk lorry. When first we bought our farm, in 1956, the job of providing a churn stand was given to a semi-retired builder, who was invaluable for such jobs as providing us with our inside toilet. "That churn stand will last a lot longer than me," he said, surveying an edifice of brick and railway sleepers. But no! A few days later, the milk lorry pulled in a bit too sharply and the new stand collapsed.

Before the days of the milk lorry, farmers round here used to take their milk by horse and cart to Winslow station, to be loaded onto passenger trains to Bletchley and beyond. Our neighbour, after unloading his churns, used to turn in at The Railway Arms, now converted into a private house, for something a bit stronger than milk to fortify him for the three mile journey home, leaving the reins hitched to a hook outside. If he became unfit to drive, the other customers would load him into his cart and leave the horse to find its own way back.

There is a similar story about the way cows were collected for milking from our farthest fields, adjoining the main road. Our predecessor had a good cow-dog. He would take him to open the field gate onto the road, and then cut back across the fields to get ready for milking. The dog would then drive the herd out into the road, past the turn to Thornton, and then right across any traffic into our lane.

What is now our garden was once the rickyard, and for many years must have held a line of corn ricks waiting for the threshing machine sometime during the winter, to thresh out the stooks of corn. When we took over, so did the combine-harvester, cutting and threshing in one operation and loading the grain, first into two-hundredweight sacks, and before long, into the grain-trailers we know today.

During the First World War, Dr Barnado's Homes used to board out some of their orphans with farm workers' families around here. We were once visited by a very spruce old gentleman, revisiting the cottage where he had spent part of his childhood. He remembered the Armistice, and the party organised for all the children in the parish to celebrate it. To his everlasting dismay, his foster parent refused to spare him the penny needed to help pay for the food. What a sharp reminder of the poverty of the inter-war years, when a farm worker might have to raise a family on ten shillings a week.'

'We remember summer days on the farm at Thornborough as being warm and sunny but they were wet at times as well.

A fine bright morning with grass in the fields, made the cows reluctant to come to the buildings for milking and they had to be called with a brisk "Come-up" call or even driven in with the help of the farm dog. They each knew their place in the cowshed and were "clappsed" in with upright wooden struts of the "browser" where the cow-cake and meal mixture was placed. The more milk the cow gave the more bowls of meal she was rewarded with. There were usually eleven or so cows to milk by hand on this smallholding, some of which produced calves in the summer and were "dried off" some weeks before they calved. This saved time with the milking while we had so much other work to do with the hay work and harvesting.

The laying hens, fattening ducks and geese were let out of the coops and sheds and fed, and some birds which didn't know that they would finish up on a meat platter were given extra rations and restricted to a run (a fenced piece of ground).

The pigs were allowed to go free range except the fattening-up ones. These had the best scraps and were viewed, poked and discussed by visitors to the farm.

After breakfast the main work of the day started. If there was hay to make and bring home it was busy for all including the horse, who was a faithful worker but enjoyed its food, shelter and understanding care like the rest of us. It was the horse which was harnessed to the mowing machine, pulling it with its rider around the field to cut the swarths of grass – and when the sun had dried it a little, the horse was put in the shafts of the swarth turner to turn the grass over to dry what was underneath; then to the machine which put two or more swarths into one, ready for the hayloaders to pitch it into the cart. Sometimes at this stage the weather was doubtful so the hay was put into heaps of hay called haycocks, to withstand the showers. When the hay was fit to put into store for winter feed it was the horse which pulled the haywaggon – a flat-bedded four wheeler with side rigging – between the rows of hay. When the call was made to the loader on top of the load to "Hold tight", the horse walked a few yards for more hay to be loaded or pitched on. Then to the rick where he stood patiently in the shafts eating fresh hay while it was unloaded on to the rick.

At midday when everyone had a rest and enjoyed a meal and drink, the horse was led to the cool stable where the harness was removed and he had a feed as well, but not a drink until he had cooled down as this would have given him colic.

More work in the afternoon for all, before the evening feeding and milking, then another load or so before the end of the day. Neighbouring farm workers would help when they could and we would help them in return. Then the dining table would groan with salads and sandwiches. During the day, refreshingly cold cider and hot tea would be taken to the hay field and rickyard.

Other jobs in the summer included hoeing the root crops, progressing along the long rows in the heat of the day, changing hands to work left-handed on the way back. One soon adapted and could use a hoe and most tools with either hand when it was needed.

The cows were mostly Shorthorn, but some had a mixed parentage in them; a favourite was part Jersey, and a large roan cow was part Hereford stock. Another, a blue-black, small and stocky, was more like an Aberdeen Angus.

They were bought or reared for production, sometimes at a bargain price, and not their looks, and were peaceful and gave no trouble. I only got kicked once, and that was not by the cow I was sitting milking, which I stopped from fidgeting by talking calmly to her and holding her back legs with one hand and pail with the other. The cows were frightened by the presence of a cat which was disturbed from its snooze by the cows eating amongst the hay in the browser. It leapt out amongst feet and hooves. Cat and cows were both scared and I got the worst of it, as the cow standing behind me lashed and caught me in the side – it sent me, pail and milk, all flying! I remember turning over in midair and miraculously landing on my feet several yards away, none the worse except for a bruise, but the milk was spilt and wasted.

It was an early start to the day when the threshing machine was working at the farm in the short days of winter.

Although the fowl could not be let out before daylight in case of a wandering fox looking for breakfast, there was the milking to be done, animals to be fed and mucked out, all before breakfast time. The two men in charge of the traction steam engine and threshing box came up the farm road through the gloom in their van which contained every imaginary spare part they might need. The boiler was stoked up and various belts were checked and driving wheels were oiled ready to start.

The "gang" was made up of neighbouring farmworkers and we helped them in return, or, later on in the wartime, a threshing gang of landgirls were employed. When these were unobtainable some DPs (Displaced Persons) were supplied. Some of these came from European towns and were not used to manual work, one could not help feeling sorry for them when showing them how to handle a pitchfork before they could start work. Eight to ten workers were needed, two to move the corn sheaves to the machine, one on the threshing box to cut the string bands on the sheaves and feed them into the drum. At the other end one worker to bag off the corn into hessian sacks, weigh and tie up. Another worker took the straw to two workers on the straw rick which was being built. I was needed to remove the chaff and cavings (short straw). This was one of the hardest jobs (and usually it was mine!), it was very dusty too. The chaff and cavings were raked out from underneath the machine onto a hessian square made from a large opened sack. The four corners were pulled together to form a bundle and carried on weary shoulders into a sectioned part of the big barn and later used as floor litter in the hen houses. As the day wore on, the heap got bigger and higher and I got dustier scrambling up to unload the bundles.

We had a break midmorning, but the machine didn't stop working. We had a few free minutes when the feeder stopped putting sheaves into the machine. The machine was fed regularly and so disgorged relentlessly, one couldn't relax in seeing to its needs. As the corn rick got lower so the straw rick increased in size.

The workers found a sheltered corner in the buildings for their packed dinner washed down with hot tea, ready to start off again. It was hard work for the corn rick men as the corn rick was emptied, as every sheaf then had to be lifted up to the feeder on the box. They tied string around their trouser legs to stop the mice getting inside their clothing and kept heavy sticks handy in readiness to strike at escaping vermin which had made their winter quarters in the corn ricks.

The machine stopped when daylight faded. Canvas sheets tied to weights to hold them down were put on half finished ricks. Tools were put away for the night and the gang thankfully went on their way. Somehow during the day, time had been found to feed the fowl, collect the eggs and secure them up again. Now after a meal it was time to milk the cows again before removing the dust and grime and so to bed.

The threshing box was booked in advance and stayed for several days threshing, sometimes to thresh wheat or oats or barley. Bean crops were the worst, being so dusty and they made more noise through the machine.

Some preparations had to be made – engine coal was delivered, hams cooked ready for hungry workers and the thatch taken off the first rick to be worked on. The corn ricks were usually built in blocks of two with a space between to accommodate the threshing machine.

Most of the animals on farms are not remembered but one or two stand out and can be recalled. Henny Penny the hen came running across the farmyard whenever the tablecloth was shaken outside. She strutted in and searched for crumbs under the dining table and as far as I know she never made a mess. One visitor thought she was well housetrained.

Another was Lucy the breeding sow, who was dutifully driven down two fields to visit a "husband", the boar. The first time two "attendants" were needed as the stiles were dismantled between fields to give passage. Not so the next time or ever after, she promptly put her large snout under the lowest rail and demolished the stile and was across the fields with the attendants running after. She was the only sow I can remember which made a farrowing bed from collected litter. One had to be careful not to leave coats, sacks or anything around or Lucy would come and take it away.

My sister and I used to cycle into the local town to visit the pictures or dances. One dark night my cycle lights failed and we only had one good set between us but we managed. I had the good front one while my sister had the good rear and we rode home in tandem. We were stopped by a local police car and we thought we would have a summons and a fine. We were let off with a caution when they discovered we were "the gals who sold the Aylesbury ducks ready for the table".'

## CHANGING TIMES

'Farming at Great Hampden in the 1920s was very different to today. The farmer aimed to have something to sell each week. The farmer's wife made butter; I can remember my grandmother turning a huge wooden churn as big as a beer keg. There were the eggs, a calf or two, sheep and maybe a pig. If there was nothing to sell, there was no money.

The farm workers seemed to have their own language. Their bread and cheese taken into the fields was a "thumbit", the threshing machine a "chine box", they ploughed a "thurrow", and when in a muddle were "aggled".

After the war things changed considerably. No more ricks were built in the rickyard, no steam engines came to thresh the corn. Cows were milked by machine and ploughs became bigger – though in my grandfather's day I had seen ploughing done by steam. There was a mobile engine each side of the field with a thick cable pulling the plough between the two. It was, in those days, quite spectacular.'

'Only two families have lived in the Kensham Farmhouse at Cadmore End since the turn of the century, when John Bird took on a tenancy from Lord Parmoor of Kensham Farm with its farmstead and 102 acres. During the First World War John's son Jack, with his friends Bert Smith and Bill Tapping, went off to volunteer for service in the infantry, and were seconded to the Dorsetshire Regiment. They served in the trenches in France, where Jack was awarded the Military Medal for gallantry. When he came back from the war he lived and farmed Kensham with his father, and after his death Jack and his brother Frank continued to farm here until they retired in 1955. Jack's son Rowley with his wife Edna and their family also lived in the farmhouse for a few years before they moved to Wheeler End Common, so in the early 1950s there were seven members from four generations of the Bird family all living in the Kensham Farmhouse.

Jack and Frank Bird's farming when I first knew them 45 years ago was the typical mixed farming of that period with a small milking herd of about a dozen dairy shorthorn cattle, some steers being fattened for beef, a small flock of about 60 sheep, and a hundred or so turkeys fattened for the Christmas market as well as some cockerels. There were also about a hundred laying hens, and two breeding sows from which the little pigs were fattened for pork or bacon. There was a stackyard in which there were two dogs in kennels, and the several small stacks of corn in sheaves each had its own thatched roof waiting for the winter when they could be threshed with the contractor's threshing drum powered by a steam tractor engine. This was a laborious task for a staff of seven or eight, with the youngest lad on the farm always being given the dustiest job of clearing the chaff.

Kensham was a typical sized farm for this area with its 102 acres, and the various fields included roots such as mangolds or swedes for the cattle, some fields of winter or spring sown wheat grown for sale, barley or oats for feeding the livestock on the farm, and a large vegetable garden. Most of the grassland was permanent pasture.

Most of the food used in the kitchen of the farmhouse was grown on the farm and was cooked over fires fuelled by firewood that came from the farm. There was no gas or electricity in the farmhouse, and lighting was either with candles or with paraffin lamps. The water system was a brick built underground tank in the back yard of the farmhouse which filled with rainwater from the gutters of the house and farm buildings, and was then pumped by hand with a semi-rotary pump into the kitchen for use in the stoneware sink. There was no lavatory, just a one-hole earth closet in a brick and flint outbuilding in the garden.

When the farmhouse at Kensham was first built in the 15th century it had been a single storey house with a high roof described as a hall house, and the roof space would have become quite smoky from the wood fire. Then in the 16th century the upstairs floor and chimney stacks were added to make it all warmer and more comfortable with more space and separate rooms. The bricks with which the farmhouse was built were made from the clay and chalk which was quarried on Cadmore End Common and fired in the kiln next to the common where bricks were still produced commercially until 1938. Some of the walls of the farmhouse are flint and brick, and the flints would have been picked off the fields of the farm.

Modernisation of the farm started in 1948, two or three years after the sale of Lord Parmoor's Estate, when my late father bought the farm and had mains water installed for the tenant farmers Jack and Frank Bird. They found this greatly improved the health of the dairy cows, who were now able to drink clean water from troughs in each of the fields. Up until 1948 the cows had always drunk from the pond in which the water was infected with Johne's disease, causing loss of weight and death of two or three of the cattle each year. So the new mains water supply was mainly for the benefit of the livestock, but the Bird family womenfolk also found the one cold tap which had been installed in the kitchen to be a wonderful modern improvement.

That really only recounts the history of Kensham Farm up until the 1950s. But farming has changed and throughout the country the land from many smaller farms has been amalgamated to form larger farm units, and these larger farms now specialise in the production of just one or two farm commodities rather than following the mixed farming pattern of earlier years. We have had to follow this general trend of producing much greater quantities of food, using more mechanisation and a smaller staff, and now my son Charlie with our foreman, (who has worked here at Kensham with me for over 30 years) and a college student at harvest time between them produce around 2,000 tonnes of grain for sale each year from the 700 acres on which we grow cereal crops. All of our cattle have gone, and in their place we provide DIY livery and riding permits for local horsekeepers. We have converted the Watercroft Farmstead into craft and light industrial workshops, and the cottages built for farm staff are now occupied by young folk who earn their living outside agriculture.'

# LACE MAKING

The heyday of the hand-made lace industry was over by the beginning of this century, but lace continued to be made in cottages, for the Bucks Cottage Workers Agency till the 1940s, and today has undergone something of a revival as we seek to regain traditional crafts. Buckinghamshire, and in particular the north of the county, was in the forefront of the industry from its earliest days.

### THE OLNEY LACE WORKERS

'Religious refugees, fleeing from the Low Countries and France in the 16th and 17th centuries, brought their lacemaking craft with them and taught the local women of North Buckinghamshire, and it soon became the cottage industry of the small market town of Olney. The poet, William Cowper, while resident in Olney, recorded in a letter dated 1780 that there were "very near 1,200 lacemakers" employed in the town.

By this time local traders had taken to stocking the thread, parchment patterns and pins that were needed for lace manufacture. These middlemen became wealthy lace dealers, making money at the poor cottagers' expense, and many of the large houses in Olney were built with the profits of the women's hard work.

Lace pillows, stuffed with straw, bobbins, bobbin winders and candle stools were all made locally.

Lace schools were set up where children as young as four were taught to make lace in crowded cottage rooms by a dame who would rub their noses on the pin heads if they did not follow the pattern correctly.

Everyone looked forward to St Andrew's Day, 30th November, known as "Tanders", for this was the lacemakers' holiday, when Olney people congregated in "one another's housen". Special Tanders cakes of dough flavoured with caraway seeds were eaten and a mead-like drink made from honey called metheglin was drunk. Games were played too, like Jumping Over the Candlestick, and a good time was had by all.

It was a sad period for this local cottage industry when the machine-made lace from Nottingham came into production in the early 1800s. Local lacemakers reduced the width of their lace from wide floral patterns to narrow "baby" lace in an effort to beat the machines. And one famous Olney lace designer, John Millward, designed circular motifs for the crowns of baby's caps, which the machines couldn't copy at first.

John Millward (who is remembered today by "Mill'ards Entry" – a narrow passage leading from the High Street to East Street, alongside his former home) won prizes for lace designs at the Great Exhibition in 1851.

Also exhibited there, for the first time in Britain, was Maltese Lace. The local women liked the look of this more "open" lace and thought it would be quicker to make than the old point lace, so a new form of lace evolved called, initially, Beds/Maltese and now termed Bedfordshire lace (though not confined to that county) with its "leaves" and "spiders" and "nine-pin edge". This became very popular in Olney and district, so much so that by the end of the 19th century the wide floral patterns of point lace (now known as Buckinghamshire lace) were in danger of dying out, so a group of ladies based at Gayhurst got together and set up the North Bucks Lace Association, persuading the older lacemakers to continue making the point patterns, and it is due to their guaranteed sales of lace that the old patterns survived.

Around the same time Torchon lace from France made its appearance – of simple geometric patterns that was easy to make. It was spoken of disparagingly by local lacemakers, who referred to it as "dishcloth" lace.

By the turn of the 20th century, lacemaking was beginning to pall with the younger women, who could obtain more money working in the local shoe factories. But Harry Armstrong from Stoke Goldington set up a Bucks Cottage Workers Agency in 1906 and guaranteed the women sales of their lace. His business flourished and in 1909 he moved to Olney to premises near the railway station, which was convenient for the transport of lace to all parts of the world.

By the 1920s he was looking for larger premises and he purchased a vacant site in the High Street and in 1928 George Knight built the lace factory for him. Lace was never made there, the women still made it in their homes, but it was used as a warehouse for sewing lace to linen and garments, packing and despatching it world wide.

Unfortunately, when this last great lace dealer of Olney died in 1943, lacemaking as a cottage industry ceased in Olney. It was continued by a few older women, but more for gifts etc, as handmade lace has always been valued as a special craft.

Examples of local lace were displayed in the Cowper and Newton Museum almost as soon as it was set up in 1900 and special exhibitions of local lace have been held there by various curators

*Mrs Nancy Ingram of Lavendon and her granddaughter, lacemaking. Mrs Ingram was one of Harry Armstrong's collection agents for the Bucks Cottage Agency in the 1920s.*

over the years. It is the interest and appreciation of lacemaking that has revived it today as a craft.'

## TEACHING THE CHILDREN

'One of the Bucks Cottage Agency workers was Mrs Barrick of Lavendon, who worked for Harry Armstrong as a girl of 16 when she couldn't get other work in the early 1920s.

A Mrs Nancy Ingram was Harry Armstrong's agent in Lavendon and Mrs Barrick took her weekly twelve yards of lace to her for collection. The pattern she worked was called "The Bud" or "Pretty Beauty" and used 26 bobbins. After helping with the housework first thing in the morning she walked down to "Aunt Lucy's" and would sit and make lace with her until six o'clock, only stopping for meals, which were taken at home. She received ten shillings a week for her lace, six shillings of which was given to her mother and the rest she had for herself. Her bundle of cream thread cost her tenpence, but there was always a little left over on her bobbins to start all over again before the next bundle of thread arrived. There were five lace pillows "on the go" in Mrs Barrick's home, as she was the fifth of seven daughters and two sons. She had been taught lacemaking by her grandmother, who had learnt *her* lacemaking at the lace school in the village, which cost twopence a week to attend.'

'A lacemaker friend of mine in Wheeler End remembers being made to visit her grandmother for regular lacemaking lessons, which she hated. She would tap quietly on the door knowing the old lady was a little deaf and then run home reporting that Grandma was out. She would have been about four or five years of age then and is now a grandmother herself and a very good lacemaker, which she took up again a few years ago.'

# IN SERVICE

**For many young girls leaving school, work in service was the only option available. Before the Second World War, even modest middle class families employed at least one servant and the 'big house' was a major local employer of staff.**

FROM PLACE TO PLACE

'After I left school in 1910 I went to my first place in Bierton, the village I was born and brought up in. It took me some time to learn how to work. Mum would not let me do any work at home because I was left handed and she said I looked so awkward, so I had to find out for myself. I remember the first morning I got up and Mrs H said, "Have you made your bed?" I am quite sure I looked at her as if to say, "What is bed?" Anyway I got on very well there and stayed almost two years. I had two shillings and sixpence a week.

I then took a job at Great Missenden, and this was quite different. The family were Sir Felix and Lady S, and three sons who were away a lot. They were a German family. He was very proud of his title and even on the phone to tradesmen he would tell them in no uncertain terms, "I am Sir Felix S, KCVO, MO, FRCP". There were five of us then – lady's maid, parlour maid, housemaid, cook and kitchen maid. We had a wonderful time as they were away for six weeks at a time and we made the most of it, so long as it was nice and clean when they returned. The food we had was the best I've ever had. I stayed there for about a year and a half. Lady S gave me a wonderful character and told me I could get a job at Buckingham Palace with it. I can remember one or two things that she mentioned – I was sober, clean and a good worker.

Next I went to Wingrave to work, to Mr and Mrs F and their three daughters. This, again, was very different to my last place with all the work to be done by myself. Up early in the mornings, light the kitchen fire, cook breakfast for the girls to get to school at nine, have my own breakfast, light the dining room fire, cook more breakfast, then do all the washing up and bedmaking. It was difficult to keep up with the bedrooms to keep tidy, as it was a large house and at that time there were lamps to fill and no hoovers or washing machines. However, I struggled on and stayed longer than I should have done because it was there that I met Reg. We had a fair and roundabouts on the village green once a year and I was going round with a fellow that I knew and Reg came up on the roundabout and told him to get off and took his place. We used to meet once a week after that and on Sundays we always went to the Methodist church. Now, every time I hear the bells ring I think back to our courting days.

After a while I tired of my job, so I left in 1915 and went to Aylesbury to work for a Mrs F and her two spinster daughters. The war was on now, of course, and I know we had to go easy with the food but when one day I had only a rabbit's head, I thought it was time I moved on again. It was there I had my last pieces of gold in wages. The daughters were proper old maids.

From there I went to a large house down Walton, to a Mr and Mrs S and two small girls. It was, at that time, not a happy family, with Mr S being away at the war. The Mrs was always complaining about something and she was continually following us about, finding fault with our work, so I stayed only two months with them. We did have particularly nice food there and when we were alone in the house we used to wander about and find little odd rooms and corners as it was an old rambling house. We came across a little snobbing room, with all the tools for mending shoes.

Then I went to Peveral Court, Stone. There was just Mr and Mrs C there, no family. There was an old cook who had been there since she was 19 and ruied the house, or thought she did, and we girls did not like her at all. Again there was a lady's maid, parlour maid, housemaid, kitchen maid and cook. We got on very well together, bar the cook. After I had been there a while Mrs C decided to do voluntary work for the war, so we had to pack up and go to London to live near Kensington, which we all enjoyed. I would have stayed longer but my brother Dennis was invalided out of the war and I asked for a weekend off to see him before he went back to Canada and it was refused. So I said, "Well, I shall *leave* and go in the morning," and that was that. I thought it very unkind not to let me go. They had no one in the war at all and I had Raymond and Dennis and Reg and a brother in law. I feel quite pleased that I did it and do not regret it.

So once more, in 1917, I took another place. This time I went to Long Marston to the vicar and was cook there. There was just the vicar and his wife, a housemaid and myself. We had a right good time there. The war was still on but we had more than our share of meat at times. It was while I was working there that I had the sad news of Ray being killed. I had sent him a parcel and it was returned to me; it made me feel very sad indeed.

The vicar was fond of his food and it was he who came out every morning and told me what to cook; the wife never knew what she was having until it was taken in. He was very particular about time and he would send it back if it was only two minutes early.

They employed a person to come and do the flues and clean the kitchen once a week and she had a shilling for it. There was quite a ceremony when she was paid – the vicar and his wife both had to be present and she had to sign for it. We girls had quite a laugh about it. The vicar always had the silver and cutlery taken to his bedroom every night and kept it under the bed, putting it out in the morning for the housemaid to fetch. It amused us very much. There were shutters to all the windows (large and small) and a bell on each of them, but whatever we should have done had one of them rung in the night, I don't know.

I found out the housemaid was not very clean, so I told the vicar's wife, either this girl must go or I should go, so she left and I stayed on a bit longer. I had my 21st birthday there and I remember Reg was in Italy at that time and sent me a lovely card and a silk scarf. I missed him so much; he joined up in 1915 and came home in 1919 and all through the years we wrote to each other. I kept the letters a long while after he came home, there were over 300 of them.

About this time I saw Mrs F again and she had no one to work for her and asked me to go back there. After thinking it over, I did – this was the place where there was so much to do, but it was in Wingrave and war seemed to be ending, so I thought I would be there when Reg came home. Finally the war did come to an end and I stayed in my last place until we married, in 1920.'

BISHAM ABBEY IN THE 1930s

'The Abbey was very large and very old, famous for its ghost of a previous owner. It was a very orderly household. We were twelve staff including a butler, parlour maid, hall boy, three housemaids (I was the second), cook, kitchen maid and scullery maid. The kitchen maid helped the cook and was responsible for staff meals. The food was excellent, all home-made and lovely cakes.

My uniform was a blue and white dress in the morning and navy blue in the afternoon, with white apron and caps. We needed to be up early, I think at 6.30, and had one afternoon off each week with every other Sunday afternoon and one day each month. On our weekdays off the kitchen maid and I went to either Windsor or Maidenhead, but on Sundays it was usually either to the Salvation Army or to friends in Burnham. All were expected to attend prayers each morning and when we could on the morning of our Sunday off duty.

My duties were calling Miss Phyllis with tea and caring for her clothes, packing and unpacking when away. I looked after the Great Hall, used as a dining room when no visitors were there. There was quite a lot of entertaining, and a special week for Marlow Regatta, and I looked after the single ladies.

We had to be in by ten o'clock on our days off. There were buses which stopped at the gate, but woe betide us if we were late. We ran up the drive and if the door was locked we had to ring the bell and Mr Harding, the butler, would look at the clock and say, "You are late." It didn't happen often. He lived in the village.

One summer the Abbey was let to an American family with all of us staying on. They were very wealthy and a sister was married to an Italian prince. He caused a lot of problems because he wanted his bed changed every day and there wasn't a lot of spare linen, especially if the laundry hadn't arrived back. I don't think we were sorry to see them go, though the staff they brought with them were very friendly.

I think my wages were about £3 a month. We were very lucky, having a very nice head housemaid.'

IN THE KITCHEN

'Born in 1904 in Gordon Road, High Wycombe, I was nicknamed Midge because I was so tiny. The youngest of the family, my mother having died when I was six months old, I was a mischievous child because I could take advantage of my being small. Even aged ten I could barely see over the table. When we moved on to the Springfield Gardens School I was part of the "Gordon Road" gang playing unmerciful tricks on a girl who split on us. I could lie in wait and signal to the boys when she was coming. This was about 1910. I could creep under the hedges to find the young shoots of the sweet briar, more delicate to eat than the usual hawthorn "bread and cheese". After one Sunday lunch I'd promised to meet my mates and after grace at Sunday lunch I prayed out loud, "Oh Jesus give me power, to shift this lot in half an hour". For this I got sent to my room, escaped through the window for the afternoon, but was caught on my return by my brother. It cost me my halfpenny pocket money to be smuggled back in by him under his big coat. But I earned an extra farthing for washing up, standing on a stool to reach the sink. That meant I could buy my usual toffee apple and my pals could hand it round as usual for them all to have a lick.

Father, who had been a rick thatcher, died when I was about eleven so I went to live with my now married sister. We moved to Longwick where her husband was the "saw doctor" at the saw mill. I learned to "snob" my shoes, soling them with discarded studded leather band-saw belts. When old enough, I went into service.

In the 1930s I was kitchen maid at Horsenden Manor, where from our rooms under the roof we girls could signal to the signalmen at Princes Risborough station. White handkerchiefs meant we could meet them, red that we could not. I worked in the scullery preparing vegetables and all the poultry and game. I could skin, pluck and clean most animals, rabbits, rooks, poultry, pheasants and the fish from the moat tossed, still flapping, in to me through the scullery window by the nephew of my mistress. I flatly refused though on one occasion to skin a well hung hare that was heaving as though still alive, and it was, with maggots.

The cook would not allow me in her kitchen when she was working so I could only peep through the keyhole to see what she was doing. Inexperience though did not stop me getting a job as cook-general with a Dr Covington in Aylesbury. Armed with a "Mrs Beaton" I managed. I had a variety of jobs, with the family of the manager of the Nestle factory in Aylesbury, the owner of a large shop in Watford, and with a builder. It was there I coped with a burglar, throwing a chair down the stairs to disturb him and alert the family.

What I liked best was to get a job as cook-general in the winter time and house-parlour maid in summer.'

'A few days prior to my leaving Lane End C of E school at Easter 1939, one of the school governors came and announced she wanted someone to work in her kitchen at Hambleden.

I put up my hand and was engaged for the job at five shillings a week, one half day off a week, to be in by 9 pm and every other Sunday afternoon off. I was just 14 years old.

My aunt with whom I lived, my mother having died when I was seven years old, took me to Wycombe to buy the uniform. First a large hard-lidded case from Woolworths. Next, to McKilroys for two blue dresses. I had two white aprons with bibs that crossed on the back and buttoned at the waist, grey lisle stockings, two white caps turned back at the front and elastic at the back to enclose one's hair, black house shoes and coarse aprons to wear when cleaning the grates and floors. We were farmers and my aunt made the coarse aprons out of sacks we used to send the corn away in. She split the sacks open, washed them and put tape on to tie round one's waist. They were very hard wearing.

The chauffeur-gardener came to collect me in a dark green Daimler, wearing dark green knee breeches, black boots and gaiters. I remember being very tearful at leaving home.

On one side of the kitchen was a huge wooden dresser, to be scrubbed by me every week. It was filled with copper pots and pans, fish kettles and jelly moulds of all shapes and sizes, looking beautiful. A lady came once a month to clean them in a large lead tray with saltpetre, silver sand and halves of lemons. On the opposite side of the kitchen was the black lead kitchen range with its fire in the centre and an oven each side.

I got up at 6 am to boil a kettle with brushwood so that I could take the cook a glass of hot water for her Fynnon Salts and a jug of water to wash with. This grate I cleaned daily with Zebra blacklead polish. It had a steel fender which looked nice if nothing got spilt on it. The floors of the kitchen and scullery were large stones, two ft by three ft, called flag floors, and scrubbed by me weekly.

In the scullery at a large sink I had two bowls of hot water for washing up, soda in one (no Fairy Liquid then) and clear hot water in the second bowl. High on the wall over the draining board was a plate rack. I wasn't very tall and my arms soon chapped from my wrists to my elbows. So painful. But I can remember well how the plates shone.

The gardener would bring in a huge hamper of spinach. I had to get all the stems and veins out. When it was cooked it was just enough to have a poached egg on it. Miss G was also very fond of plum cake so another of my jobs was to stone one pound of raisins each week. We dried apple rings for the winter and made lots of preserves as the fruit came in season.

One day Miss G called me into her drawing room. I wondered what I had done wrong. The "trouble" was that I was a teenager with a spotted face and she didn't like her staff with spots on the face.

I remember scrubbing the outside step at the front door and blackleading the large iron boot and shoe scraper. It looked nice when the weather was good but it was supposed to look nice always.

Miss G did flower arranging and what a mess she made dropping water along the polished floor, and what a job I had to polish the water marks out.

1939 was a very hot summer and with wearing lisle stockings and always on the flag floors I had galled feet, painful sores caused by chafing and perspiration on the soles of both feet. By this time I was unhappy and wanted to leave but I was afraid to give my notice in. In the end my aunt said if I didn't give a month's notice she would come and do it for me.

This was the end for me in kitchen work. I next chose nursery work with children.'

# ON THE CANALS

**The canals provided work both on the barges and in controlling the locks. Once arteries of trade, they were essential means of transport for bulky and heavy goods and the horse-drawn barges were a familiar sight only a few decades ago.**

## WORKING THE BARGES

'Now in my nineties, I first went to school at Thornborough. There were so many children at the school that there were not enough chairs to go round and sometimes the headmaster would fetch some from his house to make up the number. Children walked to school from Thornton and the Coombs on the Padbury Road.

When I was a boy of about ten and a half, I went to live with my widowed grandmother at Leckhampstead Wharf. This was midway between Thornborough and Leckhampstead. My new home was beside the canal that used to be between Buckingham and Wolverton, part of the Grand Junction. The wharf had outbuildings, stables for the horses and a coal storage yard.

I walked a mile or so to Leckhampstead Church of England school. We sang more hymns there and read stories of a moral nature, like Brer Rabbit and others that aren't read now. I was the only child who took a packed lunch and used to go to Mrs Smith's near the church, who would give me some tea to drink.

I was able to leave school at Easter when I was 13 years old with a good attendance record. Other children who didn't had to stay on longer to make up for the time lost. I went to work on a farm at Thornton where I learned to milk the cows, until the 1914 war. One of the workers on the canal barges was in the Reserves so had to report to go and fight and I took his place.

The family firm owned two barges and the horses to pull them along the canals. There was also one powered by steam, named *Jubilee* (after Queen Victoria's Golden Jubilee in 1887), the first one on the canal to change from horsepower and quicker too. The engine had been bought from a firm at Weedon in 1887 and the barge was used to transport sugar from London to Northampton for the brewery. *Jubilee* was sold later and it was then used for work on the Thames.

We were kept busy, transporting different loads. Ash poles were cut in Wicken Woods and brought to the wharf on a timber carriage pulled by horses, to be taken by barge to Leicester to be made into cotton reels. They used 18 tons of ash poles in three days.

A barge could hold 30 tons and was 72 ft long. It stood 14 inches in the water, going down one inch for every ton of cargo. They were constructed of wood and waterproofed with tar. A living area was

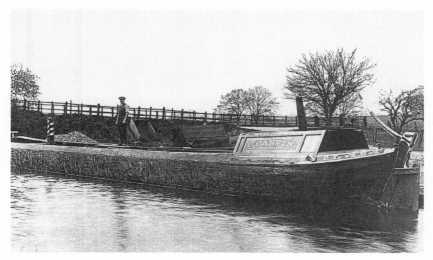

*Mr Canvin on one of the family firm's barges at Leckhampstead wharf in about 1919. Barges were still in constant use for carrying heavy or awkward cargoes.*

within its length, complete with a small cooking range and chimney. Although it was small it was warm and cosy. Beds were folded up during the daytime.

The journeys took time because we couldn't travel fast along the canal and make a wash which would damage the canal banks, so we travelled at the pace of the pulling horse. On the steam barge *Jubilee* we travelled to Derbyshire on Monday and brought back 100 tons of coal, arriving back on Saturday. We carried the bricks from Gayton to build Thornton Hall. Coke was brought from Northampton and coal from Begworth in Warwickshire. This was kept at the wharf and sold around the district by my uncle, Charlie Mellor, who was a coal merchant.

There were two sets of eleven locks and one of twelve on the way to Leicester, and three tunnels too. The amount of toll was paid according to tonnage and distance. For instance, for five miles on the Grand Union at Coventry it cost £1 7s 6d and for 24 miles at Oxford it cost £1 0s 5d.

When the railways were built they took a lot of the cargoes from the canals. Children were not compelled to attend schools then and so were able to travel with their families on the barges. All this changed after the Second World War when the Labour government made education for travelling children compulsory. Transport on the canal was drastically reduced because the bargemen who lived all the time on the barges could not afford to board out the children while they were working.

I have always attended Thornborough church, even when moving to Leckhampstead parish. I walked to Sunday school there, except when the floods were out along the river and the road bridge. I learned to ring the bells in 1914 and continued for 77 years. Sadly, I had to give up the post of verger in 1992.'


THE LOCK-KEEPER

'My father was one of two lock-keepers on the Grand Union Canal at Marsworth in the 1920s. I was born in the lock-keeper's house opposite the White Lion pub, near the bridge.

The barges were still horse-drawn in those days. My father's job was to record the cargo, making notes on whether it was wood, coal, sugar, cocoa or iron, and its destination. He worked the locks, measured the depth and generally assisted with the passage through. His beat stretched from Marsworth to Bulbourn. With the introduction of diesel the regulars who travelled from Birmingham to London made the journey in about three days, so we got to know the barge families very well.

148

In severe winters, when the canal froze, the children from the boats went to Marsworth village school. Several families settled in Marsworth when the canal traffic slowed down after the war and lorries took over the heavy haulage. Stoppages were a feature of holiday times like Easter and Whitsun. Then the canal gates were repaired or maintained and all water excluded from the lock while the men worked feverishly to complete the job before the next run of barges came through. My sister and I would take tea and sandwiches at regular intervals to the workers.

In times of drought water would be drawn from the reservoir to top up the canals, and in hard winters the village people skated on them. Sometimes in the winter a duck shoot would be arranged and even a Royal visitor was reported to be enjoying the sport one winter.

I recall sitting at my bedroom window and watching the beautiful kingfishers diving in the side locks, while herons fished the banks and otters could be seen in the reservoir nearby. Water rats, frogs, dragonflies, ducks and moorhens were all part of my childhood memories.'

# FURNITURE MAKING

**The beechwoods of the Chilterns provided the raw material for one of Buckinghamshire's most important and highly skilled industries. From the bodgers in the forests to the workers in Wycombe's factories, craftsmanship was of a high standard and can be recalled with pride and satisfaction.**

## THE BODGER

'Here in retirement in my home in the depths of the Buckinghamshire beech woods, spring is coming early. Already there is a carpet of snowdrops in flower and it would be the time of year, before the trees are in leaf, when my father would have been negotiating with a local Squire's agent to buy a stand of thinnings – the beech trees not required to reach maturity, marking the bark of those suitable with a special tool, a knife with a curved tip, called a scratcher. With a traditional forester's Hoppus Ready Reckoner, the agent would be

*A bodger working at his drawshave, a sight once common in the Chiltern beechwoods.*

able to calculate the number of trees required to provide my father with 50–70 cu ft of usable timber – a year's supply for his work as a chair bodger, work he continued until 1961, a year before he died aged 84.

My father had been brought up in Sheepridge, near Flackwell Heath and as a lad of twelve worked at Marlow Ferns learning to work a pole lathe to make chair legs, as had his father before him.

Eleven years later, Father's belongings were packed in tin trunks, and with five gold sovereigns he came by the local carrier in the waggonette here to Summers Heath for a month's work experience on a wheel lathe with his Uncle Sam. And stayed. A long month!

For a while he took a job as an "improver" in a Wycombe chair factory but wasn't happy. After five months, when he came back to the woods, he said he felt like "a bird let out of a cage". My Great Uncle Sam lived till he was 89 and even three days before his death had made three dozen chair legs. It was after eating a large Sunday lunch in September 1913 that he said to Great Aunt Marie, "I shan't be with you much longer but don't be afraid, Sammy will look after you", and with that he went upstairs, lay on the bed and died. My father said he knew it was the end. He heard the death rattle before going upstairs.

So my father continued the craft alone in the lean-to shelter by the flint cottage where he continued to live with his aunt. In 1916 he went off to France in the Army as a company cook, cooking for 200 men. During that time his aunt died. Although a big strong woman it was said she died of grief. My father was given compassionate leave and found the Squire and his family very caring, giving him a shilling, which he never spent. He kept it for luck and eventually incorporated it, bedded in mother of pearl, in the lid of a money box he made for my brother. This shilling was the equivalent of a week's rent, and with it came the promise not to increase his rent while he was away as he was fighting for his country and on their behalf. He returned on being demobbed, shell shocked, but gradually recovered and resumed his work as a bodger.

Five years later he married a local gamekeeper's daughter and we two sons grew up happily in the woods. One of our simple games was "cat and stick". With two sticks each we'd throw one up in the air and hit it with the other as far as we could. But the sophisticated entertainment which was only allowed on very special days such as an occasional summer Sunday afternoon picnic in the woods or at Christmas was our 1910 Edison phonograph with all the songs of the popular shows. We were expected to learn all the words!

In 1900 there had been 30 bodgers working locally but my father was the last, so skilled a craftsman that he could always find a market for his chair legs and stretchers. He recognised that mechanisation was taking over and that there was no future for a young man thinking of learning the craft for a living.

However, as a seven year old I learnt to shave the chair legs and have subsequently demonstrated the various techniques. But at 13 I was awarded a full scholarship, providing board and lodging and education at a craft school, set up in Thame by a wealthy local benefactor. I was there till I was 19, when in September 1949 I was called for National Service and joined the Royal Air Force, and on demob trained as a woodwork teacher. Meanwhile my father continued his bodging.

The bodgers could recognise two types of beech, "pear rind" was more difficult to work than "smooth rind". Stray lead shot which had penetrated the bark was a recognised hazard. The trees were best worked green, when freshly cut and subsequently kept moist by storing in the woods under the natural canopy or watered with water from a pond if available or even water caught in vessels from a leaning tree. Many a time I have had the job of using a watering can to water our stack by the cottage. The trees were felled by chopping

151

or sawing by either seller or purchaser and as my father worked alongside his home he would arrange for a carter to bring the logs home. A horse would drag each tree with minimum damage to the cart, pull it up, on sloping poles tied to the cart wheels, onto the cart and unload it by the workshop. As with so many traditional crafts, measurements were seldom done by rule, more usually by eye or the length of tools in use. So with the tree trunks. First the length of each was estimated using the axe handle of known length, then it was marked off for sawing into billets using an 18 inch stick marginally longer than a chair leg. These logs were split with a wedge and crab-apple wood mallet to produce eight legs with the minimum on each to be removed. The central core was discarded and the smaller rounds provided stretchers and sticks. Sitting on a three-legged stool with the chair leg trapped in the draw-shave horse my father would use a draw-shave, drawing it towards him until the middle of the leg could be spanned by the circle made with his thumb and middle finger, and the ends were tapered.

Although my father could work a simple home-made pole lathe he preferred the better quality product he could achieve on his wheel lathe made with a cast iron wheel, a yard in diameter. On this lathe the legs were turned, often with an intricate pattern of grooves and ridges as demanded by the customer – the chair factory owner in High Wycombe. The legs were neatly stacked making a four sided column, for two weeks, bagged in hessian sacks stamped with his initials and sewn up with string using the pointed horn discarded by a young buck for a bodkin. The sacks went by carter to Isaac Lords' who acted as agents or direct to a factory such as Nelson Mealings' in High Wycombe. Many factories suffered from cash flow problems and didn't survive long. One ruse was to sometimes quibble, maintaining that the leg design was not as specified, refuse to pay, then offer to pay half, "to save the bodger having to sell the legs for firewood". The bodgers made very little profit as it was, by the time they had paid for the timber, for carting to the workshop and carting down to Wycombe.

Were there women bodgers? Yes, two women in Fingest were known during the First World War to make plain legs.

A normal working day would be from 7 am till dusk with half an hour off for lunch and half an hour for tea, making a gross of legs a day, and only working on Sundays if there was an urgent order to complete. My father working at home would often prefer to work in his garden during the day when there were urgent jobs to be done on his vegetable plot, and would continue on his lathe after dark till late at night by the light of his little paraffin lamp. He would hook it on a pole wedged in a section of tree trunk and move it to wherever he was working. The shiny round metal back plate of the lamp helped reflect the light in his direction and was adequate.

He was able to insure his premises for £200 but only once was there any fire risk when there was a fire in a nearby wood.

Monday was known for some reason as Saint Monday and it was when the local woodmen met in the pub and expected the apprentices to buy some of the drinks or forfeit a tool.

Mr H. J. Massingham, the writer during the 1940s on country crafts would visit my father and refer to him in his books. In one he reproduced in full a delightful account my father once wrote to an enquiring student about his way of life. In pen and ink, by candlelight at the end of a long working day he sat writing until three o'clock in the morning about the life he loved.

An odd note:     On the 7th of May
                 The beechwoods will be
                 Half green and half grey.'


## CHAIRS AND MARQUETRY

'We were a Wycombe family involved in chairmaking for several generations. Mother's father was a seat maker in rush, cane and shaping solid seats with an adze. My grandmother's father, Mr Henry Keen, made chairs in a workshop at the back of Pineapple Cottages off the West Wycombe Road, where he lived. Chairs from Wycombe were handled by agents, carted to Windsor and there put on boats for London. So in Wycombe they became known as the "Windsor chairs" and the name stuck.

On a Sunday after morning service he taught the older local children the basic 3Rs in his front room. The Dashwoods had donated a piece of land on the main road and on it a local benefactor, Mr Henry Wheeler, had built a Sunday school room. A self taught and religious man he was always dressed in a long frock coat and top hat.

My husband's long career in working with wood started when he was a boy of 13. Brought up by Dr Barnardo's after he was orphaned when he was one year old, he spent holidays paid for by Barnardo's, as was usual then, with the Baker family who had a sweet shop in High Wycombe, and was adopted by them, as their own children had grown up.

Their son worked for a German named Graefe who after the First World War had set up a workshop in his garden employing as many as six workers in marquetry. Andrew joined them and by 18 was put in charge. The boys had to get to work an hour before the men to get the "skin" glue hot for use.

To cut the shapes one sat astride a marquetry "donkey" cutting through as many as six or eight thin veneers at once with a fine reciprocating blade. Shading of the edges of the pieces was achieved by burning the edges carefully in hot sand. The shapes were inserted in the spaces cut in the background veneer, sandwiched between glued newspaper, pressed till dry, then the newspaper on one side sandpapered away with increasingly finer sandpaper till the finished surface was like glass.

Popularity for this work began to decline in the 1930s when simple unpatterned surfaces of Art Deco furnishings were the vogue. But this brought us contracts for the refurbishment of the grander buildings such as banks and board rooms using larger attractive sheets of veneer applied to plywood. By then we had premises in Bellfield Road with huge presses. We won contracts to provide the panelling for the new Union Castle Liners and then the *Queen Mary* and it was one of my jobs as office girl to calculate the area of panelling that was supplied, to be charged per square foot. This was straightforward for clear rectangles, not so easy on the "raked" side of a stairway.

Then the war came. Andrew had been in Germany just before the war and seen the great advances being made there in research into chemical glues. We had traditionally used skin glue, make from animal waste. It tended to stain the light veneers and, being water soluble, the products needed to be kept dry, which is why the bottoms of grandfather clocks often have peeling veneers – from over-enthusiastic housemaids too free with the water when scrubbing the kitchen floor. Later a casein glue was made from milk, and being white, more suitable for gluing light-coloured woods such as beech and sycamore. Then came a special glue-impregnated tissue paper to put between the veneer and its base before going into hot presses.

The government directed Wycombe factories into making the Mosquito aeroplanes. My husband met well known personalities such as de Havilland and "Cat's Eye" Cunningham. The plywood used needed sophisticated glues of the new chemical type. A German refugee was given a laboratory at Duxford and my husband cooperated with him in trying out new recipes. We had samples of glued wood to boil up in my saucepans and out came my egg whisk and mixing bowl to whisk up the sawdust mixtures. These experiments, contributing to the success of the Mosquito aircraft, known as the Wooden Wonder, started in my kitchen.'

AFTER THE WAR

'In 1947 I started to work at the furniture factory in Princes Risborough. As I had been a fitter in the Fleet Air Arm during the Second World War and was used to handling metal I was employed to make chairs and table legs in metal.

At the time timber was in very short supply and its use strictly controlled. When it became more readily available I made bedroom suites with wood-grained plastic veneers on the surface. I had to buy my own set of tools – drills, hammers, planes, as I had to cut and assemble the parts. Later I made sideboards and dining tables in oak and oak veneers. The timber was cut to size and shape but I had to cramp and glue the pieces together with animal glue, and press on the veneers. The top of the sideboard was always screwed in position. I remember whittling away at each support for the draw-out flaps of the dining table so that they slid smoothly backwards and forwards under the table top. All furniture was marked with the Utility mark to show it was approved standard.

Goodearls Factory was one of the first to make kitchen units with oak veneers and it had so many orders that other firms in High Wycombe were asked to help out. Sink units were not included as most people had porcelain sinks in those days. The factory was very busy before Christmas with special orders from Selfridges for furniture for the January Sales.

Now part of the factory has been sold to bedding specialists and kitchen furniture is no longer made. The veneered wood is prepared in large quantities elsewhere and the cutting to shape is controlled by computers.'

# OTHER WAYS WE MADE A LIVING

**There were, of course, hundreds of other ways in which to make a living, from papermaking to watercress growing. Here are just a few!**

TOWN AND VILLAGE INDUSTRIES

'Chesham up until the 1950s thrived on family businesses and was known for its Boots, Brushes, Baptists and Beer.

There were five boot factories, four belonging to local families and one co-operative. They made heavy boots, army and industrial. These were in production until the 1950s, but only one factory remains, producing some lighter footwear.

There were six brush factories making all kinds of brushes, one making toothbrushes. Only one remains employing three or four people making specialist brushes.

Chesham, being in the Chilterns and known for its beech trees, had nine factories using local wood, so perhaps Beech should be added to that list. Here they turned wooden spoons, malt shovels, butchers' blocks, dairy equipment and butter pats, bowls for fruit etc. Toy cricket bats and stumps were also made for Woolworths. There is now one remaining employing just a few people.

The local brewery was owned by a Chesham family but after it was taken over, it closed. There were many public houses scattered around the town.

And the Baptists? There were five Baptist churches here at one time, and though two united in the 1970s, four still remain.'

'In the 1930s over 100 men and women from Edlesborough were employed at the Wallace Nurseries at Eaton Bray. The usual form of transport was bicycle. We had an hour for dinner so had to cycle home pretty smartly to have time to eat. It was a standing joke that on Mondays all we would get was "Soapsud Soup", Monday being washday.

Wallace Nurseries was an 18 acre site containing 40 very large glasshouses – from a distance it appeared to be a vast sheet of water and often seagulls and ducks would be confused and flying round trying to land. The company was formed in 1886 and finally closed in 1974. I went there straight from school at 14 and was set to work with two others in one of the houses. It was by then wartime and so most of the houses were growing tomatoes and lettuces instead of the carnations which made the nurseries famous, though some blooms were still supplied to the Court florist, they and the boxes of tomatoes being despatched from the nearby Stanbridge Ford station.

We had to start by planting the seed out in boxes and care for the seedlings till they were ready for pricking out and planting. When of sufficient size they were planted out in the main houses. They had to be selected and tied to the overhead wire, the side shoots removed and finally stopped when large enough. Then the main job was watering which was done by hand. There was a unique water tower on the site, fed from artesian wells. It had to provide sufficient water for 45,000 plants at 100 degrees on some summer days. The workers got pretty thirsty too. During the winter 50 tons of best anthracite was used for heating.

There were compensations, however. We had to change into work shoes because they got very scuffed against the sideboards of the paths and one day I found a note in my best shoes saying "See you at the dance tonight". It was from one of the young men working in the next house and the upshot was that I married him.

Other villagers were employed at the mill. There were two mills within the village boundary but only one functioned to my knowledge. From 1918 to 1988 the village centre was dominated by the large square tower of Thorn's Mill, where about 20 girls and women were employed to pack the flour known as "Eclipse" into the old cotton bags. It was known as Two Counties Mill because the stream which was the county boundary with Bedfordshire ran in a channel beneath the mill buildings.

Straw plaiting was still done in the village up to 1939. I remember both my mother and grandmother doing the plait when I was a child – and how I tried to copy the speed with which my mother worked. She would collect the straw from the village agent. Then at home it would be split into "threes" or "fives" depending on the plait required, the former being the most common.

Some men worked at the Dunstable Downs whiting works. They dug the chalk rock out of the quarry with a pick and shovel, then had to barrow it to the mixing shed where it was wetted down. Then the water was drained off and they had to shape it into "bricks" which were then set to dry. These bricks, which were rounded at the edges and looked like uncooked loaves, were used for the insides of outbuildings and then whitewashed. Other village men went to the quarries at Totternhoe, and in 1932 a large cement works was opened at Pitstone.'

'There was a basket maker at Chenies in the 1940s. I remember a long string of baskets hanging on the cottage wall facing the green. Some busybody was offended and the old lady was told she shouldn't cut in on St Dunstan's market.'

'Hyde Heath people who had to find work in the 1930s usually became farm workers, bricklayers, railway gangers, gamekeepers, gardeners or went into service at the "big houses". Those who went out of the village to work in offices were regarded by some as a cut above the rest.

Wages were very low, especially in service. My own parents received about £3 a week between them for working from 7.30 am till dusk, as cook-housekeeper and gardener at the Wick.

157

There were two brick kilns, one at Hyde End and one in Copperkins Lane. The workers came from Hyde Heath and nearby. One of our school treats was a half day at a kiln to see how bricks were made. Both kilns have now gone. The one at Hyde End became a coffin factory during the Second World War.

We had a chair bodger and a blacksmith. We used to stand and watch them at work. The bodger was Mr Sear, who turned the wood for chair legs for the High Wycombe factories; he also burned wood for charcoal in Brays and Pipers Woods. The blacksmith was Mr Stacey. His forge was in Little Missenden before the war, but later he moved to Chalk Lane. At that time you could still go to him for a gate-latch or something similar.

Two elderly sisters living at Lane Gate Cottage behind the common, took in laundry from the big houses. This was delivered in a small hand-pushed truck, beautifully clean, ironed and folded – all for two shillings or little more, depending on the load.'

## WATERCRESS GROWING

'When I first met my husband in 1927 he worked with his father in the watercress beds which were situated in spring waters between Latimer and the Mill Farm at Chenies Bottom.

They worked long hours, getting at it very early to be sure to get the cress off the same day. In very hot weather it was left in the baskets in the spring water overnight and my husband went off to Chalfont and Latimer station about four o'clock in the morning to get it on the first train to London so it arrived at Covent Garden in time for sale there.

During the war, however, the big vans came overnight (so the drivers could get some sleep) and it was taken by road in the morning.

The watercress growers wore heavy rubber thigh boots and wrapped their feet in hessian as even in cold water they got very sweaty.

The best season was always round about Easter time, and they were always busy then. They used very sharp knives and had a knack of holding a big handful in one hand, then putting the knife between their teeth while they packed the cress in the basket (or skip as they were called).

Much of the cress had to be tied in bunches in those days. They had a shed to do this in. It used to take me an hour to tie a gross. We used raffia (or bass) and each bundle had two twists round and tied with a reef knot. Rubber bands are used now. As each bed was cleared it was thoroughly cleaned out and replanted.

My husband always had to check up on a Sunday evening as even in those days there were vandals and he was likely to find his cart pushed in the cress bed, or the field gate left open and the horse gone wandering into the woods or on the road.

Unfortunately the springs got very low and they were not able to use river water as it came mostly through the Chesham sewer beds. Also the cress got a disease and there was not so much sale for it. One week in 1959 all the cress was returned so my husband reluctantly gave up and got another job.'

TIMBER AND COAL

'In the 1920s we lived at Longwick, where my father was a timber merchant. The timber yard was full of "wind" timber, mostly elm, which was felled and brought in by Latil tractors. It was then cut into planks for coffins and dried in the kiln, or stacked in the nut orchard, or cut into "bobbins" and sent by rail from Bledlow station to Grimsby where they were used to weight the fishing nets. The offcuts were sold for firewood. As a boy, I spent many hours in the carpenters' shop, watching them make fieldgates, hay racks, coffins, gateposts etc.'

'A short while ago I saw a lorryload of timber being driven by at a good speed. It reminded me of the days when the horse-drawn waggons came up Chenies Hill. They would have two at a time, each with two large heavy horses. At the bottom of the hill by the cottages, all four horses were chained to one of the timber waggons and brought it up to The Bedford Arms to be left there while the horses were taken back down the hill to fetch the other load.'

'My uncles Charlie and Fred Gates were coal merchants in Aston Clinton in the Second World War. They had a small lorry and a horse and cart. I spent quite a lot of time helping them, sometimes going to the railway station coal yard in Aylesbury, or to the station yard at the bottom of the High Street. The coal had to be shovelled from open top waggons into sacks and then weighed on scales which were carried on the lorry. This took quite a time to do and usually only one load a day could be delivered. We also went to the woods on Aston Hills and brought back loads of wood to be sawn into logs and some to be split for fire lighting. They worked from 58 Brook Street where they had a large shed in the orchard at the back of the houses. They had an electric saw bench, axes and hammers and wedges for splitting logs. I remember often chopping a sack full of lighting wood and taking it to a lady in College Road. She used to give me sixpence for it.'

# THE POST OFFICE

'In 1895 my Grandfather Jones built a house in Wingrave to serve as a post office as well as a home. Grandmother Jones was the postmistress.

Each morning a postman arrived at the post office at 7.30 am with the post, having cycled the six miles from Aylesbury. A local person then sorted and delivered the post in Wingrave. The postman cycled a further two miles to the neighbouring village of Aston Abbotts to take their post.

The Wingrave post office was then open from 8.30 am to 7 pm. The postman returned to Wingrave at 11 am to meet with another postman who had cycled from Aylesbury to bring the second post. The first postman then himself delivered the second post in Wingrave before going again to Aston Abbotts with their second delivery. The second postman returned to Aylesbury with the outgoing mail from the two villages. The first postman went back from Wingrave (to Aylesbury) at 6 pm with the second collection of mail.

In 1905 Grandfather Jones died suddenly and I moved with my mother and father to live at the post office. It was an ABC Telegraph Office and very busy with telegrams. These were delivered to neighbouring villages and outlying farms. In 1923 the post office telephone was installed. Grandmother Jones was the postmistress for 40 years, assisted by my mother.'

'In January 1940 at the age of 15½, I became, in official jargon, a temporary part time S C and T (Sorting Clerk and Telegraphist). To the people of Stony Stratford, where I had always lived, I was one of the girls behind the post office counter. There were three of us – two full time and one part time, although it was only a few weeks before I also became full time and later another part timer was added.

Our working hours were to say the least unsocial. Two weeks we worked alternate days 7.30 am–4.15 pm or 12.15 to 7.30 pm with half an hour break. The third week was split duty 9 am–1 pm and 4 pm–7 pm.

We were not only counter clerks, we were exactly what our title implied – sorting clerks and telegraphists. We worked alongside the postmen in the sorting office, sorting incoming and outgoing mail and were responsible for tying and sealing mailbags and handing over bags of registered mail to the van drivers who came out from Bletchley three times daily.

As telegraphists we received and despatched telegrams on a direct telephone line to Bedford. The ones we despatched had to be read

160

out clearly and slowly so that the girl at the other end got it all down correctly on the teleprinter. The ones we received were a different matter. We had a pad and pencil and it had to all go down in longhand. Everybody sent telegrams for everything – soldiers coming home on leave, the fish shop man ordering his fish from Grimsby, and the Steamship Company who had moved out from London and sent daily telegrams to Bombay, up to 360 words in length, all in code which had to be spelt out: A – apple, B – butter etc. Saturdays were wedding days, when dozens of Greetings Telegrams were taken down in pencil and copied in ink and best writing on special forms and envelopes. The ones we hated most were those official ones – "regret to inform you that your husband/son is missing believed killed". Often they were people we knew, although thankfully, they never concerned anyone in the immediate family of any of us.

What did we do besides selling stamps by the thousand? Well, postal orders by the hundred, and National Insurance stamps to all the local firms who sent their junior staff in weekly with endless lists of different denominations. They were all in our tills which were valued at a fixed amount. We were personally responsible for them and they had to be checked daily. Every stamp had to be accounted for, and an order made out each day to replenish the stock.

The "Balance" was a different till altogether. From that we paid allowances, pensions, National Savings Certificates, money orders, car licences, gun licences, dog licences, wireless licences and goodness knows what else. The person on early duty at 7.30 am held the balance until 12.15 then counted everything, balanced it in the book and handed it to the late duty person 12.15/12.30. She kept it until the office closed at 7 pm and then had until 7.30 to balance it all in the books. Many, many nights I have been alone in that office until 9 pm or later, trying to get it to come right!

Every day was a special day. Monday – Army allowances. Tuesday – Billeting, Widows Pensions. Wednesday – more Billeting. Thursday – Air Force/Navy. Friday – Old Age Pensions. Saturday – everybody came in for something or other, sending parcels to far away places that needed about four forms in triplicate or drawing £3 (the maximum) from their National Savings Book.

The office was warmed by a coal fire in a bedroom-type grate. It was lit by the cleaner at 7.15 am, if we were lucky, and we had to keep it going ourselves from the one scuttle of coal we were allowed each day – only 1st November to 1st May! Money is cold, dirty stuff and we all had chilblains on our fingers every winter.

I stayed there all through the war. I fancied joining the WAAF but there was no way out – it was a reserved occupation. There was hardly any time when there wasn't a queue of people, often restive, when you were alone while your colleague coped with mail or telegrams. The public always thought they had gone off for a cup of tea and said so in loud whispers. We knew everyone in the town and shared their joys and sorrows and I loved every minute of it – well nearly.

When I look back, the thing which never ceases to amaze me was the lack of security. We took it in turns to walk to the bank alone with hundreds of pounds in cash in an unlocked bag. We spent hours alone in a large building on a busy main road (A5) and when we went home, we pulled the door behind us with a yale lock – less than I have on my front door now.

Oh, there was a burglar alarm. It was on the floor by the balance till and we were constantly kicking against it and setting it off accidentally; they were so used to hearing it that I am sure nobody in Stony Stratford would have taken the least notice if there had been an emergency.'

*The telephone exchange at Chesham in 1957. Telephone users still had to wait for the operator to connect them, and would have been familiar with telephonists Rose and Olive and their supervisor Mary Joyner.*

'My first job was with Barclays Bank at Amersham where I wrote up customers' statements, and helped with the weekly balancing of accounts using a simple adding machine. Occasionally I would accompany the Chief Cashier to the post office with an HVP (High Value Parcel) of several hundred pounds in notes to be sent by post to the bank's head offices. No Securicor then!

In the late 1950s I was a telephone operator at Amersham. Telephone users could only lift their phones, which showed as a light on the switchboard, and wait to be answered by the operator. London exchanges had names then, and we had to look in a file to find the number to dial for each exchange. To ring an Amersham number we operated a key for a few seconds until it was answered, or after two minutes advised that there was no reply. I also worked at Chesham exchange which was on the first floor above the former post office in Chesham Broadway.'


## THE MILLER'S DAUGHTER

'At school we sang "Annie the miller's daughter, living beside the water" and I always felt that this was me. My father and grandfather were the millers at Longwick Mill, a water mill with a large mill pond. We five children and our parents lived with our grandparents and aunt in the mill house. I was born in 1936, just old enough to remember the end of the war and hiding under the stairs during air raids.

The mill, mill pond and stables were our playground. We paddled in the gravelly brook, building dams and searching under stones for those funny little fish called millers thumbs. In the deeper pools under banks we fished for sticklebacks with home-made nets. Especially prized were the males in spring for then they sported bright red breasts.

The pond was large, too deep and muddy to paddle, so we floated. My brothers built a punt, which we took on great expeditions among the overhanging branches of willows and sometimes right underneath the railway bank through the culvert to another pond on the other side. In warm weather we had old inner tubes which were great fun too.

In the stables we had a horse. Not a real one, because Grampy said that a horse would eat more than a cow and we needed a cow for milk. Anyway, we had a large dapple grey rocking horse as next best and on this I used to ride and ride and pretend it was real.

The cow was called Peace, because we got the first one the day peace was declared. All her successors were given the same name. The last Peace ate anything. A builder left his mac on the fence and she ate one of his sleeves. She finally died through eating roofing felt off the chicken shed.

As soon as I was big enough, I helped in the mill. Sacks of grain came in from the farms and had to be hung on the chain hoist with a special loop round a corner of the sack and sent up through two sets of trap-doors to the grain bins at the top of the building. My job was to get a sack into place using the sack barrow, hang it on the chain and pull the cord to activate the machinery. I watched the sack as it disappeared through the trap-doors, fearful that I hadn't done it right and it would crash down again, but it never did.

The grain bins were another world. They occupied all the third floor space, right at the top of the building under the rafters. Sometimes I would wade around in the grain pretending it was water. Then again it might be desert sand. I can still remember the almost liquid feel of the grain as I stirred and waded. It wasn't really allowed, but that added to the feel of it. From the top of the mill we could get through a hole into the roof of the house. This was all different levels where it had been added to over the years. We hunted up there for a box of money said to have been hidden by a previous occupant, but needless to say we never found anything.

I loved to watch my grandfather working. He talked to himself as he watched the grain trickle down from the hopper, through the damsel and shoe into the mill-stones to be ground. Then the meal had to be checked for quality. He would say, "Turned out alright seemly" or, "That lot b'aint so good".

The giant mill wheel was in a house of its own. You opened the door and there it was. The water came on to the top from the pond above, filled the metal troughs of the wheel and the weight of water sent it round. Several troughs on one side leaked, so the motion was uneven and when these were filled water would cascade down through the centre of the wheel. Below was the dark pit full of water and from there it flowed out to join the main brook. It was a frightening, exciting place and we never went there without a grown-up.

We still run the milling business, my three brothers and I, but all the old machinery has long since gone. It was too slow to process the many tons of grain we now use. The building is still much the same, full of happy memories for all of us.'


PAPERMAKERS

'My family have always been papermakers – my great grandfather, my grandfather and my father.

High Wycombe has the river Wye running through it, and along the banks were corn and paper mills making use of the water, the mills being almost alternate along the valley. Some years ago I decided to look into this to help prepare a family tree. A retired local librarian, Mr L J Mayes, has written one or two books on the paper and corn mills of the southern Wye valley. I approached him and found that the papermakers here were a "militant" company and the Paper Riots started around this area in 1836.

As far as I am concerned, I was brought to Wycombe in 1922 at the age of six months when first my grandfather and later my father were managers at Rye Mill in London Road, and at one stage we lived in Rye Mill House opposite the mill. My grandfather and grandmother lived in a small cottage in Park Street, behind the mill, and a cousin of my father's lived in Back Lane behind Wycombe Marsh paper mill, where he worked.

In my research into census documents I found that most workers, many of whom were women – rag sorters etc, lived in small streets near the mill: Easton Terrace, Saffron Platt, Queen's Road, Harlow

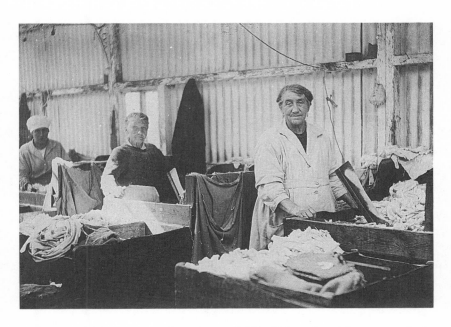

*Women sorting rags at Rye Paper Mill, Wycombe. The start of the papermaking process, the rags had to be divided into white or coloured, cotton or 'celanese'.*

Road. Some of the small houses are still in existence. No people employed at the mill lived in the west end of town.

We never talked in the family about paper-making. As far as I knew my grandfather *NEVER* worked! When the mill at Downton was sold in 1920, there were no deeds of sale in those days, just a handshake.

No paper was available at home as "off-cuts" but we did have some large pieces of felt for use on small beds instead of blankets. Felt was used in paper manufacture – the pulp was spread on it, allowed to dry and set and then rolled smooth.

The mill was eventually sold and became Thompson Mineral Waters and finally Michells Garage as it is today, and the mill race, the river Wye, now is under the floor of the show room.

My father, working for T Edmonds & T H Saunders, papermakers in High Wycombe, went to work for them during 1927/8 back in Kent at Horley near Dartford, though as a family we stayed here. (He had been born in Sunbridge, Kent. There were many paper mills in the Maidstone area and he had worked in Little Chart which was my great grandfather's mill.) As young girls, my sister and I only saw our father once a fortnight. We met him off the train on a Saturday evening and said goodbye on the Sunday evening. During 1933/35 my father was unemployed. He found the modern machine-made process was too much for him, having always been a hand-made paper-maker of high grade papers – eg the paper for bank notes, when working at Laverstock near Basingstoke.

At Helpston where one of his brothers was in sales, he made brown, coloured and marbled papers for inside book covers and also greaseproof paper. Fine quality paper for filters is still made at Helpston.

Most of the local mills – Glory, Fords Blotting Paper, Soho etc are no longer in existence and paper is rarely made by hand. Wiggins Teape has sold to an American firm though their offices are still in Beaconsfield. Our great grandfather bought the paper mill at Downton, between Salisbury and Fordingbridge, from Wiggins Teape when they decided to sell in 1897/8. Wiggins Teape had owned this mill since 1836/38. At that time they were expanding and the mill had previously had a disastrous fire which raged for over two weeks according to records I found, so it was just a shell and they had the task of building up the whole thing from scratch.'

# TALKING TO THE PAST

**Sometimes it is only in the spoken word that the true flavour of the past comes through. One man became so fascinated by the tales he was told that he began recording them.**

'Born in Watford before the First World War I only came to work in Bucks when I was 21. However, I knew Bucks well from the age of twelve.

At that time, before the days of petrol and diesel, the transport system ran on hay. My father was a horseman, handling large horses for his employer. They had a magnificent large Shire stallion, described by my father as "25 cwt of bad temper with a hide on it"! They also had Shire geldings from which one could not breed. The farmers bred from their own draught mares, so a little man, and it always seemed to be a job for little men, would "take the stallion at walk" travelling from farm to farm. He even slept with it overnight because an angry stallion could do untold damage, kicking a stable to bits. I would spend my summer holidays riding side-saddle on this great horse, seeing the Bucks countryside from this unusual vantage point.

As I said, at the age of 21 I started work – in High Wycombe library. The low wages were not enough for me to move to Wycombe, so I bought an old motor bike and travelled the 20 miles daily from home. My hours were 9 am to 9.30 pm with time off in the afternoons. I would stuff hard black chocolate in one pocket and counteracting hard black prunes in the other, adequate for my lunch and tea, and set off into the country to explore and meet people.

My first and long time friend was a roadman. They no longer exist. He'd helped me when I fell off my bike one morning on a slippery road, concerned about me but far more concerned that I might have damaged "his" road. His wages were paid by the Bucks Council but as far as he was concerned, the road was his and woe betide anybody who "messed it up". He was a great character, a long-time widower, who lived in a tied estate cottage. He poached, but only for his own needs, acquiring the occasional pheasant or rabbit. I can still recall the smell of his delicious rabbit and onion pies. He'd walk five miles if a stricken animal needed help. If the London poachers were about he'd report them to the keepers. But the keepers had strict instructions from the squire never to catch my roadman.

167

Which reminds me of the first occasion I heard his loud guffaw as he told me this tale, roaring with laughter. He was sitting in his "armchair" – his upturned barrow backing into the hedge – eating his "nuncheon" (they still called it by the old Anglo-Saxon word). He had a wedge of bread and cheese and the knife in one hand and a large Spanish onion in the other, eating it like an apple. A new keeper had arrived, a bit of a show-off and a know-all, so, he said, "My boy, I've had him, he was on his way home, midday, got three-quarter hour for his dinner, as I well know, so I got my old catapult out and kept prinking and prancing about for 20 minutes. He had to stay behind a tree all that time, he daren't come out in case he caught me poaching".

Another day he was miserable – about his rent. "They've riss it" – by threepence to two shillings and ninepence a week. The reason? The sanitary fellows had been round and condemned his old dunnekin – too near the well. So a new water closet was built, brick walls, slate roof and so on. My friend said he'd bought the wood. "What for?" I said. "Why, for my shelves, it's the driest place I've got, great for my apple crop." "But that's not what it's meant for." "You don't think I'm going to do that in there!" And he never did. When he died seven years later the wrapping paper was still on the seat.

I found that in Wycombe there was little interest in the crafts associated with the furniture trade as machines were taking over production. So I set out to search out the chair bodgers working in the beech woods, where they made the legs, stretchers and sticks for the chairmakers in town. They often worked on their own, buying a stand of trees due for thinning, 20 ft tall, twelve in diameter. These would be felled and a workshop set up in the clearing – a simple shelter under which the bodger would work on his home-made shave horse and pole lathe from daylight to dusk. I got to know well a bodger at Hampden. His idea of a "half day" would be knocking off on a fine Saturday in summer at six o'clock to watch the cricket. It was hard work and poor pay. An old account book quotes "for buying wood, making and delivering, one gross of legs and three-quarter gross of stretchers, 8/6d." A man could perhaps earn 50 shillings a week. "Why," I would ask, "don't you get a well paid job in a factory in Wycombe?" "A master would never drive me as hard as I drive myself. I like being in the driving seat," was his reply.

Provided you weren't a know-all these men who were alive to their surroundings, the wild life and the bird song, were perfectly willing to tell you all you wanted to know about their craft. I tried without success to take notes, then decided I needed a tape recorder. All that was available then was an office dictaphone, so with that, a motor car battery and convertor to convert twelve volts to 240 AC, strapped to my back, I made some wonderful tapes of local people.

For instance, I was interested in country customs. I had heard that three centuries ago it was possible for a labourer, with help from friends, to build himself a dwelling on waste village land provided he could do it in 24 hours. It had to have walls, floor, fireplace, window, door and roof. If he succeeded he could then build his cottage around it. On a North Bucks common I found seven of these cottages and the first thing I noticed about them was that the doors were hung like gates. Peering at them I was spotted by an old boy who told me this story. At No 3 lived a man who liked his midday pint. One evening when he announced that he was going to the pub for another, his wife threatened to lock him out. "That's a rum do," he said, and promptly lifted the door off its gate hooks and took it with him to the pub.

I was the last child in a family of a lot of older sisters, so I had always been interested in women's crafts. I found, to my great pleasure, a delightful old lady who was then, 60 years ago, still making lace as a paid profession. She even taught me how to make simple lace. Another lacemaker I much admired, then 75–80 years old, was in a wheelchair and had been since she contracted polio at the age of five. But no cabbage was she. She was a great character, a member of her church choir and full of interesting conversation. On my tape you could hear the regular click of the bobbins as she talked. It was said that it was possible to identify the pattern being worked by the sound of the bobbins, but I doubt it.

Eventually and with much difficulty I made a tape of a lady caning chairs in Wycombe. She was no simple caner but a specialist in her craft, able to do "double", "secret" and "spider" caning, so intricate you couldn't fathom how fingers could manipulate the cane into such patterns. She told me of a job she had done for King Farouk. This was a bedhead and footboard for a seven ft six inch wide bed. She had copied a design on the bedhead, of a camel caravan coming through the sunlit desert with its clumps of palm trees. The bed foot was of the same size but double sided – when he retired the scene showed the sun setting and the camels kneeling; overnight this was reversed and the scene which greeted him in the morning was just the same except that the sun was rising and the camels being loaded for the day's journey.

She also did work in "double" caning on chairs for the *Titanic* and was allowed ten months to complete the contract. She was unaware of world news and so it was her boss who broke the news to her of the *Titanic*'s sinking, with the words, "Alice, mate, them mermaids are sitting on your chairs."

At this time I was lucky to find a man aged about 60 who had worked in the chair trade in Stokenchurch since the age of nine, when he would get up early to light the fires in the tortoise stoves to prepare the glues for the men arriving later. He would sweep up, go home for breakfast and be back at work to spend two hours doing any odd jobs. When a little older he would adze chair bottoms (the seats), doing two dozen in summer and a dozen in winter, before going to school. He would bolt his dinner in order to go back to the factory and the men would always be pleased to see him. An old man on a pole lathe taught him how to turn chair legs and by the age of 14 he could turn a church chair leg or a Windsor leg as well as any of the men. He'd be back after school to work again and when he'd done his daily routine he was allowed to work on his own. He would be given the "slab", that is the first piece of timber to come off a log with some of the bark still on. He would split it with a "frow" and mallet, then sit at a shave horse to shave wedges, using a draw knife in the direction of the grain. When I asked him what he was paid, he said a penny a gross and it took just over an hour to make a gross of wedges. These small one inch wedges, to be used later when the chairs were assembled, would be inserted in the top of each chair leg to make a tight fit when the leg was driven into the hole in the seat. They were dried overnight and counted next morning to check there was in fact a gross. The wedges would remain in the drying stove for some months to make sure that they were bone dry when used, ideally used hot from the stove.

The miller was always reckoned to be a rogue, stealing from the corn brought to him for milling. A very old man told me this story – "Oh, ah, millers were rogues all right, my grandfather was a miller and he had an answer for the accusation – 'You can always tell an honest miller because he always has a tuft of hair growing out of the palm of his hand'. If you remarked that he hadn't got a tuft of hair his answer would be, 'Ah, but you know, that takes an honest man to see it'!"

The old man was once taking corn to be ground at a mill, some 70 years earlier, just a boy. He met the man who owned the mill, he didn't run it. "Going to my mill, boy? When you get there tell my man, the miller, to let the old black bitch out." "I got to the mill and saw the miller take two big scoops of corn out of each sack – so that is what it means, does it! So when he turned his back I put the scoops back in, ah, and three more big uns on top for good measure. Going home I met the owner again. 'All right, boy?' 'Yes sir, and he let the old black bitch out, I know. I've got three of her pups!'"

170

During the course of my tape recording excursions in Bucks I have met many interesting people, none more interesting than an octogenarian farmer, recorded several years ago. From him I got many insights into farming life in the early part of this century.

As a boy of only nine, a farmer's son, he had to take his share in the work of the farm. Up at 5 am, out to the stables to help feed and water the horses and when the carters took over at six o'clock, help with the "mucking out". In to breakfast and then a long walk to school – no school dinners then!

His father was very proud of his horses. "I like to see them dance instead of being miserable." He fed them well, "I get good grub, so should they". The standard meal was a double handful each of oats, beans and chaff, well damped down. "I didn't want to see one of them blow his nose and send his dinner flying!"

One little story of father and son. They were returning late from Aylesbury market, father driving their little cart. He had taken several three-pennyworths of whisky "to keep out the cold" and turning a sharp corner much too fast, over went the cart and horse, trapping father underneath. He called to the boy to help him out but the cart was too heavy for him to lift and father, an 18 stone man, too heavy for him to pull clear. Along came a man on a bicycle, "Lift this b..... cart off me." "Who's under there?" "Never mind whom, get this b..... cart off me." The man obliged and the father was duly grateful. "You a married man?" "You could say that, and got nine so far." "Well you ain't wasted much time have you, now you come up to the farm on Sunday morning and I'll cut you off six pound o' bacon for the kids and you can have a quart or two of good beer."

Tape records from which these excerpts have been taken, have been wonderfully rewarding. Print is good but the warmth and varying emphasis available in the spoken word is invaluable.'

# WAR & PEACE

# THE GREAT WAR 1914–18

**Shortages of food, the occasional Zeppelin, soldiers on the county's roads – all brought home the realities of war to the ordinary families of Buckinghamshire. Growing up in those years was a combination of hardship and excitement, never to be forgotten.**

## GROWING UP IN ASTON CLINTON

'I was born in Aston Clinton during the First World War. It was still very much a Rothschild village. Old Lady Rothschild had died but her daughters kept on the estate, visiting their old home for the Passover and the Jewish New Year. They visited the girls and infants schools that had been founded when they were children. New babies were inspected, and I was carried out to the Rothschild limousine for this purpose.

Less publicised than the Halton handover, the Aston Clinton estate was placed at the Government's disposal. The 21st Division from Lancashire was encamped at Catsbrains, and what is now our village football area became their parade ground. Villagers, including me in my pram, were admitted into the park when King George V came to inspect them prior to their departure for France, where they sustained heavy losses at the battle of Loos.

Soon after my first birthday my father departed on Mr Howe's horse bus to join up at Oxford. He fought in the Salonika campaign, was gassed, contracted malaria, and never once slept in a bed until he returned in time for my fourth birthday. During his absence my mother helped at the YMCA canteen in the Anthony Hall. A pound of tea had to produce 240 cups of tea at a penny a cup. There was no fresh milk and I enjoyed scraping out the Nestle milk tins. The spoons were of lead, and I remember the excitement when it was discovered I had bitten off the tip of one and presumably swallowed it.

There were concerts for the troops, at one of which a large soprano sang *Let the Great Big World Keep Turning*. I demanded to sing too and mounted the stage. The khaki-clad audience shouted down my mother's attempt to remove me. "Let her sing", was the cry, "her Daddy's out there fighting the Germans", and my rendering of *Burlington Bertie* was received with applause.

174

Mr Pullen, a young bachelor, owned the brewery, now part of the Bell complex. He departed to join up leaving his elderly housekeeper in charge. Miss Carter could manage the brewery and the brewers, but the books were beyond her. My mother, who was a good mathematician, came to the rescue and we were often there. The old off licence is now the Bell Wine Shop, and shopping there reminds me of times long ago.

Under the Rothschilds there was street lighting, with oil lamps. The Zeppelin raids – I experienced one in London from my great aunt's cellar – called for a blackout. The curtains were flimsy compared with the Second World War, since we only had oil lamps and candles.

We had an excellent supply of pure water from the Rothschild Water Works at Dancers End. Electricity, gas and main drainage materialised between the wars. Street lighting was not restored until 1949. Very few homes had water-borne sanitation. Earth closets outside the back doors were the rule.

The most hated woman in the village was a German woman employed by the Rothschilds on a variety of tasks, including Further Education. She taught German, Music and Home Economics before they were generally available in country villages. Unwisely, she insisted that children should curtsey to her as they did most willingly to the Rothschilds who were the fount of most of the good things they enjoyed. With the war obviously approaching, little girls would hide behind hedges rather than curtsey to her, and once the war started all felt she was lucky to avoid internment. She was forbidden to leave the village and had to report regularly to the policeman who lived next door. Once a year she was allowed to visit Scotland for a holiday with her friend. I was kept from contact with her, but once when she passed by on the opposite side of the road my mother told me, "She's an old German; your Daddy's fighting them". The same explanation was given when we encountered a posse of German prisoners being marched down Brook Street to work on a farm.

I remember many kind friends from those days. Mrs Vince looked after Mr Alfred Rothschild's chalet high in the Chilterns where he entertained his friends to tea. There she bred the little Chinese Spaniels which Mr Alfred gave to Queen Alexandra and other great beauties of the day. Mrs Vince invited me to tea at the chalet and let the little dogs run about for my amusement.

Mrs Ramm, head of the Rothschild's laundry (now Minshulls), had a large part in my upbringing. She taught me to iron the Rothschild dusters using a little lace iron which I still possess. Mr Smithson, Mrs Ramm's brother-in-law, kept our garden in trim. With rationing, vegetables were important. He always seemed to have some spare for us. He was a splendid gardener and kept chickens and pigs.

Mr Warren was the Rothschild's Head Gardener, whose articles in the *Gardener's Chronicle* were eagerly read by keen gardeners. The great authority on hot-house fruit, he found out how to grow strawberries for Christmas. Tring Lady Rothschild declared that his grapes had the edge over her Mr Dye's, and the best bunch of the year was always sent to her at Tring Park. I never found out in what branch of horticulture Mr Dye excelled over Mr Warren.

Mr Gurney was a painter and decorator. Finding a loose end of wallpaper I tore off a strip. My hands were slapped and I had to find Mr Gurney who was working nearby. When he had repaired the damage I was told to take sixpence from my moneybox to pay him. "I can't take it", he told my mother, "not when her father is out there fighting the Germans." "You take it," said my mother. "She has to learn." I have never since torn wallpaper.

Mr Sharp was the Postmaster. Before 1914 most women kept purses in their pockets. Soldiers wives allowances meant handbags were necessary to hold the allowance booklets. Contributing to War (now National) Savings was patriotic. "Why do you give some money back to Mr Sharp?" I queried. On being told that we were saving up for a rainy day I protested that on a rainy day people could not go shopping.

Armistice Day came and the Rivet Works hooter proclaimed the great news. My mother and I went down to the front gate just as the rector cycled by to gather the bell ringers. "The war is over; Mr Lowe will be home," he cried. Three months later my father returned having come across Europe in a cattle truck.

Sad the lot of those children I met at school whose fathers did not return and whose mothers struggled to bring them up on a pittance. Saddest of all perhaps the lot of Olive whose Canadian father, returning briefly en route for demobilisation in Canada, said he would send for them as soon as he reached home, kissed them goodbye and was never seen or heard of again.'

## AT HOME IN HIGH WYCOMBE

'I was born in High Wycombe in 1908. When the war broke out in 1914 my father joined up because, in his own words, he would never be able to hold his head up if he did not. This resulted in my mother taking his place, with his sister, in the newsagent's and stationer's business in Oxford Road which had been left to them by their father.

My chief memory of the war years is that of marching soldiers.

Hughenden Park and Tom Burt's Hill were taken over by the army and bell tents covered these areas. There were no mechanical vehicles then of course, and horses and mules were in abundance. We lived on the corner of Priory Avenue, so whenever we wanted to get to the shops, we only had a few yards to walk down to the bottom of Benjamin Hill into Temple End. It seemed that there were always marching soldiers in this area. One event which understandably stands out in my memory was that one day I was returning home up Benjamin Hill when a terrible clattering of hooves arose. A gun carriage pulled by four mules had gone out of control down the steep hill. I was frozen to the spot as they dashed past me and crashed straight into the gates of Glenister's chair factory. I have never forgotten the sight of those poor mules with the skin hanging off their heads.

In Temple End was a pub called The Fox Inn. There was sawdust covering the floor and a notice which said 'No Spitting'. I was always very frightened to pass by here, because the noise of the men shouting was terrific. Of course no women went into pubs then.

From Hughenden Road there was a pathway leading to Bellfields across which a stream ran down from Hughenden Park. At its furthest point it widened out into a nice big pond with a wooden bridge crossing it. We used to take our fishing nets and catch tiddlers there. The stream carried on into Oxford Road flowing right underneath my father's shop. There was an iron grating to

*Troops marching near Marlow in 1915. Soldiers became a familiar sight on the county's roads during the war.*

177

catch all the rubbish which had to be hauled out with a rake. The stream then crossed underneath the road to join the main stream flowing down the side of Oxford Road. Of course even this is now under concrete. In Bellfields my father had an allotment, and during the war years this went wild, but there were wonderful apple trees there and raspberry canes. We were a family of six (later eight), and we used to go there to pick fruit whenever we liked. No one else helped themselves in those days, and we were very proud to bring home enough for a pie.

I remember some of the chores which had to be done. Monday was always the day for the washing and it was long, hard work. The copper in the corner of the outhouse had to be stoked up to boil the water. We used to burn up a lot of rubbish then. This same copper had to boil up the water for our baths. We had an upstairs bathroom, but only running cold water, the hot water had to be lugged upstairs. The steel knives had to be cleaned on a knife board coated with knife powder. The daily shaking and airing of the featherbeds was a thing we avoided when possible.

Rationing of food was rather haphazard, and one day the rumour went round that a certain shop had potatoes for sale and I was sent to join the ever lengthening queue. Imagine my disappointment when they were all sold out just as I reached the end of the line after queuing for about two hours. We were very fortunate though, that my mother had a brother in the grocery trade. I remember a whole sack of porridge oats being kept out of sight on top of a corner cupboard on the landing.

This brother looked after us as well as he could but he had to be careful. We asked for 'rettub' if we desperately needed butter, and so on. One day my sister was sent to buy some herrings. These were wrapped in a paper parcel which she put under her arm as she took the short cut home through Bellfields. The dampness of the fish worked through the paper and without her knowing it, she was leaving a trail of fish behind her. When she arrived home she had just two small fish left. My mother in dismay sent her straight back to see if she could find them, but the cats and dogs of the neighbourhood were not going to let the chance of a meal like that pass them by. All she found were a few bones.

When the war ended and my father returned, he took us for lovely bicycle rides to Whiteleaf Cross and Burnham Beeches, and to the Thames at Bourne End and Marlow. We also discovered the lovely walks all around Wycombe. One thing he never wanted to miss was a visit to Disraeli's memorial in Hughenden churchyard on Primrose Day. The beautiful wreaths and crosses on and around the grave were a wonderful sight.'

# ZEPPELINS AND RATIONING

'I went to school in Quainton when I was four; my Aunt Emily, Miss Maydon, was the infants teacher. I remember school quite well, even in the infants, and I soon learned to read. There were 20 or 30 in the class, it varied. In those days you went up a class according to ability and accomplishments, not age, and I soon got higher up, away from Aunty, to Mr Ashley. Then the First World War came and we had a new teacher; we played her up dreadfully as she was not very good at discipline.

I can remember a lot about the war. The food was simply dreadful. You didn't have margarine in those days, and very little butter, a tiny bit, and we had this cocoa butter. You couldn't eat it, it was so horrible. There was very little meat – my father used to trap rabbits in the hills and sometimes we had a hare, but the allowance of meat was very small.'

'I was born in Horn Hill on 30th June 1903. During our childhood, the Boer War had not been over very long, so for a few years we had no war to disturb the peace of our rural life. I well remember the outbreak of war on 4th August 1914. My father came home for lunch, bringing the daily paper (costing a ha'penny or a penny, I forget which). I sat on his knee and read bits of the news. There was no radio of course, and we had no telephone. Quite a number of the local lads enlisted and some never came back. I remember, too, my father coming home with the news that Lord Kitchener had been drowned, and to my youthful mind that seemed an awful blow to our war effort.

My father was "called up" but was exempted owing to his work as engineer at the nearby Epileptic Colony, where he started in 1895 when the original engineer was taken ill – the engineer never returned so Father continued in this job until his death in 1965! Going back to the war, he joined the Special Constabulary, and I have an old handwritten paper headed "C Patrol" giving details where the phones were. The constables had to cycle to their rendezvous and then proceed to their duties. I remember my father coming home from his duties and telling Mother that if we had an invasion his job would be to go to The Pheasant public house and remove all the bungs from the beer barrels so that the beer would run down the gutters and drains! He had this job as he was a strict teetotaller. We thought that would have been great fun. My father used to say that he had a job to get one of his fellow constables past the pubs when they were on duty together.

The war affected us in the shortage of some foods, particularly sugar. Living in the country we had a large garden and an orchard, so we had plenty of vegetables, soft fruit, mushrooms, blackberries etc but not much sugar for jam so we all stopped using sugar in tea, cocoa etc during the war.

We would sometimes hear Zeppelins and one night one was near and we could hear the chug-chug of the engines. We were all out looking for it but when it got very near, Mother took us all indoors. We sat around the kitchen range, which was surrounded by a large fireguard. All four of us were with Mother and my brother, then about seven, said, "Read us a psalm, Mummy", and she read the 91st Psalm. We were used to having the Bible read to us, particularly on Sundays after Sunday school in the mornings and afternoons, and the evening service when we were old enough to go. There was great rejoicing in the village when the war ended in November 1918.'

# THE SECOND WORLD WAR 1939-45

**Once again in 1939, we prepared ourselves for war. This time bombing brought fear and destruction to the streets of some towns and villages, Bomber Command being just one target for the German planes. It was quickly realised that life would never be quite the same again when the war was over and the soldiers and airmen went home.**

## OUR VILLAGE WOULD NEVER BE THE SAME AGAIN

'Everybody thought the war would be over within six months. It was to be six years. Careers were interrupted, mine included. Conscription was started with the 18 year olds, and as the war progressed took in men up to 40 years old. Every young man here seemed to be in uniform. Some of the girls joined up too, and others like myself were drafted into local factories, most of which were turned over to making machines for the war. No one could refuse work when directed, on penalty of internment.

Conscientious objectors on religious grounds were interned for the duration and put to work on the roads, thus keeping open the lines of communication.

Hyde Heath had its own Dad's Army. Men joined the Local Defence Volunteers, as they were called before becoming the Home Guard. Yes, they did drill on the common, armed with broomsticks, and a funny sight it was too. After a lot of mickey-taking real arms were eventually issued. Farm workers, food distributors and the physically unfit were classed as being in reserved occupations. Flat feet got you out of the infantry. But if you wore glasses for weak eyesight you were put into the Observer Corps. Or so it was said.

When we had all been fitted into our various slots the big upheaval began. Trees were felled in Pipers Wood and other woodland in the Amersham area. Huts were erected to accommodate His Majesty's Armed Forces. At various times, Pipers Wood housed the Royal Bucks & Oxon Regiment, the King's Own Scottish Borderers, and the famous Highland Division.

A WVS canteen was opened in the hall for those off duty. Some of my evenings were spent serving tea and refreshments there. I also did canteen work at the Free Church canteen in what was St Michael's hall at Sycamore Corner in Amersham (now the site of the Amersham Free Church). I met my soldier husband there, and he would escort me home to Hyde Heath after evening canteen duty.

The village was overwhelmed with soldiers, but one could still safely cycle or walk to and from Hyde Heath without being molested. There would be a few wolf whistles, but these I found rather flattering.

The Plough became another place of entertainment. Many an evening I would help Frank Morton pull the pints, especially when he had an attack of gout. Sometimes I would play the piano for a sing-song, not too expertly I fear, and would be relieved to find that some soldier could play much better.

The village had a permanent searchlight post situated in Bullbaiters Lane. The occupants were more or less adopted by the villagers. My mother would billet their wives for a weekend, and I remained in contact with some of the wives for years afterwards.

Hyde House was used as a temporary rest home for Sir Archibald MacIndoe's "guinea pigs". These were badly-burned aircrew needing plastic surgery, and they came here between operations. Frank Morton advised me not to go to The Plough some evenings because some of these men were "not a pretty sight". I went all the same and was not bothered by what I saw.

My sister Grace eventually joined the Women's Land Army, but at this time was an ARP volunteer. She was on duty the night a string of bombs were jettisoned onto the village, believed to be from a German plane aiming to destroy the searchlight post. This was our first experience of bombing. None of the houses took a direct hit, but the explosions blew out many doors and windows. Rumour said that six bombs were dropped but only five exploded. Despite a search the sixth was never found. Rumour again said it fell in Mantles Wood. Nobody was injured but we were all scared out of our wits. It made us realise what the people of London went through night after night in the blitz.

Dances were held regularly in the hall and in the sergeants' mess at the camp. The 51st Highlanders would entertain us with pipes and drums, and they nearly went through the floor when they performed the Sword Dance and the Highland Fling. They really were a wild bunch.

Apart from all this entertainment, villagers were busy helping the war effort in many ways. The WI set up a jam-making unit in the kitchen of the hall. Some people say that it was the spoilt jam going down the drains that eventually blocked them, but, being wartime, it could have been other things. Home canning took place at the Wick (now Cedar Ridge). Here Dr Sybil Welsh set up the canning unit, and the whole thing was operated by my mother, with WI members helping during the busy fruit seasons. Most of the fruit for jam and canning was grown locally. The gardener and I picked plums from the Wick orchard until we were sick of the sight of them.

In the months leading up to D-Day, Pipers Wood camp was full of Americans. Again the villagers made them welcome. I corresponded with the wife of one of the lads, in Newhaven Connecticut, and she sent me some nylons. They were the first pair I ever wore. I took them to show the girls at work and was the envy of all. I dared not actually wear them to work then, but of course they got worn eventually and I cried my eyes out when at last they wore out. I found the Americans very polite, and none of them put a foot wrong. One of our girls went to America as a GI bride, and came back to see us some years ago.

After the Americans left, the camp was used for the rehabilitation of our returning prisoners of war. The WVS sewed flashes to their new uniforms and made what alterations were necessary so that they would look smart when returning to their regiments. I helped with this work, as I had certain sewing abilities.

It was during this time that the "Stars in Battledress" show was put on at the camp. The WVS and their helpers including myself were invited. The stars I remember best were Max Bygraves and Terry-Thomas.

Almost everything was rationed. But in Hyde Heath we did pretty well. My mother got on well with the army cooks. She met them when working in the hall canteen, and she billeted service wives for weekends. So somehow we never seemed to go really short of food. I did miss sweets and chocolate though, and I would swap my cigarette coupons for sweet coupons with the fellows at work.

During the lunch hour some of us would cycle to the British Restaurant in White Lion Road, Amersham, now the Amersham Common village hall. For fourpence I could get a fairly good meal. There was Woolton Pie, which seemed to have everything chucked into it, cheese flan, or scrambled dried egg on toast. It all went down well. The tea ration was eked out by adding a pinch of bicarbonate of soda to the pot, thus making the tea stronger.

In many ways the war did the village some good. People here became more open-minded. After all, there was a world outside Hyde Heath!'

'When the RAF decided to come to Marsworth at the beginning of the war they took over many of the fields – Wellington bombers did their leaflet raids from here. It altered Marsworth, but then when the RAF went, the American Air Force came and that altered it even more because there were so many of them. Marsworth is a little place and there was nothing here for them, so they used to run nine or ten buses every night to Luton. The Americans were especially kind to a lot of the older people – if they had their Independence Day or some other big celebration, they would go round the old folks with chickens or whatever. The kids used to love the sweets. I don't think anyone in the village bought English cigarettes while the Americans were here because you could get American cigarettes cheaper.

After the Yanks went the RAF came back again. They would put on concerts – the Ralph Reader concerts used to come down here when they were here the first time and the second time they put on several good shows in the gymnasium; I remember Brian Rix coming here.

You could say it was the RAF coming that put Marsworth on the map and brought it to life. After that the Polish people came and made their homes here, and when houses started to be built the Poles moved into them. Lots of them live around here still. But Marsworth has never been the same again as regards all the fields. Once you could walk around and say, "That's Nine Acres, that's Bratchops", and every field had its name, but that's all gone now.'

## LIFE IN ASHLEY GREEN

'It was war time. Ashley Green in 1940 had very few houses and no spare rooms. The place was full of evacuees and there were so many extra pupils at the school that another school mistress came up from Berkhamsted daily to take an extra class in the Old Memorial Hall.

On sunny days she played a little tune on a whistle and the children came out of the hot room to have lessons under the chestnut tree.

Mrs James, headmistress, had two classes in the school and Mrs Glover had the infants in what is now known as the Green Room or the Wykes Room, a small building at the end of the school playground originally built in Victorian times as a Reading Room for men of the village. There was no canteen then. The infants school stood in what was known as the Shrubberies, a lovely hiding place for children in playtime. The children liked Mrs James and made jokes about her fatness. She only laughed and told the jokes against herself. One little boy said he wished Hitler could come to Ashley Green and see Mrs James, as then he would know that he had failed and we were not starving in England.

She herself told the story that while she was having a good strip wash at the kitchen sink (there was no bathroom in the school house) she suddenly saw a helmet rising at the window in front of her, then a face of a soldier unknown to her and not of the village. He placed a warning finger to his mouth to prevent her from calling out, then disappeared again. She hurriedly dressed and went outside to find a group of soldiers cooking bacon and eggs over a fire they had made in the playground. Manœuvres were in progress. There were no houses between the shop and South Cottage, just a big hedge where voices were heard on either side – "You are dead. I shot you!" "No! you are dead. I threw a hand grenade first." There were terrible rumbling noises of tanks along the lanes.

Two girls thought they saw a German parachutist in the Glebe Meadow. They ran to tell Mrs James who hurried to the scene and sure enough it was as they had said, a hatless man in a grey uniform with a huge circle of white on the ground attached to ropes. She hurried off to Rose Cottage at the end of the green where the Special Constable lived. He was digging for victory planting potatoes, wearing dungarees and wellingtons, so had to change into his police uniform before confronting the parachutist. By then it seemed half the village had appeared on the green to peep through the hedge. Mrs James joined them when suddenly her short sighted eyes had a clear sense of vision. She ran through the gap as quickly as she could waddle shouting, "It's alright Mr Baker! This is Mrs Sommerville's nephew who was given permission to pitch his tent in the Glebe on his RAF leave."

The church had been designed and built by George Street for the Smith Dorrien family in 1873. The oil lamp hanging in the sanctuary was given by Mary Ann Smith Dorrien. It was lit every day and extinguished at about 8 pm. One day there was an air raid a little earlier than usual and the young man whose duty it was to fill, light and extinguish the lamp, forgot it, so it stayed alight. The air raid warden, seeing a light in the church, thought it was an incendiary bomb. He alerted the fire stations in Chesham and Berkhamsted, so it was not long before Ashley Green was crowded with fire engines. There were many rude and angry words spoken when they found it was only a lamp. After that the vicar, Mr Whitwell, decided to put candles in the lamp and only to light it for a service. The candles made rather a mess, so it is only lit on occasions now. Mr Whitwell had been an actor before he was ordained. He had a fine powerful voice and knew how to use it. Every Friday a sermon came through the post giving him plenty of time to learn it off by heart. People loved to hear him and the church was always full. So many said they liked to hear a man preach direct from his heart.

The Government decided farm workers needed more energy foods. Each week there was a good display of meat pies and lumps of cheese in the Memorial Hall with crowds of people going in to claim their rations. At first some unauthorised villagers claimed some, but a stop was put to this quite soon. There was an occasion when two meat pies mysteriously went missing. Nobody knew how or when but just eyed each other suspiciously. At night the Memorial Hall was used by the Home Guard.

Once a visiting officer spent the night there as no one had room to put him up. Next morning poor Mrs Baker had the fright of her life when she went to undo the blackout, clear the room for school and light the fire. She could hear a man moving around but could not see him in the dark. Once or twice a year the Memorial Hall was used for a dance to cheer us all up to the sound of gramophone music. Tea and coffee could not be supplied, so the usual drink was orange squash made up in Rose Cottage kitchen and carried across the green by men wearing wellingtons. They traipsed through the billiard room and across the dance floor with buckets of squash.

The well was still open but the shelter was taken down in 1941. The well head was sealed and concreted over. It is 185ft deep, the distance of the well to the chestnut tree opposite the church. It had become unsafe and children used to swing on the wheel and go down in the bucket. The other well, known as King Harry's, is at the bottom of Gypsy Meadow just covered by a slab of stone on the ground.

In the last century a young man stole a joint of meat from the butcher in Bovingdon. He was chased by an angry crowd along the footpath and nearly caught, but dropped the meat down the well. His name was Harry King, which was switched around and the well became known as King Harry's.

The blacksmith originally lived in the present pub with a lovely old barn at the side as a forge. It had a large horse trough outside. The wartime blacksmith lived elsewhere and only came once or twice a week to do local work here. The pub first stood on the green before the Old Vicarage was built in 1875. Parents of most of the villagers had used the pub. They were all adamant that the name had been The Golden Eagle although it had been registered by the Council under quite a different name. The villagers would not hear of it though. It was The Golden Eagle for them with the stamp of a fist. When the vicarage was built, it was put across the Chesham road along with the blacksmith and became The Eagle. Now it has changed again to The Golden Eagle.

Coming from London it all seemed very peaceful. In air raids only occasional bombs were dropped if farm workers showed a light whilst shutting in animals. We used to stand on the green and watch the raids over London. Searchlights streaked across the sky crossing each other at points, with guns and shells bursting and the whole sky lit up with fires. It was awe inspiring and quite horrific until the Warden spotted us and ordered us to take cover indoors.

The village shop was a quaint little place with a counter of heaped up square biscuit tins. Stamps for the post office were kept in a wooden fruit bowl and when larger stamps were issued, there was not enough room in the fruit bowl so an extension was made. It was a pudding bowl. There were several beautiful barns which have been pulled down in Hogg Lane and opposite Kings Pond in Two Dells Lane was a magnificent one with other barns and stables behind and a big black notice with gold lettering "By Appointment to HM" from the time there had been a pheasantry in Lane's Orchard dating back to Queen Victoria's time. Windsor and Buckingham Palace were supplied with pheasants from there and when Queen Victoria came down to inspect the pheasantry, Lane asked her permission to call his new apple after the Prince Consort, to which she agreed. Now there are still several Lane's Prince Albert apple trees in various gardens which were part of the orchard.

In wartime a policeman, Mr Topham, lived at the police house on the green, Silverdale, rented by the police from the Bakers of Rose Cottage who had recently had the house built at the end of their garden. Almost opposite was Rosie Darvil's cherry orchard which was a lovely sight in the spring, but the birds had most of the cherries. Mr Whitwell planted the laburnum tree in the churchyard opposite the Old Vicarage in memory of his son, Peter, who was killed in the first raid on Berlin. He was a bomber pilot. The vicar could easily see the tree from his study. It was still a beautiful sight this spring.'

## BABIES BY CANDLELIGHT

'War disrupted life everywhere. It came slowly but surely to us at Horsenden, by now with one child and me pregnant with a second. We were able to get away to Bognor for a holiday, where there were a few newspapers only, for the residents. We queued up outside the newspaper shop to hear the BBC bulletin at six o'clock. One day we found soldiers sitting on the pavements as far as we could see, their heads in their hands. Dunkirk had happened. We could plainly hear the guns and explosions across the Channel but no word of defeat did we hear.

The second baby was born during the air raid at High Wycombe Nursing Home, hastened on by the hideous siren which reverberated all around the Thames Valley. "What will you do if there is a blackout?" I asked. "Deliver baby on the kitchen table," was the cheerful reply, "by candlelight." Not all of us had been able to get material to black out our windows and wardens patrolled at night looking for any chink of light that might guide the enemy and betray the towns.

I thought back to my mother's stories of the First World War, when her first reaction was to dig up the garden and fill it with potatoes and to buy a sack of sugar and another of flour. Armed with these iron rations we faced the uncertainties of the future. In the Second World War rationing was a fait accompli from the start.

The local Boy Scouts covered up the famous Whiteleaf Cross carved in the chalk on the Chiltern hills above Princes Risborough with greenery and bushes, as Chequers, the Prime Minister's country retreat, was too near for comfort and easily recognised.'

## BOMBS AND GAS MASKS

'About an hour after war had been declared there was an air raid warning in Nash. Selby Harwood, the air raid warden for the village, came round in his car with his head out of the roof, blowing a whistle. Everyone naturally went outside to see what all the noise was about only to be shouted at by Selby to get back inside. Fortunately, the all clear went before he had got round the village!

Defence precautions involved putting tree trunks across the roads. One end of the tree was attached to a cartwheel so that it could be rolled across the road if we were invaded.

Wartime entertainment in Nash was made by the fortnightly whist drives run by Wilfred Varney in the school. The prizes were mainly bought from the proceeds and most of the profits went to the Red

Cross or to the Christmas party for the children which was looked forward to with great excitement. There was also the Saturday night "Picture Bus" into Stony Stratford, costing one shilling return. This was a big outing of the week for the younger generation.'

'When the war came we were living in an evacuable area at Ealing, so back to Bucks we came to stay with a colleague of my husband's, at Farnham Royal. By this time we had two little boys. Shortly after we arrived in Farnham Royal we heard of a house coming vacant in the same road as our kind hosts and we were fortunate to persuade the owner to let their house to us for the "duration" as he was called up for the Army.

Although we were aware of the war, especially as my husband was on duty at ICI in Slough and away from home every eighth night, we had pleasant neighbours, with whom we remained friendly later when we moved to Blackpond Lane and round the corner.

Our younger son soon settled into his own little house, a spare coal bunker into which he took his toys, refusing to share it with his older brother, only giving it up when they both had chicken pox.

By this time the eldest had started school and seemed happy enough going off with his gas mask over his shoulder every day. Children were not allowed to come home except with an adult and spent a large proportion of their day in the air raid shelter. Parents used to collect them at 4 pm unless there was an air raid warning when they were kept in the shelter until the all clear. We all shared this accompanying of the children, bringing home any that lived near us.

Of course, it was nothing like being in London and we were very fortunate. The grocer came up with his van from Slough, the butcher from Farnham Common, the milkman came in a cart and measured our two pints a day with my jug. We had a neighbour across the road who kept hens, as we ourselves did, and the butcher in the village taught me how to kill one when necessary. We swopped our cheese coupons for sugar and a friend with only one boy gave me clothing coupons when she had some to spare. Fruit and vegetables I was able to buy from a bothy in Burnham after walking across fields. When the grocer had tinned fruit he would add it to my weekly order. I used to buy day old chicks in Slough Market and the boys loved to watch them grow.

Going into Slough and coming away in the evening was not always pleasant as large oil burners were placed at intervals all up the Farnham Road. They smelt terrible but were there to blanket the town as a hindrance to German aircraft. Another hindrance to the aircraft were the balloons which floated above the Ford works. At

ICI Wexham Road were the rocket batteries which were only fired once, except for practice, and that very night my husband was given leave to be absent from duty. One of his crew bicycled to look for the nose of the shell and found it beyond Stoke Poges and we had it on our mantlepiece until the war was over.

Two or three other events I remember were not so pleasant. Days were designated for collecting various necessities to build ships and aircraft and we were urged to contribute our railings, fire irons, pans and any other metal we possessed. We parted with a very nice brass fender and fire irons.

We had the daughter of a friend with us one weekend and on the Sunday morning two or three bombs fell on nursery gardens just up the road. Several house doors were blown in – our roof and our neighbour's were lifted off by the blast and all our pans fell off the shelves. Fortunately no one was hurt but we were all a bit shocked and the neighbouring house was looking odd as the roof had come down crooked.

Another night I was looking out and could see fire burning on what looked like ICI ground, but when my husband came home and told me it was a small store of oil that had burned itself out, I was very relieved.

At the end of the war we were faced with the problem of finding a new house. Tribunals were held where there was any difficulty, to decide who in their judgement had the better claim to the house. As we had probably said we wanted the house for the duration of the war we felt we must go, and before the end of 1945 we had found a suitable house in Datchet where we lived for 21 years and where our boys grew up.'

'High Wycombe was a pleasant country market town when first I came to live there in 1928. Until 1941 I taught mathematics at Wycombe Abbey School. When war was declared, staff and girls joined us from St Paul's School, London and all the Abbey staff moved to live in the school.

A plan was made to dig trenches for the girls at Wycombe Abbey School to use during air raids. Then someone in the town remembered the inspection tunnel for the private sewage system at Daw's Hill. This was opened up and provided with a number of access points. Here it was thought we could be safe (we never tried it).

Tree trunks were put at random on the games field to deter aeroplanes and parachutists from landing.

I trained as an Air Raid Warden and when war was inevitable we were called to fit gas masks. There were few masks available but for hours, one evening, we fitted people and made lists of their names, addresses and sizes. None could be issued, we had so few. But perhaps the exercise gave confidence. When war came in reality, many people enrolled as blood donors and were called in after bad raids in London.

Refugees from London were given emergency accommodation in the town and traffic increased greatly. Amazing forms of transport took partly built or damaged aeroplanes to factories. By the time I left High Wycombe in 1941, great changes were already taking place and the quiet country town had gone for ever.'

'When the war started, dozens of evacuees arrived at Hughenden. Small children with gas masks, looking bewildered after taking nearly all day to come from Marylebone (about 30 miles away), they were left at their various new homes. They settled into country life well and were very good children, except for a few who played truant from Sunday school!

One night about 15 bombs were dropped in the valley, evidently meant for Bomber Command. One fell into a garden which luckily was very wet from much rain and dived into the chalky soil. The indentation was seen the next day and the squad came and detonated it. It was quite large and a good way down. Relatives staying for safety never came again but the evacuees stayed on. On another occasion a doodlebug shattered the east stained glass window of Hughenden church, but in time it was all beautifully replaced.'

'Taplow suffered little damage from enemy action, only one bomb in a field of kale, which damaged the rear of the row of houses in which I lived. No one was hurt, just shocked.

The nearest I came to danger (by now I was a teenager) was when I decided to wear my long blonde hair in the Veronica Lake style. She was a film star of the era whose hair hung provocatively over one eye. This made seeing where I was going not only difficult but dangerous with the increase in traffic.'

'I became a member of the Women's Voluntary Service during the war and worked under the guidance of Mrs Dorothy Rothschild of Waddesdon. I was put in charge of "Salvage". The village Guides went round Quainton with a handcart, collecting any old newspapers, rags, and any other rubbish suitable for recycling. I got together a team of ladies, and we had to sort the rubbish into sacks of each kind – some of it, I might add, being pretty filthy. To do this we were given the use of an old stable at the vicarage. What one would do for England's war effort was nobody's business.

190

As an Air Raid Warden I was on duty several nights a week. At the beginning of the war it was very quiet, but later on we did get the odd bomb dropped. Mostly we watched the many aircraft going over to Germany, and the others coming to London, and of course the searchlights picking them out. One night I had just got home from duty when I heard a terrible noise. Thinking it was a bomb, I opened my door, only to see flames a short distance away. It was a plane that was just coming back to our local airfield. There were eight young airmen killed in that crash, and some of them had been living in our village. It spread a feeling of gloom around and I for one will always remember it.

The war went on. We had rationing of food but always seemed to be adequately fed. The country folk grew lots of food and we preserved what we could – it was bottling in those days for we had no freezers then. There was even a fresh egg sometimes as many people kept chickens. The years passed until to everyone's great relief, the war ended. In May 1945 I went with several other ladies to our local airfield – Westcott – to receive plane loads of prisoners of war who were being released as our troops entered France and Germany. There were all nationalities and we fed them before they were transported to other parts of the country for sending on to their own homes. I especially remember those wonderful little Gurkhas. There were a few tears, but oh what joy those days brought.'

'Norah and Douglas moved to The Lee in 1937, when Douglas was a policeman attached to Wendover. They lived in the police house in Lee Common, and Douglas travelled round his wide area on a bicycle. A good deal of Douglas's work was in tracking down poachers. In those days there was no difficulty in getting the men to hand over their guns when caught – they had a healthy respect for the Law!

The police house had a bath in the kitchen, and there was a boiler to heat the water, which had to be transferred to the bath in a bucket. The bath had a table-top lid, and Norah slept on this during the war when Douglas was called out – this happened when the phone rang, announcing a red alert. The Home Guard had to be called out by phone and Norah had to issue the men with their firearms and ammunition when they called at the house. Then she had to be up at six o'clock in the morning to take in the arms and ammunition when they came off duty. She received no pay for this duty.

The first bomb of the war is said to have fallen at the nearby village of Ballinger, setting a bungalow on fire. Winston Churchill came to see the crater.'

'I came to live in Farnham Common as a young bride just as the war was about the start. My husband was in charge of the largest switchboard in the world (at that time) at Pinewood Studios. We had a house built in One Pin Lane – a quiet country lane called after the public house, a "pin" being a barrel of beer holding four and a half gallons.

Woods and fields surrounded us. The house was the first to be built in the lane for a very long time. In the mornings the dawn chorus was deafening and we never dared to leave a door or window open as the birds flew frantically in and out. We had taken their territory! This went on for some time each spring. Sheep wandered down the lane and round the house until we built a fence. The local football team, managed by the butcher, played in the field behind us.

But war came even here. The lovely beechwoods were commandeered and a "big gun" put there, which of course became a target for the enemy. A cottage near us was hit and I helped to rescue an elderly couple and retrieve their treasures. My husband was called up and I slept nightly on the dining room floor with my evacuees. When the bombs fell we got under the table! Years later an unexploded bomb was recovered from School Wood in front of our house.'

'Towards the end of the war, in about 1944, the Germans developed a long range rocket which could be aimed over the Channel. Older folk in Chesham will remember these doodlebugs well, visible and noisy in the dark, but only dangerous once the engine cut out and they swooped silently to earth, there to do a lot of damage.

However, on this occasion it was in the middle of morning service at St Mary's church when a tremendous explosion startled us all, blowing open the heavy door, swinging it backwards and forwards and forcing in the windows, then sucking them out again. Owing to the glass held by the lead, nothing was broken.

The congregation, sitting at the end of the first lesson, began jumping up; the vicar then stood in the middle of the chancel steps and firmly announced, "We will now sing the Te Deum." Up we all rose as one, as if about to sing the National Anthem, hands to attention, not looking to left or right, and we sang it quite certain that our own particular home was blown to bits.

Away in the woods of Chesham Bois, a man was picking wild raspberries. He heard the rocket and its engine cut off and pressed himself against a large tree. After it had exploded harmlessly amongst the trees, he hurried home to find his wooden house nearby pitted all over the inside walls with glass, and his Sunday joint had been blown out of the oven and was lying on the grass outside (his wife had gone to Chesham Bois church). The only things undamaged were six eggs in a wooden egg stand, the blast had flowed all round them.

We used to think that perhaps the doodlebugs were aimed at Chequers there being no other place of importance, such as a factory making war weapons. The few bombs that fell were dropped just anywhere by German bombers chased off by our fighters.'

FIRST AID?

'Although life took on a different meaning during the war in Drayton Parslow, there was still laughter in the village: the arrival of the evacuees with their London voices, the forming of the Home Guard and the First Aid classes.

These First Aid classes provided useful knowledge but the best entertainment was provided by "field work". "Patients" were placed in a field, complete with tags stating the type of injury to be attended to. Finding a casualty in a blackout, with only dim torches allowed, was difficult enough but bandaging and splinting arms and legs was even worse. Getting the poor bruised patient on a stretcher and back to base was almost impossible. Carrying a stretcher over a ridge and furrow field is in itself a work of art and strength, and add a liberal amount of freshly deposited cowpats and the exercise became even more hazardous. If the patient was still on the stretcher by the time the fence was reached they were very lucky. Getting over the fence was another matter. The stretcher balanced, then wobbled on top of the fence and finally shot its poor trussed up victim into the ditch. The First Aid given to this patient at base had nothing to do with his tags and a lot to do with "injuries received on active service". Volunteer patients were difficult to find after the first exercise and not without good reason.'

HELPING THE WAR EFFORT

'Although only ten when the war broke out, I joined my mother in many WI activities in Edlesborough. My friend and I collected salvage every Saturday morning, pushing our tea chest on wheels round the houses for any paper or magazines which could be spared. Like all good refuse collectors we had our "perks" in the shape of comics and foreign stamps (from soldiers serving abroad), though naturally the comics were returned when read.

That was the easy part. The real labour took place in a very damp and mouse-ridden outbuilding at the vicarage where the paper had to be sorted, weighed into 14 bundles and tied ready for collection.

Another grimy activity dreamed up for us was making camouflage netting. The basic nets were spread out on the village hall floor. They were marked with the patterns required in various colours. We had to thread strips of dyed hessian into the appropriate places. As both nets and hessian were soaked in creosote, protective clothing was essential – but getting rid of the smell was more difficult.

A really helpful idea was that each WI should be provided with a hand-operated canning machine and a supply of cans so that as much food as possible could be preserved. All the fruit and vegetables were canned in water – we had no sugar to make syrup. The food was heated in large pans, the tins filled and topped up with water, then placed in the machine for the lids to be sealed on. Labels were then applied, but as these sometimes fell off later some strange

*Women were exhorted to do their bit for the war effort by following government advice to 'Make Do and Mend'.*

meals were concocted. Also a faulty can would occasionally blow up in one's larder – never a dull moment.

I can't remember who organised it, but jamjars were a valuable commodity during wartime. Children scoured the ditches and hedge bottoms for them, collecting a ha'penny for the pound jars and a penny for the two pound.

A rather bizarre activity dreamed up by the local "squire's" wife of the next village was to collect the cabbage white butterflies as their caterpillars were foes of the cabbage. We caught them, removed their heads and presented them to her. I can't remember the rate of pay but it was evidently worth the mile or so to walk.'

'In order to conserve the county fruit crop, the government made an allotment of sugar to the WIs rather than increasing the personal rations, with the intention that they would open village "Jam Centres" where everyone with any fruit could take it in to the Parish Room, have it made into jam or canned and buy it back at cost price. All the labour was provided voluntarily by the WI members.

The Queen, as a WI member, got to know about the scheme and wished to see it in action. My mother was controller of the local centre at Penn and Tylers Green and one day she received a message from the WI County Secretary that, on the next jam making day, there was to be a special inspector from Windsor coming to see how the system worked. It was to be completely secret and no one was to be told. So she had to spread the word that there would be a lot of fruit that day and all helpers would be needed! The visit was a great success and the Queen was very interested in all the stages of preservation.

The Queen was continuing her trip with a visit to Hyde Heath to see another centre and I suggested to the detective that, rather than drive down the newly constructed concrete road to Amersham, it would be much more enjoyable for the Queen to go through the country lanes and beechwoods. He said they didn't know the way so would I pilot them.

The outcome was I headed a convoy of four cars through the lanes. Because of petrol rationing cars were fairly infrequent in those days and I caused some consternation to a couple of farm waggons which I had to get out of the road by hooting violently. Through an oversight I was not presented to the Queen at either end of the journey but she sent a special message to the "pilot" that she had very much enjoyed the drive.'

## A LIFT FROM 'BOMBER' HARRIS

'I shall always remember when "Bomber" Harris gave me a lift during the war. I was waiting for a bus to take me to my wartime job at the bottom of a steep hill, but when it came instead of stopping it went straight on. Behind was an official car, flag flying, with the Air Marshal driving and an officer sitting bolt upright in the back. The Marshal stopped and asked me to get in saying, "We'll catch that fellow."

He asked me about my work and my husband who was serving abroad at the time and followed the bus. This had to pass the road where the Air Marshal was living and had stopped at a bus stop a short way further on. Instead of my just getting out of the car the Marshal went out of his way, drove in front of the bus, spoke to the driver, and saw me off the car and on to the bus, to the amazement of the passengers, before turning and going on his way. A kind act in the middle of the war from the head of Bomber Command. I did wonder, though, if the bus did not stop because the driver may have thought the Marshal should have preference!'

## A MOMENT OF MAGIC

'During the war my sister and I used to cycle from Monks Risborough, where we then lived, to the weekly dances at the village hall in Butlers Cross. At that time soldiers of the Brigade of Guards and the Royal Artillery were stationed around Chequers, so there was no shortage of dance partners.

I vividly recall a clear, frosty, starlit night on one of these occasions. As we alighted from our bikes outside the hall we could hear the chatter coming from The Russell Arms opposite.

Then someone began to sing *Guide me Oh Thou Great Jehovah* to the tune *Cwm Rhondda*. Soon others joined in, until we were listening to a veritable male voice choir. Of course, it was the Welsh Guards. We leaned on our bikes and listened enthralled until the singing was over.

Fifty years have rolled by since that night, but whenever I hear that beautiful hymn I relive that magical moment. I feel again the frosty air on my face and picture the bright stars. I think of those lads from "The Land of Song" and wonder how many of them survived the war, and indeed of those who did how many are alive today.'

# A CHILD'S WAR

For children, wartime life rapidly became quite normal and many Buckinghamshire children were spared the traumas suffered by those in counties more heavily bombed. Evacuees arriving here found relative peace and security, and some were so happy that they didn't want to go home.

### 'GET INDOORS, THE WAR'S STARTED'

'At the outbreak of war we had just come home from Sunday school and were leapfrogging the white posts that lined the church path in those days, when Mr Enos Pusey came along and told us to get indoors because the war had started. I don't think it made much impression on an eight year old but it certainly changed the village of Lane End.

We had the day off school when the coaches came from London bringing evacuees and their teachers. They came tumbling out of the buses carrying gas masks and clutching little bags or cases and many with a doll or teddy in their arms. They went into the village hall where kind ladies from the village had gathered to take these poor children into their homes. How traumatic it must have been for some of these children and what a wrench for their parents not knowing for some days where the children were.

By now the village school was not large enough so the LCC took the Methodist Sunday school building over so that the children could continue their education with their own teachers. Even so there were too many children so for some months we used to go to school for half days only.

In the preparation for D-Day we had the troops going through the village for three days and school was cancelled because we couldn't cross the roads, so we stood watching and waving and cheering the soldiers. Some of them threw us sweets or money as they passed by. On D-Day itself, 6th June 1944, the skies were full of planes and gliders going over to France and this went on nearly all day.

"Booker Bill's", as they were called, were the planes that used to fly in formations of six threes day and night, training our young men between the ages of 18 and 24 as pilots to fly on bomber missions. We didn't complain about the noise they made, we were so indebted to them and to others who gave their lives so valiantly.

After the war when I was working in High Wycombe, my journey home by bus passed Booker Woods. I often used to look at one tall fir tree standing above all the others and to me it was a memorial to ten brave Canadian airmen whose plane crashed into those trees in Widdencox Park Woods. Their plane had been hit and they were making for Booker airfield but didn't quite make it. What a disaster – it could have been the village if they had crashed into it instead. We were told not to go anywhere near the scene but still went and what a horrible sight it was.'

## CAREFREE DAYS

'I was born in 1934 in the lovely village of Long Crendon. Both my parents came from Long Crendon; my father, Willis Hawes, was a dairy farmer, and my mother, Dorothy Shrimpton, came from the well known family of needlemakers.

We lived at Friars Dairy in the Chilton Road, and I remember helping my father fetch the cows in for milking, watching him sit on his stool milking the cows, then carrying the bucket of milk, tipping it in the cooler, through the strainer and into the churn. The milk was taken around the village in a pony and cart, some in bottles but most in the churn which was then ladled out into people's jugs. The fields and dairy no longer exist, houses now cover the whole area.

We were living at the Friars when the war began, though we soon moved to Woodway Farm, and I had started school. Dozens of evacuees came to Long Crendon and everyone with room took in one or two children. Relatives from London came to stay with us, and we had an evacuee and also an old couple who had a bed-sitting room downstairs. After a while the army took one of my father's fields for a searchlight camp and we had several soldiers and officers billeted there, mostly Londoners. They were very friendly and helped with the haymaking when not on duty; a couple of them married girls from the village.

We had chickens, pigs, cows, sheep and a good vegetable garden, so were never short of food. Mum made butter and Dad occasionally killed a pig; Mother would salt it down and hang it on a rack in an outhouse. We also had the lambs inside after they were first born and bottle fed them until they became stronger. One night we heard a doodlebug overhead. Its engine stopped and the Londoners were very scared but it dropped in the field across from the farm, trying to hit the army camp we guess.

Eventually we moved back into the village and my friends and I were intrigued by the American airmen, both black and white, who came to the village dances and went out with the village girls; again some married village girls. There was also a packing station in the Church House and many women worked there. A hostel was built for displaced persons who helped on the farms with the Land Army girls, and this later became part of the village school extension.

My sister Margaret was born during the war years and my mother and Grandmother Shrimpton, who had always lived with us and was a widow from the First World War, bought a parachute and made us all lovely clothes from the silk. Grandma worked in the village shop in the Square during the war and I would meet her at night and walk home with her in the dark. I liked to go early and watch her and Mrs Betts weighing up the rations for the customers' orders and sometimes I was allowed to help.

During this time my father joined the RAF hoping to fly aircraft, but his eyesight failed him, so he became an airfield controller instead.

These were carefree days for us children. We spent our summer holidays in the fields, always in a group, sometimes with Mrs Grace Pearce, the wonderful mother of a friend. She would take us for picnics over the "close" and we would walk on to Notley Abbey, the home of Laurence Olivier and Vivienne Leigh at that time. Sometimes we went swimming in the brook at "Bailies", this again was across the fields on the way to Thame. My memories of Mrs Pearce and the vast amount of time she spent playing with us will never fade. Her husband was the village cobbler, a crippled man, who for years was the scorer at all the village cricket matches.'

'When the war started I was nearly four years old, and nearly ten when it ended, therefore the years 1939 to 1945 neatly span my early childhood. Was a young child aware of the war, you may ask. Yes, indeed. I could not fail to appreciate its importance in adult conversation, and on the radio news. The newspapers were full of war reports – I wondered what items could possibly fill the papers in peacetime.

In a period of insecurity, I enjoyed a secure life. Not for me the separation from parents, destruction of home, loss of relatives or lack of food which unluckier children suffered. At Holly Green Farm, Bledlow, we had our own supplies of poultry, eggs, milk, vegetables and fruit. Also, our butcher was a great personal friend of my father. The economies and modifications which my mother no doubt had to make were not obvious to a child. Only two unobtainable items did I dream of – ice cream and bananas. In the dim recesses of my memory I could see an ice cream man selling from his bicycle cart in Chapel Lane. Of bananas I had no recollection, so I always wished for these when stirring the Christmas pudding.

None of our close relatives or friends was in the Forces, nor in the Home Guard. The hut in the rag pit, on the way up to the woods above the village, from which the Bledlow contingent operated, was an exciting mystery to me. I felt confident that they were up there every night defending the village from any possible enemy attack. The men in uniform I saw were usually from Halton Camp, near Wendover. When visiting our grandparents at Tring, we persuaded my father to go via Halton, so that we could play the war-time version of the counting game for car journeys. My sister and I took turns to count soldiers and airmen, which left mother to count sailors. Needless to say they were not very numerous in Bucks, but she sometimes caught a glimpse of one home on leave. Her score never exceeded three.

One appointment which my father held during the war was that of Billeting Officer for the village. This meant that mother went to people's houses asking if they had room to accommodate child evacuees from London, which the government mistakenly believed would be bombed in the early stages of the war. Many residents had spare rooms and thought they could manage a quiet girl evacuee – when the children arrived the majority were boys. We had a large farmhouse and only two children in the family at that time, so we had our share of evacuees. First we had a boy in his teens, who attended the village school for a time, then worked on the farm, and as soon as he was old enough joined the Navy. Then we had two young school teachers, and later a man and his wife, the manager of a factory which had been evacuated to Princes Risborough. This latter couple had two rooms in our house and lived separately as far as possible. These additions to our household were no doubt inconvenient for our parents, but we children welcomed new people to talk to. The married couple, in particular, were fond of children and introduced us to new books and games.

The evacuees, both children and teachers, brought added numbers and stimulus to the village school, which then had pupils from five to 14. We were happy and well taught, though sadly lacking in equipment by modern standards. The infants wrote on little slates, though whether this was the normal practice or due to a paper shortage, I am not certain. Some of our work was for the war effort. For instance, I knitted a long navy blue scarf for a sailor – older and more experienced knitters made socks in airforce blue or khaki. The headmaster was justly proud of the school garden, tended by the older pupils, so the Dig for Victory campaign was a boost to his enthusiasm. The paths of the garden were edged with boards a few inches high and, in the absence of an air raid shelter, these wooden edgings were to be, amazingly to us, our protection from the blast of a bombing raid. The air raid drill was hilarious, when we had to lie face down across the garden paths (most of us were short enough) our heads protected by the wooden edging. Fortunately there was never a real raid. We always carried our gas masks to school, on a strap like a satchel. Practice in putting them on was good fun. Some small children had models decorated with Mickey Mouse – I was proud that mine was all khaki, like the adult version.

A memorable time during the war was when a regiment, or was it just a platoon, of soldiers came to our farm for exercises. They camped round the edge of Home Meadow, and some groups installed themselves in farm buildings. Thus the cart shed became the cookhouse, and nearby the vehicles were parked, covered with camouflage netting; would they really look like trees from an aircraft, I wondered. A loose box near the house became the radio post, and the officers occupied a spare downstairs room of the farmhouse. The men in the loose box appeared to do their work at night, for the hours when we were all asleep were punctuated by the crash of the heavy front door, the clomp, clomp of army boots on the tiled hall floor, and voices from our back room as the messages were relayed. The troops in the meadow were friendly and chatted to me as I passed that way to and from school. One afternoon, a group showed me their iron rations, "bully" beef and hard biscuits – how unappetising it looked. What they were really longing for, they said, was a nice fresh loaf of bread, but as they were not allowed to leave the camp, perhaps I could buy one for them? I took the money and willingly trotted across two meadows and along to the bakery in Sandpit Lane. When I returned with the loaf, the grateful soldiers cut it up and ate it straight away – I went home well satisfied that I had contributed to the war effort.

During the second half of the war I became aware that many normal activities were curtailed. We could not go on holiday, and many commodities were in short supply, such as clothes, shoes, furniture and paint, but none of these things worried a child. Even the shortage of toilet paper was overcome at our house, since mother had a large supply of old dressmaking patterns and the pieces, though of odd sizes and shapes, were ideal in quality. Looking at the pictures of the impossibly long, thin ladies on the packets was an added interest.

For many people, the war brought unprecedented opportunities to travel and work in different parts of the country, or abroad. Some young Bledlow people met and married partners from distant counties, and these marriages were a happy subject of adult conversation. Everyone was surprised when the stationmaster's shy youngest son came home with a wife from Belgium.

201

Anyone writing about adult life in Bledlow between 1939 and 1945 would probably write a different account, remembering the difficulties and perhaps the sorrows. For a child, however, and particularly for me, those years were happy and interesting.'

## AN EVACUEE'S STORY

'I'm a Londoner. My father died when I was five and my mother, as a single parent, brought up three children in a London suburb – we had a pretty tough time. We belonged to an "extended family", so when we were evacuated it was a very traumatic experience.

We were evacuated on the day war broke out. I had my sister with me – I was 13 and she was ten, and we left from Ealing Broadway in a double-decker bus. We'd had our bags packed for some time as we'd known that something was going to happen. I was at Ealing County Girls School and the previous year there had been two girls from Czechoslovakia there, so we knew this war was coming. I don't think anyone suspected it was going to be such a big thing, they thought it would all be over in a very short time.

First of all we went to Aylesbury. We had to be sorted out and people came and collected you and took you to the various homes. Of course it was a bit difficult for us because I had to stay with my sister and look after her, that was my last instruction, so we were among the last to be chosen. Eventually there were only the two of us and another girl in the same form as me, so the three of us went to a very old lady, a spinster, on the Wendover road. I don't think she knew what had hit her, actually. We arrived, just like that, and we had bars of chocolate, biscuits and tins of corned beef, that's all we had to give her.

She was quite a character, this old lady, though it must have been absolutely overwhelming for her. Possibly she was 60 but to me she seemed ancient. She coped very well really, but she used to cart us off to chapel three times on a Sunday, morning service, afternoon and evening. She would walk in front and we would trawl (sic) behind. I wasn't a churchgoer at that time, so it was quite interesting.

There's one thing I'll never forget. In London we didn't live *in* the city but we had an upstairs flat. My aunt lived downstairs so she had the garden and we didn't have any garden of our own as such – the park was the only outside place I knew. There was a lot of countryside round where we were on the Wendover road and the old lady had a big garden too. I in my innocence collected a lot of caterpillars and put them in a jamjar. My friend said, "Well, you ought to let them have some air", so I made some holes in the paper

202

over the top of the jar and left it on the mantelpiece. When we came down to breakfast next morning all the caterpillars were crawling up the wall – the old lady was *not* amused. She also had a harmonium and my friend used to play it, with me pumping it with my hands.

We couldn't stay there long, though, because Ealing County Boys School had come as well and we overwhelmed the local school premises. So after six weeks we were trundled back to High Wycombe. There wasn't a lot more space there for the schools, but there was more than at Aylesbury. We used mainly a chapel which had a big hall and lots of small rooms, and we also used some of the facilities of the girls high school.

I was billeted with my sister at West Wycombe, with Mr and Mrs White, who had no children. She could easily have been 50 but again to me they seemed quite elderly. It was soon obvious that we were going to settle in, so Mrs White said that they were now "Auntie" and "Uncle", and so they remained to the end of their days. We kept up with them until they died, and they lived into their nineties.

We were there for nearly four years. It was something that changed my life – I became part of a family whereas at home there was just Mother and she was working all the time. They were both what I would call "country folk". Uncle was born in Turville and his father had had a wood business. He used to tell us many tales of the wood trade and of fetching the timber down to High Wycombe with the horses and cart. The horses knew their own way back home as the drivers would often stop off for a drink and get back on the cart worse for wear. Uncle worked for a firm called Castles which would normally have been making furniture, but during the war they made parts for aircraft, mainly the propeller or "air-screw", as they called it. He cycled from West Wycombe to this firm near Booker, and it was a tremendous uphill journey, in all weathers. Auntie made him milk puddings to take with him for lunch, a half-pint size in a little dish.

Auntie was born in Postcombe, near the border with Oxfordshire, and she'd been in service. Though they were only 30 miles out of London they really *were* quite countrified. High Wycombe was a market town and very few people had cars – or in any case any petrol – and everybody came in by bus, so Friday was definitely "Market Day". Auntie always came in on a Friday and did some shopping, but even during the war the Co-op used to deliver most of her heavy goods. The Co-op man would come and you'd have a little book with your order filled in, and he'd bring it the next week.

They were completely self-sufficient for garden produce. Uncle had a long garden and he grew all the vegetables to see them through the whole of the season. I saw vegetables that I'd never seen before –

broad beans, leeks, things that were strange to me. I suppose Mother just had to have whatever she could get. Auntie was a good cook, but she'd present these things to us children and we'd turn up our noses at them. But she soon got round that because she used to cook them and then sieve them laboriously, so every day we'd have thick vegetable soup. We gradually acquired these different tastes and then later on we'd try out the vegetables. It must have been awful for her, preparing all those meals and then these children saying, "Oh, I don't like that!" She'd make wonderful puddings, spotted dick in cloth rolls with string at the end, and bacon and onion in a roll. It was an eye-opener.

Auntie taught me so much of cooking and sewing, and my love of gardening also came from there. She wasn't allowed much of the garden, though, because Uncle considered that all of the garden was for vegetables. She was allowed just a little strip down the side, but she cultivated all she'd got, with rose bushes and sweet peas and other flowers. She used to make a lot of wine too – dandelion, potato – that was quite potent, I remember. She had a wonderful larder with an enormous marble slab – no fridge, of course, so all the fats were kept on this slab. During the summer she had to boil her milk when it came and we had to drink boiled milk. That wasn't very nice. Her sister-in-law cycled to Turville each week and in the spring she brought back eggs from a farm there, not black market but extra to our ration, and Auntie would preserve them in isinglass. There's a pot in my garden now with plants in it, and that's the pot that used to stand in the larder, full of eggs in isinglass, so that during the winter we could have eggs for making cakes.

The radio was our lifeline – Auntie and I loved to sit up on a Saturday night and listen to the play. Uncle wasn't very keen on the idea but she finally got his permission for me to stay up – "late", according to him! The radio had batteries and we had to take the accumulator to the village to have it charged every week.

I remember the seasons there in West Wycombe – the change of seasons and the weather affected me more there than in London. There was much more going on at different times. I remember the first spring, when the beechwoods were all out in leaf, just up the lane, and Auntie took us up – and there was this mass of bluebells. We'd never seen bluebells before and we could hardly believe our eyes. Auntie said, "You don't pick them, you leave them there for other people to enjoy", but we couldn't resist picking a few. We took them back and she wrapped them very carefully in a box and tissue paper and sent them to my mother.

We always went for a walk on Sundays. Uncle was a very strict person and had been a very strong churchman but when he came back from the First World War and they settled in West Wycombe, he found the services too "High". His faith was there but he couldn't go along with the church. On Sundays we had very strict rules, we weren't allowed to sew or to knit or anything.

Uncle was rather aloof in lots of ways but he was "a presence". He joined the Home Guard – that was a bit hilarious but he enjoyed it. They used to meet at the top of the hill but I don't think they had any guns, though they did have uniforms, dreadful things really. I think he did duty at night sometimes. Although we were only a short distance from London we never had any bombing as such except for one afternoon, I remember, when a stray plane came over and dropped its last bomb, I suppose, over in the far wood. It shook people up because until then they hadn't had anything at all.

We really had no idea what was happening in London. We did go home occasionally – at the beginning we went back for the school holidays – but when the bombing started Mother felt it was better for us to be away. Auntie was very kind, she used to invite Mother down for a weekend and Mother would come, so we didn't lose contact.

I must confess that I became very close to Auntie because we were there all the time with her and she was home all the time, and those are impressionable years when you're 13 to 17. She was very strict, though, and we weren't allowed to stray or go out. You had to tell her where you were going and she kept us on a tight rein, but when I think about it I realise what a responsibility she took on with two teenagers.

Originally all Ealing County Girls School came out, but then a lot of them drifted back and after about 18 months there were so few left it was difficult to organise lessons, so I joined the High School at High Wycombe and took my School Certificate there. My sister went to the local secondary school and finished her schooling at the same time as I did, when she was 14. We both went back to London then, in 1943, and I took quite a time to settle down. Eventually I picked up a social life and began to gad about quite a bit. As I said, we'd led a very quiet life in West Wycombe. But we still missed Auntie and we still went down there quite a lot, partly for a break from the bombing. She saw me through two or three boyfriends I took down there!

Auntie was more like a mother to me really and we always visited her. My husband and I called in on our way back from our two days' honeymoon near Henley and my sister went to live in Oxford after she married, so she would visit Auntie and Uncle. When my daughter was born I took her down there – we always came back with a jar of jam or something! Auntie really changed my life.'

'I cannot start my story by saying it was a lovely day, or pouring with rain, the day I arrived in Princes Risborough in September 1940. Neither can I say what the exact day was. I suppose it is not surprising as I was only ten years old and very frightened of what was happening to me. I know I arrived by train with my mother and that it was a Sunday.

I could not technically be classed as an evacuee as the boundary for evacuation in Wimbledon ended down in the town and we lived up the hill on the edge of the common. I went through most of the Battle of Britain there; our school was closed as children had been machine-gunned and killed coming home from school one day. Our days were spent like street urchins, seeing who could collect the largest pieces of shrapnel, and at night we were bombed. Many is the time I was blasted from my bunk bed in the air raid shelter onto the three people sleeping on the floor below. It was important that I should be "got away" and friends knew friends in Princes Risborough, so that is how I arrived in Buckinghamshire.

After a short period to settle in with my new-found family, I had to go to school, which was held in the local village hall. There were four classes, each screened from the other, so only one oral lesson could take place at a time. It must have been a nightmare for the teachers. I seem to remember going over to the playing fields opposite for long periods of lessons if the weather was suitable.

Nine months passed and in the June of the following year, the daughter of "my family" got married. I played my part in the preparations, but unfortunately I got measles three weeks before the wedding and the bride-to-be hadn't had them. Oh dear! say no more – but all was well on the day.

I later moved with the family to Saunderton and thus to Bledlow Ridge school for a time. Finally, to end my schooldays, I was back at Princes Risborough primary school without a scholarship, the paperwork for which never caught up with me – I was still classed as a Londoner. I left school at 14 and the first year of my working life was spent with the Norwich Union Assurance Company, whose three main London offices were sheltering at Horsenden Manor, but in 1945 they moved out and returned to the city. I was adamant that I would not go back; I had made friends here and, most of all, had a caring Aunt and Uncle (so duly named) to look after me. I never gave it a thought that my mother, who was a widow (and I the only child), would ever like me back. I found out later she was only too grateful that "Auntie and Uncle" could give me a good start in life.'

# ON THE LAND

As men were called up into the services, the need to get women onto the land and helping to produce the country's food became essential. This took a great deal of organisation and tenacity, as a County Organiser of the Land Army remembers. They were happy times for many of the land girls. A special section of the Army was the Women's Timber Corps, the enthusiastic 'lumberjills'.

## ORGANISING THE LAND ARMY

'The Women's Land Army was formed in 1939 in conjunction with the War Agricultural Committee to enlist, and as far as possible train, girls to work on farms in place of the men who were about to be called up to fight.

I joined the Land Army in Buckinghamshire in October 1939 just after the outbreak of war. On arrival I was appointed a County Organiser under the first County Chairman, the Hon Mrs Heywood Lonsdale. I was given a list of all the farmers in a large section of the county and told to visit each one and tell them that their workers would probably be called up, and to establish what extra help they might need, so that the county organisation could have some idea what the requirement might be.

I did not always have a happy reception. Most of the farmers declared that they would never employ a girl. I felt quite triumphant on the rare occasions when a farmer who perhaps already had a daughter working on the farm admitted he would be happy to do so.

Our office started life in the converted stables at West Wycombe Park, but later on we moved to a redundant pub at 6 St Mary's Street, High Wycombe which was much more accessible. There we had the bare necessities – a waiting room, a switchboard, a tiny interviewing room, the County Secretary's office, a records room (a file had to be kept on every land girl) and the largest room which housed the stocks of uniform.

By 1940 girls over the age of 17 were being called up to do a job, and they could elect either to join the forces, go into a factory, or work on the land. The ones who chose to work on the land came to me for interview. The basic requirement was that they were in good health and reasonably strong, and willing to go wherever they were sent. By 1941 we were importing girls from other counties. Sometimes a farmer would send us a girl whom he wished to employ and ask us to enrol her in the Land Army, but that girl still had to undertake, once enrolled, to go where she was appointed if and when that farmer had no further need of her help.

One day a farmer sent me a girl for interview whom I thought seemed very unsuitable, so I painted a rather black picture of the job hoping to put her off. However, at the end of the interview she asked, "There is just one thing I would like to know; could I have one day off a month to continue my present job". She turned out to be chief mannequin at a big London store, and she went on to be a very good land girl.

Sometimes we would get a draft of 50 or 75 girls arriving on a Monday morning at Aylesbury station. They all had to be interviewed (we had a small office in Aylesbury near the station for this purpose), and then found lodging for the night. We had a clearing hostel near the station in Aylesbury where the girls usually went for their first night, before being moved to another hostel or to private employment on a farm.

Buckinghamshire was one of the largest employers of land girls in the country. At the peak in October 1943 there were just under 2,000 girls in training and employment in the county. This posed considerable problems for uniform, housing and general welfare. We felt very responsible for the girls who had left home, often for the first time, mostly from towns and cities, and were expected to adapt almost overnight to working in the countryside. They were lonely, young and inexperienced. I recall an occasion when I visited a farmer and asked where the girl was, to be told that she was "up the field putting the horse into the cart". I found the girl in tears, having no idea how to go about the job, being totally unfamiliar with both horse and cart. Fortunately, I was able to help!

Often I was on "uniform duty". Each girl on arrival was allocated a pair of corduroy knee breeches, two shirts, cotton overall, dungarees, green jersey, hat, overcoat, wool stockings, shoes and gumboots. Stocks had to be held to accommodate all shapes and sizes, and frequent requisition orders had to be sent to the Land Army Headquarters in Sussex. Once I had to put in such a large requisition order that headquarters felt obliged to telephone to ask if I really meant it. I did!

Housing was another headache. We preferred the girls to be billeted with families but it became increasingly difficult to find places for them. After I had spent a day visiting 46 houses and succeeded in obtaining only two billets we realised we would have to open hostels. Many well known houses were used as hostels, and there were one or two purpose-built hostels. Mentmore Towers was used, as was Waddesdon Manor, where the grounds were turned over to growing tomatoes. Between eight and ten girls lived there in a cottage which was normally used for the garden boys. They were cared for by a Mrs Johnson, who was wife of the head gardener, and at one time these girls were sending over two tons of tomatoes to market each week. All but one of the orchid houses were turned over to tomato growing, the rose beds were dug up, and tomatoes grew against clipped yew hedges.

Winslow Manor was used as a hostel, as was Linfords Manor and Tingewick, where the hostel was upstairs and the owners, the Gore-Langton family, lived downstairs. At Tower House near Slough 70 girls lived and worked at the market gardens around Wraysbury and Eton Wick, and at Thame Colonel Ashton, who later became Chairman of the War Agricultural Committee, made available two cottages at Scotts Grove Farm, where about six girls lived. The first girl to arrive there stayed on to train many others who followed.

Coppins, the Iver home of the Duke and Duchess of Kent, had a hostel in the stables. Often the Kent children could be found in the hostel kitchen looking to see what was on offer.

Food was short, of course, but extra rations were issued to the hostels and the girls were always given sandwiches to take for their lunch at work. One girl complained that her sandwiches were uneatable and I went to see what was going on. "If you don't like them I will eat them," I said, and sat down and ate her lunch. She looked very glum. Then I relented and gave her my lunch.

Providing uniform and suitable housing was difficult, but not impossible. Providing for the girls moral welfare presented greater difficulties. A girl came to me one day to say that she and her friends wished to use the service canteen in Aylesbury, but were not permitted to do so because the Land Army was classed as industry, and not services. The manager of the canteen had told the girls they could come in if they first went out onto the street and picked up a serviceman to accompany them! I had sharp words with the canteen manager and the matter was put right, but the same thing happened at other canteens, notably on railway stations, where the service canteen was the only one available. Eventually a report was sent to the National Chairman and the matter was put right nationally.

On one occasion there was a big in-draft of American soldiers who had a lot of spending money. When the GIs took our girls out they were often offered alcohol for the first time, and had no idea how to use it. One day we had a phone call from the Metropolitan Police to say that one of our girls and her boyfriend had been arrested and were being held at Paddington police station in a drunken state. A very sad little soul was sent down to Aylesbury next day on the train. I gave her some strong black coffee and asked her what she had had to drink.

"Well, he had a bottle of whisky in his pocket."

"And how much did you drink?"

"About so much," indicating about four inches.

"Well you know, a man will pour out a little whisky in a glass and mix it with soda water or water."

"Oh, but we did mix it."

"What did you mix it with?"

"He had a bottle of champagne in the other pocket."

Another day I was sitting in my office and I heard three girls talking in the next office about how they were going to go out and get drunk. "Is this a good idea?" said I. "Oh, that's all right", they said, "not dead drunk, or merry-drunk, just happy drunk!"

My chief job, when not in the office interviewing or handing out uniform, was inspecting farms as to suitability of accommodation, and visiting the liaison officers, of whom we tried to have one in each village – a woman to whom the girls in their area could go if they had a problem or needed more uniform. Telephones were not so readily available as they are now and it was not always easy for a girl to get in touch direct with the office in High Wycombe. I also visited the hostels regularly to see that the girls were all right.

Many problems arose, and some could be quite difficult to handle. I inspected one farm, and put in a report to say that no girl should be sent there because the accommodation was highly unsuitable – the farmer's three teenage sons had to go through the proposed girl's bedroom in order to reach their own. However, there was a slip-up, and while I was away a girl was sent there. Inevitably, she complained, and I had to go in and tell the girl to pack while I informed the farmer she was leaving. I then packed girl, luggage and bicycle into my car and took her to a hostel. The farmer was not pleased at having his farm labour removed on the spot.

On another occasion I went to a farm in Waddesdon where the girl had complained that she was being asked to do domestic work, which was against the rules. I was first met by a ferocious dog. Having got past the dog I found a very angry farmer in the milking shed who knew why I had come, and informed me that I was one of those "useless people who work in offices and can't even milk a cow". Happily, I was able there and then to prove him wrong!

Then there was the girl who got much too friendly with the farmer, to the annoyance of the farmer's wife. I had to go in and remove her but she took to visiting the farmer in the evenings, and so she had to be posted to a farm a long way away from where she could not keep in touch. Unfortunately this kind of thing happened more than once.

Many of the girls who lived in hostels and whose work was either too far to walk to, or who were not being picked up in groups by lorry and taken to work, were issued with bicycles. Frequently these city girls could not ride bicycles, and I spent many an hour running behind a girl holding the saddle while she tried to keep her balance!

Farms at that time were very labour intensive. Most jobs were done by hand. Horses were still widely used, although tractors were coming in. The girls turned their hands to everything. They were best at milking, and caring for the cattle and horses, but they did a lot of heavy work and had to be shown how to do it without injuring themselves. The last thing we needed was bad backs! Some of them even drove tractors, which were very heavy – no power steering in those days! At harvest time threshing gangs were organised and taken by lorry from farm to farm as required, since combine harvesters were a rarity. The girls worked very hard for long hours, and managed wonderfully well.

When our second County Chairman, Mrs Fellowes, took on the job she was keen to see as much as possible of what was going on. I took her one very hot summer's day to a farm to see a combine at work, as they really were a novelty. I remember she was wearing a beautiful pale pink linen dress and picture hat to match. The farmer invited her to ride on the combine with him. When she came down her lovely outfit was pale brown.

Life was tough in the winter. It was hard on the girls, and travelling by car was difficult. My little Ford coped wonderfully well, but it was certainly primitive by today's standards. There was no heating, so I used to fill a hot water bottle before leaving home to give me some warmth, and then fill it again at the office before setting out on my visits. There were no automatic windscreen wipers. They had to be operated by hand. Many of the country roads were gated, and driving home at night after a long day was not easy.

My car carried anything and everything, a lot of which it was not designed to carry and it was frequently overloaded. On one occasion the hostel at Brill had to be evacuated owing to infection. The bunk beds the girls used had been made from wood collected from the bombed areas in London, and it turned out to be infested with bugs, so everything had to be fumigated. Unfortunately the girls' rations were all sent to Brill, since that was where they were registered, so every day I could be seen with my car laden with food, coal and other

211

provisions transporting them from Brill to the temporary hostel. On one of these occasions I had a puncture on a hill!

We always picked up men in uniform who wanted lifts. On one occasion I saw five RAF personnel thumbing a lift. I stopped and explained I had not room to take them all. "That's all right," they said, "we'll manage". And manage they did, four in the back and one in the front!

The work was hard and there were many difficulties, but we had a lot of fun and excitements. There were rallies at intervals when armlets were awarded for long service. On 9th July 1943 three Bucks land girls were thrilled to be invited to Buckingham Palace for a Garden Party to celebrate the fourth anniversary of the Women's Land Army, where they met Her Majesty the Queen and the two Princesses. I was not there on that occasion, but my turn came later. On 7th December 1945 I was present with 17 of our girls at a party given by the Lord Mayor of London at the Mansion House, at which Her Majesty the Queen presented six-year armlets. One of our girls, D.A. Buckmaster from Penn, led the milking section of the parade through the City before the party.

Saturday 12th May 1945 was a very exciting day. Victory in Europe had just been announced and there was a big rally of Bucks land girls in the school hall at Eton College. Seven hundred girls were present, and 51 received scarlet armlets from the Duchess of Kent for four years service. The Minister of Agriculture and Fisheries and the Minister of Food were present at the rally and made speeches. I could not do better than to close with some of their words.

Lord Woolton said, "As Minister of Food I should like to send to all of you my congratulations on the important contribution which you have made to Victory. Without the immense increase in the production of food from our homeland, my task of feeding our people during the attacks from sea and air would have been impossible. The Women's Land Army have played a great part in securing the increase."

The Minister of Agriculture & Fisheries said, "I would like to take this occasion . . . to convey to you and all other members of the WLA my deep thanks and admiration for the splendid work the Land Army has done during the past five and a half years. Every member of the Land Army can feel proud to belong to a force which has done so much to ensure that the people of this country and our fighting men abroad have not gone short of food."

Both Ministers also reminded us that the war in the Far East was not yet won, and even when it was the Land Army would still be needed because food would be short for a long time. This turned out to be very true, and in March 1946 a recruiting campaign was begun, the numbers of girls employed having dropped considerably with the ending of the war. For six weeks during my final year with the Land Army I drove a horse box from town to town, village to village, market to market, throughout the county recruiting new members.

Eight hard working but happy years came to an end with my retirement on 31st January 1947.'

## HAPPY MEMORIES

'On 8th June 1942 I joined the WLA and along with five other girls I was sent to a large dairy farm in Wing where we were taught to do general farm work.

Our day started at six o'clock when we did the milking. It was a very hot summer and hay work was in full swing. I remember the huge blisters on my heels caused by new boots.

At the end of the month's training we were all dispatched to various farms and I came to Swanbourne. The first few months I spent at Moco Farm doing field work as there was no milking. I was very happy working there but during the winter there was very little work for me so I moved to Home Farm, where they already had another land girl. Her name was Joan and we soon became good friends. I think she was pleased to have someone to share the milk round with her; we did alternate weeks, but of course we had to milk the cows first! There were five of us hand-milking 28 cows – "Old" Will, "Young" Frank, Bill and us two girls.

We worked seven days a week, with a half day off unless we were doing extra time during the busy seasons. We delivered the milk daily by pony and float. The village was full of characters and we got to know everyone pretty well. Some of the old ladies still wore long black skirts and crisp white aprons. The price of milk was fourpence a pint and I remember one of our customers held me personally responsible when I told her that it had been increased to fourpence ha'penny! She said that "it would be dear at a penny a pint."

Most of the implements we used are now museum pieces, like the horse rake, the binder which cut and tied the sheaves, the elevator that carried hay from the trailers up into the ricks, and many more. Hay ricks were thatched to make them weatherproof and this was a specialised job – I only did the "yelming", getting the straw into bundles and carrying it up the ladder to the thatcher. The corn was kept in the big dutch barns until the threshing box came from the Ministry of Agriculture.

There was always plenty of field work to do, one of my least favourite jobs being to hoe endless rows of sugar beet or mangels. We cleaned ditches, cut down thistles and drove the tractors, and after each milking session the sheds had to be mucked out. The cows were fed on farm produce: hay and oats which we crushed by machine, and mangels crushed by a hand-operated chopper, but they also had cow cake, which was delivered in sacks. Cows, like humans, have their own personalities; some kind and gentle, others with a streak of malice. I loved their large soulful eyes.

There were twelve milk-producing farms in the area and now there are four. Swanbourne was a pretty village, with lovely old elm trees lining the roadside. It was also a community, where there was always something going on, from whist drives to socials and dances. There was the sound of hens clucking in back gardens, the sight of cattle or sheep being herded along the road to pastures new and the drone of the Wellington bombers from the airbase nearby. It's very different now, of course, but I have many happy memories of my Land Army days.'


## THE WOMEN'S TIMBER CORPS

'My earliest memories of Buckinghamshire go back to the war years, between 1943-1945. I was one of a dozen or so 19-20 year olds, newly-trained volunteers in the Women's Timber Corps, a special section of the Women's Land Army.

We had reached conscription age and had opted to work as "lumberjills" with the Home Timber Production Department, in order to keep up supplies of pit-props for the coal mines, Army telegraph poles and so forth. At its peak, the Corps had around 4,000 members working all over the country, plus 1,000 in Scotland.

We arrived in Slough, then part of Bucks, in late January 1943, full of enthusiasm for our new way of life. We were taken to our billet, the YWCA hostel, and from there we were taken by lorry each day to the woods, usually larch plantations about 30-40 years old. Our first job was to trim off the lower dead branches, called "brashing-out", then, with axes, we cut the "fall", the wedge-shaped cut at the base, facing the direction in which the tree was to fall. Then the cross-cut was used, with great cries of *"Timber"* for even the smallest specimen.

When a number of trees had been felled we would then lop the branches and pile them in a long row forming a "drift" of about ten trees width, between one pair of "fellers" and the next, to be burnt at a later date. The next operation was cutting the pit-props into varying lengths of between three to six ft.

Thicker six ft lengths were sometimes cut for use as "wood-wool" (packing material), and very straight, suitably-sized trees were destined for use as Army telegraph poles. These, and the wood-wool had to be peeled with a "paddle" while the sap was still fresh, a pleasant, relaxing job.

The remaining thinner top branches were then cut into lengths and called "Cellotex" for making into wood-pulp for the paper industry, so every part of the tree was used. It was the work of the measurer (also a WTC girl) to select the timber for its various uses, and to measure our day's output. She also carried out office duties, costing, wages, etc.

We took packed lunches, prepared by ourselves after breakfast, and, being land girls, we had extra cheese rations. Not being a lover of Cheddar cheese, I would dearly have liked to swop for a slice of ham or even Spam occasionally, but one gets used to anything in time, and we certainly all had good appetites! We made our tea in a billy-can on a brushwood fire, first boiling the water, then throwing in the loose tea (no tea bags then) and National Dried Milk. Quite a dreadful-looking concoction really, often with bits of burnt conifer floating on the top, but a very welcome cuppa, nevertheless. After all, it was pretty strenuous work, but we all enjoyed it tremendously and we acquired the most wonderful tans, even as early as February, when we started to roll up our sleeves, *and* our dungarees, which became shorts when the knees wore out.

At the end of the day we travelled home covered in dust and resin, which had become almost black and was well-nigh impossible to scrub off. Afterwards, we would soon demolish our evening meal, relax, perhaps write letters, or go out on the town.

*The Women's Timber Corps enlisted young women to work with the Home Timber Production Dept, and they tackled the task with enthusiasm and good humour.*

215

Six of us had become friends at the training camp in Suffolk, and subsequently shared a room at the hostel. We always went out together, but after a few weeks we decided this wasn't such a good idea, as not one of us had found a date. One evening we had a plan. We would split up into pairs, and after about an hour or so we would all meet up in the Forces Canteen in the High Street, with (or without) our conquests. My friend Gwen and I, being perhaps a little bolder than the others, arrived first with two soldiers from the Pioneer Corps, one of whom (Gwen's) had been a grave-digger in civilian life. Two girls turned up "without" and the other two also arrived with two soldiers – almost everyone was in uniform at that time so there was no shortage. Thereafter, all we girls could do was giggle – oh! the cruelty of youth – but we had at least achieved our goal and restored our self-esteem. Our escorts must have thought us all pretty silly but of course we couldn't share the joke, and one girl actually married hers, so some good came of it after all!

Another time we were burning bracken and brushwood at Bulstrode Park near Gerrards Cross and discovered we were next door to an Army camp. Several soldiers appeared driving Bren-gun carriers and offered us rides which we promptly accepted, girls (and boys) being what they are. I accepted a ride on the pillion of a despatch rider's bike and had the shock of my life when our foreman, our nice Mr Lingwood, chose that moment to arrive, to see how we were getting on. He was very nice about it but we did feel a bit ashamed of ourselves.

We stayed in the area for about 18 months, felling woods at Black Park, Stoke Poges, Iver Heath, Fulmer and Denham etc.

It was then time for us to move on and we were taken by lorry to our new home at "Cokethorpe" near Witney in Oxfordshire, now an independent boys school, where we spent the next 18 months, until the end of the war.

I stayed on in the WLA and returned to Bucks as a trainee tractor driver at the Bucks War Agricultural Committee depot at Turnfurlong, Aylesbury.

I was sent out with Dorothy, an experienced driver who became a good friend and taught me to plough, disc, harrow and generally cultivate the land. Later we were given the depot's first new Fordson Major, much easier than the old Standard Fordsons. Haybaling and harvesting with the old binders were jobs I enjoyed but the ploughing (with only a two-furrow Ransome plough) was a job Dot took great pride in and I suffered a few tickings off at first for messing up her work with the "trip-rope"! Sadly she died in 1954, at the early age of 30, but I'll always remember her as she was then – a tall, dark, very attractive girl – and with great affection. We lived at the WLA hostel in Stoke Mandeville, behind Strouds Garage and near the County Farm, on the Wendover Road, and from there we were taken (by lorry, as usual) either to the depot or to our current place of work on one of the various farms in the Aylesbury Vale, ie at Stoke Mandeville, Wendover, Bierton and Hulcott, Quarrendon, Whitchurch and Hardwick etc etc etc!

One day I was sent out on a very unusual job. My "Major" and I were transported to the new housing estate under construction at Southcourt. The firm laying the drainage (or possibly water supply?) needed to hire a tractor and driver to haul the long, black steel pipes into position beside the previously-dug trench. I was given a "mate" – a pleasant Irishman, who attached the pipes to the drawbar, rode with me and released them at the other end.

A group of German POWs who were working on the new road close by, seemed to be taking a great interest. Maybe it was the sight of a girl engaged on such an unconventional task (maybe it was just the sight of a girl!). I must admit I was pretty surprised myself at the job I was doing. However, later, whilst sitting eating my sandwiches, one of them, who was the mechanic on the site, came over and started to chat – in fairly good English (self-taught, I learned later, from reading the newspapers). After lunch, he took over from my Irish friend for one or two trips and I well remember the Irishman remarking that he could see me going back with him to Germany as a "GI bride".

Little did he realise the significance of his words, as, although I didn't go to Germany until 21 months later, we did get married, in March 1948!'

# THE WAR ENDS

At last it was over and we could start to get our lives back to normal. Celebrations took place in towns and villages all over the county after VE Day, though some did not quite go as planned, and ways of commemorating those who had played a large part in the war effort were considered. For young couples setting up home, however, housing was in very short supply and some resorted to squatting in old army camps.

## CELEBRATIONS

'VE Day, 8th May 1945, was a day of celebration in Lane End and so was the next day, Ascension Day – as ours was a church school we all went to church at nine o'clock and then had the rest of the day off. Friday we went back to our classes only to learn that King George VI and Queen Elizabeth were coming to Wycombe Abbey School to meet General Doolittle. Miss Noble, a very gracious lady who lived at Fingest Close, paid North's Garage to take 24 of us to go and see them pass by and we had a marvellous view. It was truly a memorable week.

There were always plenty of activities going on in our village and one that attracted a large gathering of girls was the Girls Friendly Society, which used to meet in the school. We took part in many competitions within the Oxford Diocese. For the Victory Parade in 1946 we entered into a procession of floats. Mr George Thomas kindly loaned us his lorry and we transformed it into the Queen Mary liner taking GI brides to America. For days we were making portholes or sewing and when we had finished the ship was 30 ft long and we won first prize. We sailed down The Row and rolled about a bit over Wheeler End Common, and then disaster struck along the narrow tree-lined Bolter End Lane. Our mast snapped in half and our funnels were damaged. Coming from The Peacock back to the village it rained heavily and put the smoke out in the two remaining funnels. We went to The Chilterns, which had been a wartime sugar store and is now Elga's, and Mr Percy Bishop our lorry driver got out of the little back window through which he had climbed into the cab and promptly fainted and fell on the floor from the fumes!'

'Anticipating the end of the war, the local firemen at Wendover constructed an enormous bonfire ready for VE Day. Before the official celebration some boys lit the fire prematurely. The Wendover firemen, who soon found the culprits, ducked them in Whitchell pond. Everyone thought they got their just desserts.'

## SQUATTING AT THE VACHE

'I was born in the gardener's cottage at The Vache in Chalfont St Giles, where my father was head gardener, supervising an under-gardener and the "bothy boys", lads straight from school who lived in a special house. The Vache was then a private house belonging to the Hawkins family but they used to let it to the Maharajah of Patialia while they went to their house in Bexhill. The Maharajah was only allowed to bring one wife with him but he could bring as many daughters as he liked, and I remember seeing all these girls in their brightly-coloured flowing robes walking through the gardens. I also remember seeing my father "potting" rabbits with a shotgun through the bedroom windows of the cottage.

When I was five we moved to Welling in Kent where Father set up his own nursery gardens, but I returned to Chalfont St Peter on the day war broke out, 3rd September 1939, to stay with relations as an evacuee. As we lived quite near the Arsenal at Woolwich, it was thought safer if a member of the family came to Chalfont, so I stayed with my brother's in-laws who lived at Fairview Cottages, which were quite old, on the main road just before the village.

I'd just left school so I got myself a job with Davis's the drycleaners, which was part of Sturleys, the cake shop, in Gerrards Cross. It was one big shop divided in two, Davis's had one half and Sturleys the other. I met lots of well-known actors and actresses who were associated with this area, coming from Denham Studios and Pinewood – Googie Withers and John Mills and so on. A film star, Conrad Veidt, who played spy parts, lived on the Windsor Road, in one of those "modern"-type houses. A lot of them were pulled down because they had flat roofs which caused trouble.

The very first day I was in St Peter I met Doug, who was to become my husband. He was with two other young fellows, I was with a relation, and of course the young men thought, "Oh, there's a new bit of stuff in the village! We haven't seen her before!" So I got to know him and we went out together until he got called up and then whenever he came back on leave.

Meanwhile there were a lot of soldiers at Whann Cross Farm in the area of Narcot Lane and Welders Lane, and they had an ack-ack gun there. The Devons were there, and the Gordon Highlanders, and

219

others whose names I can't remember. During the war a parachute bomb fell in Maltmans Lane. While I was working at the drycleaner's I had to do fire-watching duty. Blankets and camp beds were provided in an upstairs room above Savory and Moore the chemist's, and we could sleep there between duty periods. We used to have to go on the roof and patrol the streets too, though the girls and women weren't supposed to do that. Doug was in the ARP when I first knew him, and in the Home Guard too. There were lots of Yanks round this area and later on, just before D-Day, you couldn't move for lorries in some parts of Chalfont St Giles and St Peter.

St Peter village was very different then. There was a cinema – the building started off as a Memorial Hall for those killed in the First World War. You got in for about sixpence and we called it "the fleapit". That was where the Victoria Wine shop is now. Gerrards Cross cinema was an eye-opener too. I was taken there and I said, "Have we got to sit downstairs? What's it like upstairs?" (I was used to sitting in the balcony at home). I was told, "What do you mean – upstairs? There's no upstairs!"

Where the precinct is now, opposite the church, I used to go with my future mother-in-law who did a lot of shopping at Honeyball's, the grocer's. She would ride down from Gold Hill on her old upright bike and then push it up the hill again with all the shopping. There was Forbes & Pullen's, the chemist's, Howard Roberts the grocer's, and a sort of retreat with cottages and the Misbourne running through. Windsor's shoe shop was there and in Church Lane was the blacksmith, Bert Kingston, and another blacksmith, David Brown, just in Joiners Lane. Ellwood House, which gave its name to the flats built on its site, was a beautiful old house, with lovely trees. It was a really lovely spot. Hill House was privately owned then too, and Chalfont Park was a private hotel. Where the new buildings are now in the Market Place there was the Old Curiosity Cafe and a garage and an ironmonger's called Nash's.

There were very few houses in this area where we live now, just a few odd cottages at the end of Monument Lane and the bigger, old houses there. There was a fish and chip shop in Chalfont St Peter, at the bottom of Grassingham Road, and a hairdresser's, Christabel's. In the Market Place, towards the top end, was a shop which during the war we called the "Bomb Shop". Not that it had a bomb put in it. They sold groceries and seemed to be able to get all sorts of goods – they always had plenty of things to choose from. Apparently they'd been bombed out in London, hence the name of the "Bomb Shop" given by the villagers. Where Barclay's Bank is now, there was a sweet shop, Harriss's (sic). Instead of a farthing in change, you sometimes got a packet of pins from some shops. Food seemed much cheaper then, but it's no good thinking of that when you go shopping now. Mr Willoughby, who later had the shoe shop, worked for Telling's the ironmongers then, and he'd bring you anything you ordered or wanted. The goods were brought to your door so it didn't matter so much when you didn't have a car.

When Doug my husband came out of the Navy – we'd married in 1944 – we "squatted" up at The Vache, so I went back to where I was born, in fact. The Vache was an army camp during the war and the rumour was that it was going to be given to foreign troops, Poles and such, in the area. All the local fellows had come home, there was nowhere to live, so one by one they drifted up and we were two of the original squatters up there. There are people in Chalfont St Peter and St Giles now you wouldn't believe had been at the Vache at that time. A lot of the local girls married the soldiers stationed in this area and likewise a lot of the local fellows married girls from outside the area, so it started what we know so much of now, people marrying out of their villages and towns. When I first came back to St Peter, people knew that I was a stranger and they'd ask, "Who's she?"

Doug knew nothing about our going to the Vache. We'd been living with his parents but we wanted a place of our own, so I went over to Chalfont St Giles and staked my claim. In September 1946 we moved in and lived in an army hut. Doug divided it up as it was one big room at first. Right from the onset we always put money into an account so that if we were ever called upon for damage or anything, we'd have some money behind us. Eventually, of course, the Council did take it over and put water in. At the beginning there was no water and no toilets, only the latrines the Army had used, so they were divided off and the men used one half. I remember them going up in the evening with their buckets and their wellington boots and their brooms and disinfectant to keep the latrines nice and clean. They did a rota system and of course the men and some of the women had been in the Forces so they were quite prepared to do the work. Our two children were born while we were living at the Vache; I used to boil the nappies in an old-fashioned copper. We had an outside tap which Doug boxed in, and in the winter people would come and use our tap as it didn't freeze up. It was hard then. I know the youngsters have it hard now but we had it equally as hard. You'd have nightmares about someone knocking on the door and saying "You're not supposed to be here! Out!"'

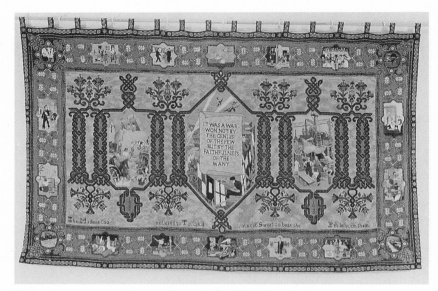

*The tapestry woven by members of the WI after the war, to commemorate the work and sacrifice of women in the services and on the home front. It is now in the possession of the Imperial War Museum.*

## THE COMMEMORATION TAPESTRY

'Women's Institute members, who took part in so many co-operative activities during the war, decided in 1945 to take part in one on an even greater scale than ever before – to embroider a hanging depicting the Work of Women in Wartime.

After much discussion and the overcoming of many difficulties it was agreed that the type of embroidery should be the canvas work stitches at which WI members had always been so good.

Miss Sybil Blunt, a well-known Winchester artist, was asked to design the embroidery in such a way that it could be worked in pieces by members in different parts of the country and joined together later.

The design of the framework and background of the panel was worked out on squared paper by Miss Blunt – the pictures were watercolour sketches and these were redrawn on to squared paper by Miss Foster before she and other members worked them in petit point.

222

In the framework from the top right-hand corner clockwise there are 18 medallions showing the NFS, evacuation, women railway porters, hospital transport by ship and plane, bus conductresses and policewomen, canteen workers, FANYS, nursing sisters, WVS, WRNS, a Women's Institute Fruit Preservation Centre, a housewife, ARP, forestry, rest centres, radar, the making of camouflage nets and postwomen. The three larger panels represent work on the land and in industry and the three Services.

WI members from every county in England and Wales took part in the work, some doing little more than a few stitches and others large portions; but before it could be begun two-day schools were held at Winchester so that all the stitches required could be learnt by one representative from each county who then went back and taught other members in her county. The schools were held in 1946; in 1947 every member who was to take part worked a sampler to ensure that she had command of the stitches. The work on the actual hanging began in March 1948, and was completed in January 1952. Approximately 400 workers took part, all anonymously, and in this Mrs Parnell played an important part, visiting practically every county to see that the work was being done on the right lines.

The work was done in 15 separate pieces and these were finally all joined together at Winchester. One of the most remarkable points is the accuracy with which it was worked. One join of 66 inches in length necessitated 1,200 threads of canvas being threaded through the corresponding holes in a second piece of canvas and this was accomplished without a fault.

The quotation,

> ". . . . . . the madams too,
> Not used to toil, did almost sweat to bear
> The pride upon them, that their very labour
> Was to them as a painting, . . . . . . ."

is from Henry VIII Act 1, Sc1 and was chosen as being both appropriate and amusing. The quotation in the centre panel "it was a war won not by the genius of the few but by the faithfulness of the many", comes from *Memory Hold the Door* by John Buchan.

It has been calculated that there are 2,000,000 stitches in the hanging: there are about 3,000 in each small picture and 145,000 in the centre panel. Thirty-five pounds of mothproof wool have been used; the foundation is single mesh hemp canvas 100" wide. The hanging measures 15'3" × 9' and weighs 47 lbs.

The project was finally completed in 1952 and presented to the country, and the tapestry hung for a while, certainly until the late

1960s, in the Imperial War Museum in London. After about 20 years it was lost sight of by the general public but in 1987 I started to make enquiries of its whereabouts and eventually discovered it in the Museum's store in Duxford. Interest in this celebration of the work carried out by women during the war was revived, and the tapestry was returned to the Imperial War Museum in London and once more put on display.'

# HIGHDAYS & HOLIDAYS

# MAKING OUR OWN ENTERTAINMENT

**In the days before television, and even before radio, we made our own entertainment in towns and villages and in our homes. From singing to sport, there was something for everyone in even the smallest community.**

## FROM CONCERT PARTIES TO CRICKET

'Before the Second World War social evenings were held once a week in the hall at Hyde Heath, costing adults sixpence and children threepence. This included refreshments, which were laid on by members of the Women's Institute. Mrs Flint played the piano. She and her husband later formed the Hyde Heathens Dance Band.

There were games and raffles. Anyone was welcome to get up and do a "turn", and it didn't matter whether you had talent or not. It was more a question of nerve. Mrs Hobbs used to sing *When The Angels Play Their Harps For Me*, Harold Shirley would play a tune on his one-string fiddle, and my mother would sing *Danny Boy* and reduce everybody to tears. Afterwards we played Musical Chairs and Pass the Parcel. Then Connie Flint would play a waltz like *The Blue Danube*, and everybody would get up and dance. That's how I learned to dance. During the war I moved on to the Jitterbug . . .

The Hyde Heathens consisted of Connie on piano, husband Tom on drums, Henry on violin, Maurice on banjo, and last but not least Jack Redding from Chesham on trumpet. Not at all a bad combination.

Dances were held once a month, and everyone seemed able to dance. The women wore long dresses and the men their best suits. Most girls wore home-made dresses reaching not quite to the floor. There were other functions attended by the so-called gentry, who were obliged to wear full evening dress. Not having the required attire, we didn't go to these.

I was about 14 then, and if there was no dance at Hyde Heath a crowd of us would cycle to Ballinger with our long dresses pinned up to the waist to save catching in the bicycle chain. I was dance-mad, and if there were not enough boys to go round, girls would partner one another.

Once a year a travelling theatre came to the village, the actors taking lodgings with the local people. Twice weekly a different play was put on. *Sweeney Todd* was a big draw, as was *East Lynne*. They would ask a local girl or boy to take part, thus guaranteeing a good audience. I remember one girl playing Little Willie in *East Lynne*, who was supposed to be ill. She was plump and robust, but she really did do a good job of dying.

A concert party sponsored by the newly-formed Chesham Co-operative Society came to the hall twice a year. They called themselves the Fol-de-Rols. We children endured two hours of songs, sketches and jokes, just to get free samples at the door, usually sauce or tea. I tried the dodge of going round twice, and was told to ask my mother to join the Co-op. Eventually she did. The Co-op van delivered groceries here on Fridays. All purchases were tied up with string around brown paper parcels. My mother always kept the string and brown paper, which would one day "come in useful", she would say.

An outing to the seaside was usually organised by Mrs Hampton, president and founder of the local branch of the Women's Institute. The open-topped charabanc would draw up outside the Memorial Hall at 4 am, and mums and kids would pile into it for the long trip to the seaside. Destination was usually Bognor Regis. It was Mr Hampton who donated the hall to the village as a memorial to the fallen of the 1914–1918 war, so it is properly called the Memorial Hall.

In 1938 a sports club was formed. My friends and I were in our teens, so it was probably one bright idea aimed at keeping us on the straight and narrow. The yearly fee was half a crown, and sixpence was payable on attendance to subsidise the evening snacks and drinks.

There were dart games (for a small trophy), pocket billiards, card games, shove-ha'penny and table tennis. I was "shooter" of the ladies' netball team, and we played teams from other villages. Alas, wartime brought the end of the sports club.

Whist drives were held fortnightly, alternating with other villages. Little Missenden still run theirs to this day. Many a partner's master card has been trumped in error.

Then there was cricket. The teams played on a pitch that didn't resemble in any way the almost plastic-smooth pitch of today. Matches were played in Howell's field lying beyond the common towards Hawthorn Farm. Never on Sundays – that would have been sacrilege. After completing our Saturday morning chores a gang of us would wander towards the meadow, hearing the sound of leather on wood echoing through the copse. "Cor, that was a sixer!" we would shout, and hurry along to see the play.

The outer field was bordered by a wood on one side and a hedgerow on the other. Beyond the hedgerow lay the cornfield. Wild bee-orchids grew in profusion in the outer field. We would pick them by the dozen, discarding those that drooped before we got home. No one ever imagined that these beautiful wild orchids would become so rare as to be classified as a protected species.

There was a small hut where the cricket score was kept by Margaret Darvell and another young lady. To qualify for this role you had to have been a grammar school pupil. That ruled me out. Anyway, I was too small.

It was at the cricket matches that I learned that "Wal clart olt on, Arfer!" meant "Well caught hold of, Arthur!" And other Bucks expressions and swear words unfamiliar in our household.

Cricket teas were served by the players' wives, with Mrs Howell the farmer's wife presiding. Fresh cream from the farm went into the huge scones, and cucumber sandwiches and cream cakes were the order of the day. I learned the dodge of standing around looking soulful and longingly at the table laden with goodies, and someone would soon hand me a cream cake. That someone was usually Mrs Alfred Howell herself. "Run along now", she would say, and I would sit beneath the horse chestnut tree licking out the cream. Happy days!

After the war, the cricket field was no longer used for the game. Most of the land had been given over to arable farming to feed us in wartime. Cricket was later played for a while in the field which now contains the Chiltern Hundreds Housing Association estate.

Later still, everything to do with cricket seemed to fall apart for years. But somehow it revived, and now we have a thriving cricket club with a fine pitch and a smart pavilion on the common.'

'In the first 25 years of the 20th century, Wolverton, though comparatively small, was quite a lively place.

In those days, with no TV, video etc (not even radio until the mid 1920s) entertainment had to be home-made or at any rate local. There were eventually two cinemas and even a weekly concert party during the summer months, but not even those for the first few years.

There was, however, a flourishing choral society and a town Silver Band. The band competed each year at the band festival at the Crystal Palace and often were winners in their class. They played at many local functions, gave a Sunday evening concert in the park in summer, and on Christmas Eve went round the town playing carols all night long.

Most of the other music and drama was provided by the three chapels and their Sunday schools. There was generally one adult concert or play and a children's concert every year. The Church Sunday school also gave a yearly concert or produced a play. Each chapel Sunday school had an anniversary when we all appeared in our best white dresses and sang to our parents and friends and to the other two Sunday schools. Ours was held in the Works Dining Hall, which held a lot of people, so was quite a big affair.

All the Sunday schools had a "treat". Ours was usually in the grounds of Claydon House. After tea Sir Harry Verney and Lady Rachel joined us on the Terrace. In my mother's day, Florence Nightingale would be there as well. The Co-op also provided a treat for members' children as did the top and bottom clubs. As my family were teetotallers I did not, of course, go to the two club treats, but I had the advantage of magic lantern slides shown by the Band of Hope! The Methodist mothers had a sewing meeting (and gossip) every week, culminating in a two-day sale of work for church funds. They generally had a theme. One year all helpers were in Japanese dress – a most colourful affair. In addition, the Sunday school ran a weekly class leading to the Scripture examination at the end of the year. There was another course of lectures on the evils of strong drink. (At the age of nine or ten I could have told you all about cirrhosis of the liver and fatty degeneration of the heart!) There were prizes for weekly essays.

Sport was well catered for, with two tennis clubs, a bowls club, cricket club and football team. On Whit Monday there was always a big sports meeting on the track in the park, with many well known athletes competing in the running, walking and cycling events.

The only things in short supply in Wolverton were books. The County Library did not open a branch until 1925. Before that there was only the Sunday school library and one run by the Co-op, neither free and both rather limited. Still, better than nothing.'

'There used to be a cinema at Chalfont St Peter, and if you called at the back door and helped stir the ice cream, you could have some. Sweets could be bought at the back door at any time. Cinema seats cost a penny, Saturday afternoons a ha'penny. Wellingtons were worn for crossing the fields, then left in the hedge and shoes put on for the visit to the cinema. The building later became a roller skating rink and today is a brush factory. A second, smaller cinema was built in the 1920s in the heart of the village, as a memorial hall to the First World War. As well as films, dances were held there, and Gilbert and Sullivan operas too. It was demolished in the 1950s and shops built, continuing the long line built in 1923.

A swimming pool was built in a gravel pit and filled from the river Misbourne, but the springs soon pushed the thin concrete off the bottom! Radios were few and far between in the 1930s but my father made one and when we opened the window on Boat Race Day a huge crowd gathered in the High Street.'

'Lantern slide shows were held at the Salvation Army Citadel in High Wycombe in the years after the First World War. This consisted of a big white sheet pegged up at one end of the hall. At the opposite end a huge lantern was erected and slides were inserted, and the scene on the slide was projected onto the sheet. All this cost us a penny for the show. The evening ended when we got home, and were searched for the inevitable flea that had come home with us.

Cinemas progressed from silent films, with the pianist thumping away at the base of the screen, to talkies with recorded music. Children were allowed in for threepence and a Mr Green in control at one cinema ejected them by the scruff of the neck when they misbehaved!'

'On Saturday afternoon the treat for children at Farnham Common in the 1920s would be to go and buy a bag of stale cakes from the baker, which cost us a penny of our pocket money, and sit and eat them in the local cinema, The Beacon. There would be a pianist who would play appropriate music to fit the film, fast and furious for cowboys, dramatic for detectives and romantic for the love scenes.'

## A GIFT TO THE VILLAGE

'The second Sir Thomas Chaloner, tutor to Charles I's brother Prince Henry, gave Steeple Claydon its most interesting secular building, which is still a centre of social life today. He built a school, which flourished and decayed, and was restored to use by Sir Harry Verney of Claydon House in the 19th century. At one time my grandmother was headmistress there before her marriage. Later Sir Edmund Verney added a concert hall and was the first to adopt the Free Libraries Act and opened the Chaloner Library, believed to be the first village public library in the country. The building became known as "The Library Hall". Florence Nightingale, who often stayed at Claydon House, donated £50 towards the cost of books – her cheque is framed and mounted on an interior wall of the building. The hall has on its gable a shield with the motto, "Liberty is the best of all things".

There were many books on shelves from floor to ceiling during the 1920s and 1930s. The reading room was open daily and as a girl I can remember using it on cold or wet days, reading some of the books or the newspapers which were delivered each day. Another room in this building was something of a mystery to we girls, because only men were allowed to use it. Open every day, the young men of the village gathered there to play billiards and darts.

The concert hall was also much in use, for all sorts of functions. I spent many happy hours there. When very young there were children's parties and the occasional travelling film show. The church Arts Club held their meetings there, where we were taught drawing, painting, needlework and folk dancing. We learned such dances as Gathering Peascods, Rufty Tufty, Black Nag and Durham Reel to name just a few. We would then give displays during the summer at local fetes. These were danced to the accompaniment of gramophone records. Then there were the concerts themselves, enjoyed by all, both on and off stage. The acoustics were excellent, and so was the block parquet floor, always highly polished for the weekly dances which I attended in my teens. These were eagerly looked forward to and many a romance started and flourished during the waltz, quickstep or slow foxtrot. When the Second World War started we saw a sprinkling of khaki and blue uniforms amongst the dancers and this created an added interest for the local girls.

After the war most of us returned from service life and married, and raised our families. The hall then became the venue for the baby clinic. In 1951 I joined the WI, so I continued to use the hall for WI meetings and their various activities.

In the early 1960s the Verney family gave the building to the village, and then sadly the reading room was closed as a library, the books were transferred to Aylesbury and the billiard room was made available for the Aylesbury County Lending Library. It was from that time that the building became known as the village hall, no longer the Library Hall.'

'The Guild Room, opposite the manor house at The Lee, was lent to the village by Mr (later Sir) Arthur Liberty, as there was no village hall. The Guild Room was a great boon, and every kind of activity flourished there. There was an excellent library (probably stocked by the Liberty family) with very good books, which could be borrowed for nothing. There were also sixpenny hops, and ballet classes – in spite of the atrocious surface of the floor. Musical evenings were popular, arranged by Dr Stainer, a musician who lived at Sly Corner, Lee Common with his family, who between them provided songs and violin, cello and piano items. The Youth Club was opened on 30th April 1949 and WI meetings and village events are held there now – the Guild Room is now a private house.'

## SUMMER AND WINTER DIPS

'Lord Desborough was the patron of the Polytechnic Ladies Swimming Club in the 1930s and he offered a standing annual invitation to the members, which included myself, to a Half Mile River Swim in that part of the Thames which flowed near his beautiful estate at Taplow Court. He made a striking figure when in blazer, flannels and straw hat he greeted our bus, and we saw him striding across the lovely lawns which formed the estate.

When I was told he was a notable swimmer and sportsman in his youth and had swum the river Niagara twice, I could quite believe it.

It was an unforgettable day, warm and sunny, and his hospitality and the tea we afterwards enjoyed have stayed in my memory all my life.'

'At Chesham's open air swimming pool the water was changed on Sunday and Wednesday. Children who helped to clean the pool earned a free swim – when the pool was refilled with icy cold spring water! I recall swimming in 49 degrees Fahrenheit and being blue with cold and my teeth chattering afterwards – but it was fun.'

## MUSIC AND THE OVALTINIES

'Like many homes in the 1930s, we had a radio and also a piano. My father had a double bass, a piano accordion and also a harmonium! He was a great lover of music but couldn't read a note or play any of the instruments he owned. My brother and I both had piano lessons in the village, Wheeler End, but we were very bad at practising and so didn't make the headway we should. Eventually my father got tired of paying for lessons for two very uninterested children.

I can't remember listening to the radio very much, except of course at the start of the war, when all news bulletins were avidly followed. We also enjoyed the comedy programme *Itma* very much.

Oh yes! We did like the Ovaltinies programme – I think on Radio Luxemburg. I joined the Ovaltinies Club and had a brown badge. I probably had a certificate as well, and a list of rules which all Ovaltinies should obey. I think I tried very hard at first but after the novelty had worn off, I'm pretty sure I didn't bother much. You had to promise to be kind and helpful at all times, do all sorts of good deeds and certainly drink plenty of Ovaltine.'

# MEMORABLE OCCASIONS

Wandering through West Wycombe caves with a candle, taking the
old folks on an outing in 1949, or being 'weighed in' as Mayor
– a handful of memorable high days. Royal occasions were, of
course, joyfully celebrated all over the county, whether jubilees
or coronations.

## VISITING THE CAVES

'The West Wycombe caves were in their natural state when I visited
them as a child. They were cold and damp and as the ground was a
wet chalky mess it was difficult for us to stay on our feet.

The "uniform" for such visits was wellington boots and a fleecy
lined mac. We paid a halfpenny for a lighted candle on entering,
which was a waste of money because it was invariably blown out
by the boys.

Once I was allowed into the Golden Ball on the church at the top
of the hill. After climbing many steps it was like sitting on top of the
world.'

## THE MAYOR MAKING CEREMONY

'The first lady mayor of High Wycombe was Grace I Reading during
1956/7. Some time before, Dame Frances Dove, the founder of
Wycombe Abbey School and a Charter Trustee in Wycombe, stood
for mayor but was narrowly defeated. It was said that the vote went
against her because she would not admit the townspeople's girls to
her school. However, she bore the town no grudge and indeed was a
great benefactor, donating a silver gavel to the town and the "Dove"
window in the church.

When Councillor Elizabeth Barratt became mayor in the 1980s,
the ceremony she took part in, and which she describes, had not
changed since the early days.
"As the civic procession slowly proceeded along the High Street to
the ancient Guildhall I was feeling both excited and apprehensive yet
humble at the thought of the honour to be bestowed upon me. The
Mace-Bearer proudly bearing the 300 year old golden mace led the
procession closely followed by the current mayor resplendent in a

red cloak edged with ermine. Attending the Mayor were the Beadle, the Town Crier, representatives of the armed forces and the black robed Charter Trustees which included myself.

As we reached the Guildhall we could see the beautiful old scale, a comfortable looking chair suspended from a fine brass tripod, which was to be our weighing machine after the Annual General Meeting. My apprehension increased by the second. Nevertheless, there was the meeting to be held first with speeches and the changeover from the old mayor to the new. I had already planned that my speech would contain references to our ancient traditions and the installation of High Wycombe's first mayor in 1285. I was also aware of the goodwill surrounding me, the support of the Charter Trustees and the encouraging shouts from people who were already beginning to arrive to watch the Weighing-In Ceremony.

The ensuing 45 minutes went all too quickly and descending the wooden stairs I was the one now wearing the lady's tricorn black hat, the white Buckinghamshire lace jabot, the glorious red robe edged with ermine and the magnificent golden chain of office with many previous mayors' names inscribed. I felt warm, comfortable and very happy. Fortunately, the new mayor is weighed first so the agonizing wait for my name to be called was not too long. Assisted by the Mace-Bearer, Beadle and Town Crier I was escorted to the scales and duly sat down. Then I became aware of eager young faces and necks strained where children were cramming to catch a glimpse of what was happening. There were schoolchildren, Cubs, Brownies and their leaders all smiling and waving. It was a tremendous thrill for anyone. Through my mind went the thought that this ceremony had actually taken place in the Middle Ages and had been revived again in the 19th century and that I was one of so many who had sat there and lived this wonderful moment.

All too soon the moment passed. Now for the declaration of my weight. Dare I say I cannot remember but I do know that the robes weighed heavy and as I said to my colleagues, "That is my excuse". If one gains weight the Town Crier shouts, "And some more"; if one loses weight or stays the same he shouts, "No more". Though embarrassed, I was rather pleased that he did shout "And some more" because the children just booed until the echo could be heard in the surrounding hills and then everyone laughed and cheered. What a happy glorious moment. My daughter, my Mayoress, followed and my husband, my escort, the other Charter Trustees and many dignitaries were weighed that day; not forgetting the outgoing Mayor who also had put on weight much to the crowd's delight." '

# THE OLD FOLKS' OUTING

'The 15th annual outing of the Wycombe Marsh Old People's Committee was held on Wednesday 10th August 1949 as this extract from the Minute Book recounts.

"To start with it was a lovely fine day and it was a very pleasing and encouraging sight to see the old people collecting together in King's Square. The journey to Oxford was very enjoyable and it was a grand sight to see field after field of lovely golden corn, some of which was cut and some already carried.

On arrival at Oxford we turned right and made a tour of St Giles which the old people enjoyed very much. After turning back and crossing over the Thames we had a pleasant journey to Abingdon which was reached at 3.50. Tea was arranged for four o'clock but the chairman and secretary experienced trouble over this. Owing to another party of 100 being booked also at four o'clock, the caterers wanted us to alter our time to 5.30. This we refused to do as it would interfere with our other arrangements. Owing to this we were a scattered party sitting down to tea, being divided into three parties. Apart from this a lovely tea was provided and it was a very pleasant change to see the waitresses going round persuading the old people to have a bit more, not that some wanted any persuading.

There were 160 old people, 15 visitors and helpers and six drivers making a total of 181 sitting down to tea. About five o'clock we were in the coaches again, on our way to the Grove Fruit Farms where we were welcomed by Mr and Mrs Jim Aldridge and their daughter Jean.

Here we split up, the main party of ladies going with Miss Aldridge to see the house with its lawns and gardens, also six houses which had been built at great cost for some of the employees. They enjoyed this very much and no doubt more than one old lady made up her mind that she would see that her old man had the garden at home looking better in the future than it had done in the past. The men went with our chairman and his brother Jim in the coaches on a tour of the orchards and many saw fruit farming as they had never seen it before, absolutely par excellence.

The time came when we had to climb in the coaches for the homeward journey and say goodbye to Mr and Mrs and Jean Aldridge, but before we went all the old people had a big bag of choice fruit, a gift from our chairman. One coach party insisted on him and brother Jim getting into their coach while they gave them a big cheer and said 'Thank you', which they meant.

On the way home we were taken off our route to see the Atom

Station at Harwell where they are planning the wonders of Science for the next generation and which is famous the world over.

The journey home via Didcot, Wallingford, Henley and Bourne End was enjoyed by all in the quiet of the fading day and we reached King's Square soon after half past eight.

As the old people were met by their children they were full of what they had had and what they had seen and said it was the best outing they had ever known. Those who had worked so hard to look after them during the day felt amply repaid and as they looked on the happy faces of the old people and realised that for some it would be their last outing with us, they forgot how tired they were and gave thanks for the health and strength and privilege to give one day of their lives for the old people."

A Saunders   Hon Secretary'

## ROYAL CELEBRATIONS

'At the Silver Jubilee of George V, I was among the local school-children who celebrated in the Market Square at Princes Risborough with dancing and a maypole. There was a procession in which I and many relatives and friends took part. We all dressed in Victorian clothes and rode in my uncle's cart, which we decorated with red, white and blue ribbons and paper. There were twelve of us packed in, so it was a good thing for the horse that there were no hills to negotiate.'

'The Jubilee was a wonderful day for everyone. There was every entertainment imaginable on the common at Hyde Heath – teas, races, fancy dress and all the fun of the fair, with every pram, bicycle, wheelbarrow and horse and cart decorated. There was maypole dancing, and the winner of "Riding the Greasy Pole" was given a new five shilling piece.

In 1937 Hyde Heath Memorial Hall committee had a jolly good pow-wow to sort out how to celebrate the new king's coronation. Plans were made for a fancy dress parade, and prizes were to be awarded for the best fancy dress, the best dressed vehicle including bicycles, and the best decorated house. The procession was to start at the top of Keepers Lane and end at the post office, and Robert Redding would lead it on foot.

It seemed the whole village turned out. There were prams, bicycles and carts as well as people. My mother had been widowed almost a year, but she was told off severely by two very religious ladies for dressing up so soon after my father's death. "He's not even cold in his grave," they said.

*Towns and villages throughout the county celebrated George V's Jubilee in 1935 with enthusiasm. At Wendover a procession of decorated carts and floats was a highlight of the day.*

There were two Britannias. I was one of them, and was mounted on a horse drawn cart with other children, each representing one of the Dominions of which Great Britain was the Mother Country. Myself as Britannia was my mother's brainchild, and she borrowed a fireman's brass helmet for me to wear. I felt so embarrassed that I wasn't really a happy exhibit at all.

One rather large lady dressed up and intended to ride a donkey the whole way. But such was her weight that the poor beast could hardly move, so she had to get off and walk the best part of the way.

Everybody was happy. Children were presented with Coronation mugs. If you were lucky you got a china mug, if unlucky an aluminium one which when filled with hot tea burned your hands and left a black ring around your mouth. Somebody's bright idea, no doubt. It seemed that prizes were won by all. My mother got a first for Best Decorated Bungalow, the Dominions Cart, and one for fancy dress.'

'On a glorious early summer day in May 1935 Chesham celebrated the Jubilee. There was a procession through the park, with all the little girls in their prettiest frocks, and flowers in their hair. The old

237

fire engine was in the show, pulled along by the firemen. Later on in the day we walked through fields thick with buttercups and daisies – a magical day out for a London child.

Two years later, at the Coronation of George VI, there was a procession from Chesham up to a field which is now Penn Avenue, with everyone carrying torches to light the bonfire on top of the hill. Others were lit in a chain right across the country.'

'There were great celebrations in Wheeler End on Coronation Day 1937. Many houses and cottages were decorated with red, white and blue bunting and flags.

The main event was a fancy dress parade. My little sister of two was dressed in a Union Jack dress and matching bonnet, "Little Miss England". I won first prize wearing a green dress with red poppies dotted over it and a red poppy in my hair, all made with crepe paper. A wide sash worn crossways from shoulder to waist had the words, "Lest We Forget".'

'The first television set in Wingrave was hired for the Church Room by the village Coronation Committee in 1953. Mrs Allen was delegated to cut the sandwiches as she could cut the loaves of bread straight!'

# THE VILLAGE YEAR

**Every year certain events could be counted on to brighten our lives and provide welcome relaxation from day to day worries and work. Some celebrations still have a place in our lives, but others, such as Empire Day, once celebrated on 24th May by every schoolchild in the country, have passed into history.**

### SHROVE TUESDAY CONCERT AND CLUB FEAST DAY

'The two biggest events in village life at Grendon Underwood were the Shrove Tuesday Concert and the Greyhound Club Feast Day, the latter on 29th May, Oak Apple Day. The concert was meant to be a last fling before the serious season of Lent and was organised by the rector and the schoolmaster. All such things were held in the village hall, which was a large corrugated hut left over from the First World War, heated by two tortoise stoves – you roasted in close proximity to them and froze in the draughty bits between. The stage was of loose planks on trestles, covered with a heavy carpet, none too safe for galloping about. Another girl and I once sang a plaintive duet, "Won't you buy my pretty flowers?". We were meant to be poor little flower girls, with bare feet and ragged dresses, and we carried baskets containing bunches of snowdrops which we later sold to the audience. Mr and Mrs Phipps from the nearby village of Ludgershall usually "entertained" with husband and wife sketches. He always seemed to wear a silk scarf tucked into his open-necked shirt, and their main props were a rickety bamboo table with a pot plant or teapot, according to the action. The village band did their best to raise the roof and the audience applauded everything with much clapping, whistling and stamping of feet. After the war and marriage, I was roped in once more to "do a turn", and took part in a playlet with the burgeoning bump of my first pregnancy carefully hidden under a frilly pinafore. We kept quiet about such things until they were obvious in those days!

The origins of the Greyhound Club Feast Day, or Club Feast as we always called it, went back to 6th October 1788, when a group of bellringers formed their own Friendly Society to provide insurance cover for sick members, based at The Greyhound inn at the west end of the village. Proper Articles and Rules were drawn up, which still hold good to this day. Members paid two shillings per quarter, "one shilling and ninepence to the box and threepence to be spent", which must have been quite difficult to afford in those days. At times of sickness members could benefit from six shillings a week – but not if you were suffering from venereal disease. "Employees only" seemed to be the rule, so farmers and their sons never joined. In spite of hiccoughs during the two world wars, "The Club" is still thriving, though hardly anyone takes advantage of the benefits these days – worth 30p.

The Feast Day started early, as it still does, with members peeling great quantities of potatoes and lady helpers preparing the rest of the food. This was the only time women had anything to do with the Club – well, it would be, wouldn't it? The village hall was a hive of activity. At 10.30 am all members marched from The Greyhound to church behind the band, with banners flying and staves clutched in the officials' hands. After a rousing service, probably the only time in the year when the church was full, members and the band returned to the feast in the village hall. Beer flowed freely all day, and the horn mugs and big blue and white jug held together with metal bands are still in use today. After appetites were satisfied, came a certain amount of speechmaking, and officials for the following year were voted in. After dispersing and drawing much needed breath, the band toured the village, playing and collecting for band funds.

In The Greyhound yard and spilling onto the triangle of green outside, was the fair, which was really all we children were interested in. One year the much loved Galloping Horses roundabout was superseded by a Noah's Ark, but after the war the horses reappeared. Swingboats gave the half-grown boys a chance to show off, and there were the usual roll-a-balls, darts and coconut shies. Mr Tack brought his sweet stall, making some of his wares on the spot, and we always bought his big humbugs which had to be broken into little pieces before you could begin to eat them. But what we loved most of all were the infamous squibs – a toothpaste-type tube filled with water from The Greyhound, costing a penny a tube. We ran around squirting each other, preferably down the neck if anyone was silly enough to let you, and running away. But woe betide you if you squirted a grown up by mistake – retribution was swift. These did not reappear after the war, and just as well.'

'For many years, Miss Muffet, Bo-Peep, Boy Blue, mounted redskins and cowboys and many other characters would be seen processing down the main street of Chalfont St Peter, usually led by a brass band, and followed by beautifully decorated floats. Bringing up the rear was a huge "Bucks Swan" on a well camouflaged lorry, and Miss Chalfont and her ladies in waiting would smile and wave to the crowds that had turned out to applaud. This was always on the Saturday nearest 29th June, St Peter's Day, and was known as Feast Day. Hours had been spent the previous day covering the framework for the swan with cotton wool, and WI members also sold raffle tickets and made the crown for Miss Chalfont. This annual event was postponed during the Second World War, and HRH Princess Marina came as the official opener when it got off the ground once more. Unfortunately, from a happy day out for the locals, it gradually turned into a money making day for spivs who came out from London, crowds came from far and near, and there were even bouts of rowdyism ending in court cases. Sadly, Feast Day was abandoned and is now just a memory.'

OLNEY PANCAKE RACE

'Each year on Shrove Tuesday, come hail, wind or snow, the world famous Pancake Race is run in the small and historical town of Olney. The race originated in 1445 when a maiden cooking pancakes, which were popular even in those days, and using up her fat before fasting during Lent, heard the church bell calling people to the Shriving Service (a service held for confession of sins before Lent) and ran to the church still holding her frying pan. It was revived over the centuries from time to time and there are photographs taken in 1921 and 1926. It was again revived in 1948 by the Rev Ronald Collins, then vicar of Olney, when the BBC Radio Service were researching for a programme on ancient customs on Shrove Tuesday and came across papers relating to Olney Pancake Race. More papers were found by the vicar in the old vicarage and so the race was revived and run in that year, 1948 by 14 women from the congregation of the parish church, St Peter and St Paul.

The race runs from the Market Place when the church bell rings out at 11.55 am and finishes at the side entrance of the churchyard. Each girl entering must be 18 years or over, have lived in Olney at least three months, must wear a headscarf and apron and of course hold a frying pan with a pancake. The pancake is tossed at the beginning of the race and the end and the winner must have a pancake or part of one in her pan at the finish. The runners are expected to attend the Shriving Service after the race at which many of the Olney hymns are sung. The traditional prize for the race is a kiss from the verger and a prayer or hymn book, but the runners nowadays receive many more beautiful presents donated by local shops and firms in the area. The course is 415 yards long and the record time in which it has been run is 59 seconds. The whole morning and early afternoon is great fun with lots of activity going on in the town and pancakes, approximately 700 of them, sold in the church hall.

In 1950 the town of Liberal, Kansas, USA challenged us and have run against us ever since. The present score is 20 wins by both sides making us equal. They have sent representatives most years and on two occasions two of our committee have visited Liberal.'

## MAY DAY AND EMPIRE DAY

'It was during the 1930s that the headmistress of Padbury village school revived our May Day celebrations. For weeks before May Day we schoolchildren had been asking the village people for flowers to decorate our May garland. No one ever refused.

The frame of the garland was constructed of thin willow wands bent to form a bower with two handles for carrying. This was made by the older boys. It was the girls' task to collect the flowers. Cottage gardens were depleted of their choicest blooms; a few late daffodils, scented gillyflowers, forget me nots, polyanthus and, the most coveted of all, beautiful vivid orange Crown Imperials. One special

*Padbury girls carrying their decorated wands for the May Day celebrations in the 1930s. May Day was once far more important in our annual calendar of events and children spent weeks planning for it.*

lady, Miss Finch, gave us these, and once as a Maid of Honour, I carried a Crown Imperial for my own wand and wore a crown of polyanthus flowers.

All the girls carried their own decorated wands but the centrepiece of the procession was the bower of flowers carrying a large doll. The day before May morning we assembled in Mrs Clarke's kitchen at Bennet's Farm and bunched and tied the flowers onto the wooden frame. When completed it was sprinkled with water to keep it fresh. For weeks we had been practising our May Day songs. *Wake, Wake, Wake, For It Is Sweet May Morning* and *Come Lassies and Lads* were everyone's favourites.

Whether or not May morning was fine, the girls all wore their prettiest dresses. Leading the procession would be the garland carried by the two older boys. Then came the May Queen escorted by four Maids of Honour and accompanied by her consort wearing his crown of gold. Then we marched up the village street singing our May Day songs. All the villagers came to their doors to watch and put a copper or two in our collecting box.

Our first call would be to Mrs Raikes at the Hermitage, who after listening to our songs would give us some coins. We would then walk up to Padbury Lodge, then occupied by Mrs Gorelangton. We formed a circle on the lawn singing of May Day and gazed expectantly on the upstairs bow-fronted window. The maid would then throw down a half crown on behalf of her mistress.

Our next calls would be to the Vicarage and Dunsty Lodge along the Thornborough road. We would then go home to our mid-day meal. After our break we walked to the outlying farms, Mr Roper at Lenborough and Mr Crooke at Padbury Mill. By then we were rather tired but thoughts of lemonade and chocolate biscuits awaiting us at Mrs Stagg's grocery shop would spur us on.'

'We had no village maypole at Edlesborough but on May Day we would decorate our dolls prams with flowers and go "Maying", which involved showing off our prams at neighbours' houses and gathering a few pennies. We also made what we called garlands. This involved fastening a carefully arranged head of flowers on a broom stick adorned with ribbons. The flowers were arranged in concentric circles – I remember using forget me nots and the white flowers of large garden stitchwort. These garlands were carried with the prams.

There were other flower gatherings, and we also, in the appropriate season, went violeting, primrosing and leasing. The violets were gathered for Mothering Sunday, tied into bunches and presented to our mothers at a special Sunday school service.

"Leasing" had me wondering when my friend suggested I should accompany her on this activity. It proved to be gleaning. We visited the harvested fields and collected the odd heads of corn which remained on the ground. This was winter food for my friend's hens.'

'Red letter days at Lower Winchenden included May Day when the schoolchildren toured the village singing songs with their garlands, finishing at the Priory where we each received a bun, an orange and twopence.

On Empire Day Cuddington and Chearsley schoolchildren joined us at the Priory for a sports afternoon and tea, ending with the singing of *Land of Hope and Glory*, *God Bless the Prince of Wales*, and "The King".'

'The May Days which I remember were approximately between 1955 and 1960, when my brother, sister and I attended Longwick primary school. I cannot remember the number of pupils at that time, but at a rough guess it would have been about 30 and as far as I remember every one of us carried a garland on May Day. My family lived about two miles outside Longwick on an isolated farm.

May Day was definitely something to look forward to and every day we eagerly watched the Crown Imperials. Would they bloom in time? Might they bloom too early and be faded? Sometimes we would get up in the mornings and they would be drooping with frost, but miraculously they always seemed to be just right for May Day.

The Crown Imperial was so important because it was the only essential flower for the garlands. Our friends in Longwick supplied the polyanthus and wallflowers and anything else that was in bloom, we supplied Crown Imperials and cowslips. Together we made two crowns for the four girls (two children to a crown) and a sceptre for my brother.

I think that one of my parents must have made the frames for the garlands; I have no memory of doing so and yet when I was asked to make a frame a few years ago I found that I knew exactly how to do it. I do remember how much we enjoyed scavenging in the hedges and ditches for moss to cover the frame (when damp it kept the flowers fresh) and also bunching the flowers to attach to it. The Crown Imperial was first placed at the top of the crown or sceptre. There was a story attached to this. At the crucifixion of Jesus every flower bowed its head and wept, but the Crown Imperial was too proud; afterwards it realised what it had done and ever since it has bowed its head and wept, and you can see the tears or pearls inside the petals (Crown Imperial or "Crown of Pearls" as we called it).

The bunches of flowers were carefully attached to the frame, which had been already covered in damp moss. A doll was needed for the centre, and she had to be dressed in white or white with a blue cloak. Over the garland was a veil, in our case a net curtain, then it had to be kept in a cool damp place – the farm dairy was perfect, until May Day.

May Day morning we rose early. I remember one year when a neighbour who worked in London had particularly asked us to call with the garlands. We walked across the fields to his house at six in the morning, the grass still crisp with frost. It was quite a long walk to Longwick, we didn't have a car (we usually cycled to school) and the other children had usually been round most of the houses before we got there, so we concentrated on the outlying houses and on at least one occasion Ilmer. I regret to say that we loved to arrive before people were up and to take them by surprise. We would go up to the door and knock, then uncover the garland and sing to them "Good morning Ladies and Gentlemen, we wish you a happy day. We've come to show you our garlands because it is May Day. We only come here but once a year so please remember our garlands." My father did tell me that when he was a boy there was another verse, but I cannot remember it. Sometimes we were given money, but I don't think we ever collected much. I certainly don't remember being able to buy anything afterwards, so perhaps we were made to give it to a charity, I don't know.

One of the best things about May Day was being allowed to be late for school. This was unheard of for the rest of the year, but the school seemed to really encourage us. In fact without the enthusiasm of the two teachers (Miss Wootton and Mr Wood) I am sure that there would not have been anywhere near as many garlands.

Once we were at school the garlands were put in the church part of the school to keep cool, and we carried on with our lessons until the afternoon. The school finished early and we paraded to the village hall where the WI had organised refreshments and judging. We all marched round the hall singing, and the smell of the flowers was delicious. Once the judge was the author Alison Uttley and she later incorporated May Day in a book.

It was a wonderful day, as much fun as Christmas, but in a different way. May Day was a celebration of Spring.'

## THE FLOWER AND PRODUCE SHOW
## AND THE SUMMER FAIR

'The Hyde Heath Produce Show usually took place in June or July, when a huge marquee would be erected on the common to house the exhibits. I use the word "common" instead of "heath", because that is what my generation called it.

Entrants competed for the Hampton Trophy and the Brodie Rowe Cup, the latter being given by a stockbroker who then lived at Hyde House. In later years Dr Sybil Welsh of the Wick also contributed a cup. Dr Welsh was my mother's employer, so it was considered infra dig for my mother to enter the competitions. But enter she did, and won several prizes over the years until an almighty row blew up over this. She was an excellent cook, but unfortunately her culinary talent did not rub off on this particular offspring.

Rivalry abounded among the fruit and vegetable entrants. The main section was for the cottage gardeners. Weeks beforehand, neighbours were spying on each other to wheedle out the secrets of what vegetables were being grown and what they were treated with. Old Mr Turney got away with loads of prizes. He lived in a cottage in Brays Lane, one of a row of four where the only sanitation was bucket lavatories. We can only guess at his cultivation secrets.

On the big day, competitors bustled and pushed to get their vegetables into the best display position to catch the judges' eyes. Embroidery was my mother's speciality and over the years she won many prizes. I was made to enter the children's wild flower display contest. Once I just shoved them into a jar, and blow me if I didn't win a prize.

Outside, the travelling show people erected a roundabout, all brass and painted horses such as you find at the steam fairs today. There were swinging boats and coconut shies too, and penny water squirts to annoy the adults. These people were eventually barred from the common, as their attractions were too popular and took money from the villagers that otherwise would have been spent on the side shows organised by the village hall committee.

There was also bowling for a pig, a real live one at that. Other attractions were hitting the flitch, pillow fights on the greasy pole, knobbly knee contests, and races for adults and children.

The real highlight was the Gurning, where one tried to pull the ugliest face through a horse collar. No one ever beat Jack Fountain at this. Out would come his false teeth and he would swallow his nose with his bottom lip. Real 'orrible, he looked.

Somehow, the Produce Show eventually petered out, and is now no more.'

'Seer Green Flower Show in the 1930s always took place in August – we could never go on holiday until September in order not to miss the show. It was always held in Mr Boddy's cherry orchard. The week before the show you would see the men going along with their scythes and what were then called bagging hooks to get rid of the rough grass and nettles, and they would have buckets of whitewash ready for marking out the races.

On the Saturday morning of the show at about nine o'clock along would come the WI ladies. Mrs Watson organised the helpers and they would arrive with a clothes basket full of bread, cakes and fillings for the sandwiches, large carving knives and china. There was a large copper and a fire was lit underneath to heat the water.

There were three tents, one for vegetables, one for refreshments and the other for flowers one side, ladies exhibits (cakes, pastries, bread, jams, pickles etc) the other. There would also be what we now call handicrafts, such as knitting, needlework, rugmaking and so on.

At two o'clock there was a grand opening by Admiral James – he was the original "Bubbles" in the Pears Soap advertisement. Then there was a dash to see who had won prizes. You could hear the discussions – "Mine looks as good as the first prize winner!"

After a long look around the tents it was teatime, so off to the refreshment tent. Then came the races; youngest first – running, sack race, three legged, followed by the ladies' egg and spoon. The men's races came last. Finally there was a "marathon", round Mr Boddy's orchard, starting at the stile by The Horseshoe right across to Long Grove, then to Boddy's farmhouse which was opposite the chapel. I remember Mr Inskip always determined to finish, when he must have been between 60 and 70.

After the grand prizegiving by Mrs James, who was always very fashionably dressed, the day ended with the rush to the tents to retrieve the exhibits.'

'For many years after the Great War Padbury had its own Flower Show, held during August in a field around Old End.

A marquee was erected to hold the exhibits. As most villagers cultivated vegetables both in their gardens and on their allotments, there was keen rivalry over the largest onions or the heaviest marrows.

There was also a section for the children for the most varied collection of wild flowers. It was a ritual that on the Sunday before the show, parents and children collected as many different kinds of wild flowers and grasses from the fields and the railway embankment as they could find, to enter in the show.

During the day of the show, sports were organised for adults and children, ending with the traditional tug-of-war.'

'After the Second World War the old custom of having a fair on the green at Wingrave was revived, to take place on Feast Sunday at the end of July, the patronal festival of the village church of St Peter and St Paul. This was also the Sunday on which other customs took place, when grass was laid in the church nave and parishioners tried to surround the church with pennies.

Smith's Fair and Rose's Fair alternated, having obtained permission to use the green from the parish council for a cost of £2. The vehicles were not allowed to assemble on the green till after 8 pm on the Sunday evening, but the neighbouring roads were full of caravans and lorries much earlier in the day.

The fair was a highly organised assembly, soon setting up suspended lights and starting the steam engines. The greatest area was taken by the dodgem cars. Owing to the unevenness of the green the platform had to be levelled with wooden blocks which were carried by the children – even toddlers could carry a block. Old and young, boy and girl each had a job to be done in sequence. Stalls for rifle shooting, darts, hoopla, coconut shies, fish and chips and candy floss were set up, and the swingboat stands erected overnight.

Next day they were furnished with the necessary apparatus and the glittering prizes were displayed. The fair opened at 6 pm for two evenings, on Monday and Tuesday, when the young people from the neighbouring villages found their way to Wingrave, guided by the sounds of the fairground music from the steam engine organ.

Wednesday was dismantling day when each one once more had his job. By teatime many had drifted away and by midday Thursday the last ones had gone, leaving neither damage nor refuse.

The fair people were Londoners and when old Mrs Rose died her sons took over and went to Hampstead Heath for the whole season. This was in the early 1960s. They wintered between Cublington and Whitchurch. An application was made to the parish council to change the date of the fair to August Bank Holiday Monday but was refused as the council felt there were too many events on about that time. The fair could return, but only on the original feast day. Then between 1963 and 1967 the green was levelled and in 1966, when Mr Bunce was at the Rose and Crown, posts were put out. And that was the end of the fair at Wingrave.'

'There were a few highlights during our year at Great Horwood after the war, which the whole village joined in. The Whaddon Chase used to meet on our village green in the spring and we all turned out to see the horses and the hounds. The rights or wrongs of hunting didn't come into the picture, it was just a form of entertainment to us children. Then there was the church fete, which was held in the rectory grounds. The Great Horwood Silver Band would play all afternoon and there would be teas on the front lawn and games and stalls on the side lawn, including bowling for a live pig which our family was lucky enough to win one year. There was also a Field Day which was organised by our school headmistress, Mrs Griffin. We had a Field Day Queen and her attendants and every child in the school was dressed in fancy dress – whether they wanted to or not. We all met up on the green with the queen and her attendants in a horse and cart and we would be paraded round the village led by the band. This day used to raise funds to take the village schoolchildren out for a trip to the seaside or a local amusement park.

Then would come Great Horwood Feast, when the fair would come to the village. For weeks beforehand we would be saving our money to spend in two glorious nights of entertainment. It was the tradition that the fair wasn't allowed on the green before 7 pm, after the evening service had finished, so all afternoon the fair lorries would be queuing up along the Little Horwood road ready for the big moment when the Great Horwood Silver Band would play them onto the green. Then the band would play for the rest of the evening whilst the fair people began to erect the stands.

It really was a great day in the life of the village, and all the villagers would stand down the Little Horwood road and around the green. It was also a good night for the two pubs in the village, as it was thirsty work watching the fair people build the dodgems. Every year the fair would bring dodgems, swingboats, hoopla, a coconut shy, candy floss, sweets, penny slot machines, rolling the ball stalls, darts, and a wonderful stall where you could win really good prizes – a half teaset, dolls' prams or pushchairs, baskets and a whole host of other goodies if you just had that lucky name that flashed up.

I don't know how they managed to fit so much onto our small green. Then on the Wednesday they had to leave by midday, and how empty the green looked after they had gone.

The only sad thing about the fair coming was that it would soon be winter. The fair came at the beginning of August, not before the 6th or after the 12th, and then it was said that you could draw your curtains and light your fires as winter would soon be upon us.'


## GUY FAWKES NIGHT

'Guy Fawkes Night was one of the big events of the year at Hyde Heath. One year, in the 1930s, we had all hands on deck to build the biggest bonfire ever. The news even spread to London, and the *Evening News* sent a reporter and photographer to get the story.

The bonfire was sited on the common directly opposite The Plough. This didn't please landlord Frank Morton, as he had two petrol pumps right next to the pub. But eventually he relented and donated a barrel of tar and a pile of old tyres for the bonfire.

My blood runs cold when I think of the trees and furze bushes that were cut down to feed that fire. The bonfire was built so high that a cherry-picking ladder was needed to reach the top. One local resident had her birthday on 5th November and her father could be relied on to provide a good display of fireworks. What a night that was! There were no mishaps and the bonfire smouldered for more than a week afterwards. The Chesham Fire Brigade made an appearance just in case the petrol pumps blew up. These days such a bonfire would never be allowed.

We kids next day searched the common for dropped coins, and we found some. I found a silver tanner (6d), and for the next week I had more friends than I ever knew of.'

'A very large bonfire was built on the common at Wheeler End every year in the 1930s, ready for Guy Fawkes night. It would start to be built by the local boys and men well in advance of the 5th, some time in October. One particular year the bonfire was ready for the big event, when, to everyone's horror, it was set alight late at night. I don't think the culprits were ever caught. A new bonfire, just as big, was hastily built and the men took it in turns to guard it during the night.'

CHRISTMAS

'I came to Penn in 1946, and just before our first Christmas a knock on the front door heralded the local Mummers. Unfortunately we did not have the space to let them perform their whole play – but they sang their Mummers song. I wish I had been able to take down the words. They never came again.'

'At Christmas in Nether Winchenden in the 1920s there was a party at the Priory, with Father Christmas and presents for everyone. A Servants Ball was held each year which older children were allowed to attend. Nearly everything was then centred round the Priory, which is now known as Nether Winchenden House. Colonel and Mrs Bernard were then in residence and took an interest in the village. There was always hot broth for the sick and milk puddings twice a week for those with big families and for old people.'

'The most wonderful part of Christmas in the 1930s for my brother and me was very early in the morning, feeling with our feet the full pillowcase of toys, which we could make bump on the end of the bed.

At a reasonable time we were allowed to look at all our presents: crayons, paints, books, perhaps a doll for me and a train set or Meccano for my brother, sweets, clockwork toys, and all manner of exciting things. We usually had a jigsaw each, made of wood and very strong. They were called GWR jigsaws – were they manufactured by the Great Western Railway?

The day itself was, I suppose, rather quiet, but there was a definite magic about it. For one thing a fire was lit in the front room, where my brother and I played all day. Normally this room was never used, only on Christmas Day and Boxing Day.

We always had roast chicken for dinner, which was a very special treat. It's strange when I think of it, because like many families we kept our own chickens, primarily of course for the eggs, but I really cannot recall eating roast chicken except on Christmas Day.

To follow, of course, was home-made Christmas pudding with custard, and then in the afternoon a sumptious tea with Christmas cake and mince pies which were filled with home-made mincemeat. As a special treat, I was bought a bottle of blackcurrant cordial and my brother a bottle of ginger beer.

We never had, or expected, a Christmas tree. We didn't know anyone who did! We had a truly magnificent tree at our school at Wheeler End which we thought was wonderful, and never longed for a small one in our living room.'

'In the 1930s the school at Drayton Parslow provided a yearly Christmas concert. This, the highlight of every scholar's year, was performed on a very unsteady stage which creaked and groaned as children danced their way through the evening. Tiny children played their way through *Christmas Eve is here*, pinning their socks to the mantelpiece of a very unstable fireplace, while the more mature members of the cast performed songs, solo and choral, and acted pieces from well known books such as *Alice in Wonderland* and *Uncle Tom's Cabin* etc. The school would be packed for the three or four nights of the week. The VIPs had reserved seats at the front and proud and enthusiastic parents sat or stood in the rear. Every item on the programme was cheered and "Encore, encore!" could be heard from all round the room. Consequently, the concert lasted twice as long as scheduled. The activity in the dressing room was unbelievable and the frantic hunting for costumes, repairing rips and tears, giggling with nerves and being shushed by the teachers, had to be seen to be believed. Both teachers must have been exhausted.'

'At Quainton in the 1930s a chapel choir always sang carols round the farms and villages at Christmas time. In the early days Mr Jim Ayres was the choirmaster, who took along his violin, and later his daughter Dorothy accompanied the choir on her piano accordion.

Usually it took a week, starting at the outlying farms, the highlight being when you were asked to partake of refreshments. On Christmas Eve the carol singers went round the village and were well received, calling for a deserved break at Mr Ayre's house for refreshments, and usually finishing on the green at about eleven o'clock, by now competing with the bells which were ringing for the midnight service at church. On Boxing Day the handbell ringers started early going round the farms and finishing with visits to various homes in the village.'

# Index

252